Embracing Persephone

By the Same Author ☙

Woman Changing Woman:
     Feminine Psychology
     Re-Conceived Through Myth
     and Experience

Celebrating Girls:
     Nurturing and Empowering
     Our Daughters

Embracing Persephone

HOW TO BE

THE MOTHER

YOU WANT

FOR THE DAUGHTER

YOU CHERISH

VIRGINIA BEANE RUTTER

CONARI PRESS

Conari Press books are distributed by Publishers Group West.

Cover illustration: *The Young Shepherdess* (detail) by William-
Aldolphe Bouguereau, San Diego Museum of Art, gift of Mr. and
Mrs. Edwin S. Larsen/Bridgeman Art Library

Book design: Jaime Robles

Library of Congress Cataloging-in-Publication Data
Rutter, Virginia Beane.
Embracing Persephone : how to be the mother you want for the
daughter you cherish / Virginia Beane Rutter.
p.   cm.
Includes bibliographical references.
ISBN 1-57324-563-1
1. Parent and teenager.   2. Mothers and daughters.   3. Teenage
girls.   4. Parenting.   I. Title.

HQ799.15.R87 2000b
306.874'3—dc21   00-010735

Manufactured in Canada.

00 01 02 03   TRANSCONTINENTAL   10 9 8 7 6 5 4 3 2 1

And when [Demeter] saw Persephone,
    she leaped,
    like a maenad
    in the woods
on a shady mountain.
            And Persephone,
from where she was . . .
her mother, descending . . .
    she leaped down
          to run . . .
       and to her . . .
         stopping . . .

    "My child,
you should not have . . ."

    "Well, mother,
I will tell you everything
    precisely . . ."

    They spent
the whole of that day
    with hearts united
and they warmed
each other's heart
with many gestures
    of affection,
and her heart stopped
    grieving.

    They gave
and received
    joy
from each other . . .

from "The Hymn to Demeter,"
Homeric Hymns,
translated by Charles Boer

Acknowledgment is gratefully made to Charles Boer for permission to quote from his translation of "The Hymn to Demeter," in *Homeric Hymns,* revised second edition, Spring Publications, Dallas, copyright 1980.

The names of the mothers and daughters whose stories are told here have been changed to protect their privacy.

Contents ↝

Acknowledgments ᔓ

Embracing Persephone: How to Be the Mother You Want for the Daughter You Cherish is a tribute to the vitality, insight, and awareness of the adolescent girls and their mothers I spoke with while researching this book. The young women were willing to be honest and open about their experiences—both light and dark—in order to help others. Their mothers enthusiastically participated and wanted to learn. It has been a joy for me to interview and work with these women. I have been moved, delighted, and awed by the stories they have told me. I want to thank all these dynamic, spunky, young women and their loving, committed, wise, and adventuresome mothers for their contribution.

I am equally grateful to the therapists and teachers who agreed to be interviewed about themselves, their students, and their clients. Without three special women, psychotherapists who are devoted to working with adolescent girls, this book would never have come to fruition. Corisa Baley Aaronsen, Jan Berry-Kadrie, and Beth Hossfeld have my heartfelt thanks. My agent, Barbara Moulton, and my editor, Deborah Baker, deserve the credit for bringing the book into the world.

My daughter, Melina, and my son, Naftali, were teenage muses behind the scenes and gave me unfailing emotional support. And my husband, Peter, bless his heart, remained the bedrock of the family as I wrote yet another book.

Introduction ∽

*I*n the ancient Greek myth of the seasons, beautiful, teenage Persephone is picking flowers in a meadow when the earth opens and Hades, god of the underworld, snatches her up and carries her off to the land of the dead. In a different version of the myth, Persephone voluntarily leaves her idyllic life with her mother to go into the underworld and become Hades' bride. Her mother, Demeter, grieves so prodigiously at her loss that the landscape withers into barrenness.

Zeus, Persephone's father, tries to persuade Demeter that Hades is an appropriate son-in-law. But Demeter is inconsolable, and Zeus orders Hades to return the girl to her mother. Hades agrees but secretly slips Persephone a pomegranate seed, food of the underworld, which seals their relationship. By this cagey move, he ensures that she will have to spend time with him each year. In the winter, when the earth is dormant, Persephone is with her husband in the underworld; each spring she comes back to Demeter, goddess of grain and plenty, who ecstatically embraces her and brings the world back to life.

This myth directly invokes your relationship with your adolescent daughter as you brave her exciting but terribly risky passage to becoming a woman. In the last ten years girls have been liberated as never before, to master skills, set goals, and dream beyond even what their liberated mothers might imagine. Girls are raising their voices in every sphere of life: excelling in math and science, competing in sports, traveling to learn languages, and taking up social causes. High schools are responding with forums for girls to air complaints about sexism, harassment, and prejudice against minorities, and school administrations are sponsoring gay and lesbian groups. In the wake of Title IX, counselors, coaches, teachers, and mentors are being trained to meet girls' needs. With this tremendous shift in attitude, girls are increasingly empowered even as they confront their tumultuous peer culture.

Despite all the new opportunities that have come out of the girls' movement, middle schools and high schools continue to be risk-taking environments loaded with danger for girls. Parents have to face the hard facts of the world our daughters are growing up in. Drugs and alcohol, reckless driving, sexual harassment, promiscuity, guns and violence, and eating disorders are part of hallway conversation. Girls are sexually active at earlier ages, and violence against girls is pervasive. Television, movies, and computer games continue to produce images that sexualize girls, often in profoundly sadistic ways.

Inevitably, whether your daughter chooses to liberate herself or is carried away, she, like Persephone, will descend into high school life. And you, like Demeter, must worry and wait to embrace her each time she returns: after each emotional upheaval, each scrape with the law, each unwise judgment call, each narrow escape from harm, and each failure or triumph. In your embrace, you need to be aware of who she is and where she has been. When Persephone returns, she is no longer an innocent child but a queen, fertilized by experience. Or at least so we hope, against the many obstacles, for our daughters.

Opportunity and risk will always go together. We know that our daughters, like willing Persephones, need to take risks as adolescents.

Healthy risk taking is part of the way they grow. High school is a place to try new sports, to take new classes, to meet people whose backgrounds are different from their own. Some girls feel overwhelmed by the high school milieu; others jump right in without a thought for the consequences. As a girl begins to take more chances and make decisions on her own, she gains a sense of adventure, expands her personality, and finds satisfaction in assuming new responsibility for herself and others.

The dilemma for us as parents is that today's risks border on life and death choices: the risk of HIV infection from even one unprotected sexual encounter; the number of deaths resulting from drunk drivers; the emergency room visits for drug overdoses. Yet adolescence need not be an impossible time for families. Girls are more resilient than we think; they are strong as well as vulnerable.

With both dangers and opportunities swirling around your daughter in high school, it is all the more important that you, her mother, be in touch with her life and relate to her needs. You cannot leave her education to the school alone. As mothers, we can help our adolescent daughters take advantage of the new awareness in our culture. We can engage with them in ways that support their inner resources by giving them a positive self-image, social skills, self-protection, core self-worth, and healthy self-interest, by imbuing them with messages that will serve them during this difficult passage. Their high school years can be a chance for us to prepare them—through our expanding, not diminishing, relationship with them—to go out into the world.

Girls are challenged internally by the entrenched patriarchal attitudes toward women and externally by the current dynamic, yet often destructive, teenage culture. This culture is radically different from what most parents experienced. Understanding ourselves and our daughters is the key to both mothers and adolescent girls learning to negotiate these challenges. I hear girls' longing to be met by their mothers in the heartfelt refrain, "I wish someone would tell my mother that!" Those who manage this period with more grace accomplish it by maintaining an alliance with their mothers, even in the face of their need for rebellion and separateness.

Although your teenage daughter's increasing independence will often be dramatically played out in various forms of rebellion, she also wants to stay connected. How will you handle her having her own life, separate from yours, as her privacy and her peers become increasingly important to her? What will you do with your wistful feelings about this change even as you understand that, like all teenage girls, she wants less scrutiny? Will you know when to leave her alone and when and how to be involved with her?

A girl's separation from her mother at adolescence is daunting for another reason. As she becomes an adult, her questions about her femininity and her path in life stir up similar questions for you, her mother. Your daughter's development challenges you to redefine yourself as a mature woman and reexamine questions touching on your own coming-of-age. This can be uncomfortable.

As you remember your own high school and young adult years, strong feelings well up. If you pay attention, you can begin to identify your own conflicts, and see how your feelings and experiences influence your responses to your teenage daughter. You may see yourself through your daughter's eyes, you may hear echoes of the arguments you had with your own mother. Use these experiences as tools to explore issues in your own life. If you turn away from this opportunity to gain self-knowledge, you will lose a chance for your own growth. And you may fall into unconscious conflict with your daughter, and find yourself at an impasse that forces her to act out against you; perhaps you reached a similar impasse with your own mother. Finally, facing this inner tension will test your feminine strength and prod you to change.

Most mothers are seeking a different way for their daughters; they do not want their girls to experience what they went through at adolescence. We want them to succeed where we failed, to surpass us. The girls' movement has narrowed the gap between parent and child by further enlightening mothers who came of age aware of feminism. We have thought about, read about, and struggled with gender issues our whole lives. We bring that awareness to our relationships with our teenage daughters, for better or worse.

Sometimes this era of girl power can feel threatening to mothers who were raised in less liberating or supportive environments. Our own feelings of resentment or anger toward our mothers, fathers, or bosses may come out in unrealistic expectations or punitive actions toward our daughters. We have a lot to teach them, but we also have much to learn from girls who are becoming catalysts for change in their families and communities. How can we recognize these deeper currents in our relationships with our daughters and give them our support and insight so that they can embrace their opportunities and confront their challenges in healthy ways?

Even if you did not have a positive mothering experience yourself, by taking up your unresolved issues, you can still change the way you treat your daughter. Confront your own anxieties as you mother your adolescent and you will enlarge and deepen the bond between you. This involves a certain amount of self-knowledge and self-questioning. Watching her, you will be confronted daily with memories of yourself at her age. Your daughter's journey in these years is also a journey of self-discovery for you. How can you grow as a woman, as an individual? Who are you becoming? Entering the fray of your connection with your adolescent daughter will energize your own life.

Being aware of yourself and your daughter does not mean that you will handle every situation perfectly. There is no absolutely right way; no expert can tell you the exact limits and freedoms that you should impose on or give your daughter. Each girl is unique within the context of her family's and community's values. But the value that all mothers and daughters can share is the value of an ongoing relationship.

Mothers and daughters go back and forth in conversation with many variations on the theme: "You don't understand" and "I can't talk to you anymore; you criticize everything I say and do." If your relationship with her as a young girl has been good, you will feel the loss of each other. As yearnings stir in your daughter for a wider horizon, she misses the secure identity of the years when you, her mother, were her whole world. And you feel the absence of your willing companion and feminine soulmate.

If your rapport with your daughter has been problematic in her younger years, the power struggles at adolescence will intensify. It takes sensitivity and a willingness to change your mothering strategy in order to be close to her in new ways. It is never too late! Don't despair because your daughter is already sixteen and you wish you had done things differently; know that you can start to change your tactics any time and build from there.

But there is no easy course through the emotional muddle of a girl coming into womanhood. Eventually, she will be independent and you both will let go, either gracefully or furiously. Although you as the parent set the tone, meeting the challenge takes a lot of energy, love, and dedication on both sides. The joy that you both will feel is well worth the effort.

However you have reached this crossing, the question you now face is: How can you as a parent stay calm and centered in the midst of your girl's push and pull, back and forth, affection and rejection? As one confused eighteen-year-old said to her mother, "I hate it how I need you so much!"

Embracing Persephone shows you, as her mother, how to participate in the pattern of loss and return in your daughter's development. This book will help you identify the issues that trigger conflict with your daughter, provide you with strategies for keeping your relationship open, and give her a touchstone in you that will see her through the tempests brought on by her changing body, her academic demands, and, above all, her social demands. It will help you deepen your relationship with your daughter through her high school and college years.

In this book, girls' stories reveal the reality of teenage life and teach you how to stay connected so both you and your daughter get what you need. Mothers' (and fathers') stories deliver the other side: being the loving, worried, helpful, well-intentioned, exasperated, sometimes misguided, and often stressed adults responsible for girls' well-being.

Direct, down-to-earth communication and feeling is one way to stay connected to your teenage daughter. Chapter 1, "'You Don't Understand Anything!' On Connecting," illustrates some of the typical, seemingly unresolvable conflicts that arise when she enters high school (if not before) and throughout those four years and shows you how to resolve them. It defines what you can do when, despite your best attempts, your communication breaks down, and teaches you to recognize when your daughter is ready to take another step in growing up. It gives you skills to use in anticipating and supporting her new, fluctuating personality.

Being grounded in her body is at the core of your daughter's identity. Chapter 2, "Body Language: Food, Piercings, and Clothes," shows you how to support her positive body image, teach her to appreciate her menstrual cycle, and help her to meet her own physical needs. Girls' feelings about their bodies are often expressed through the clothes they wear, and through adorning themselves with makeup, jewelry, body piercings, and tattoos. This chapter shows girls in conflict with their mothers about self-image and discusses ways to settle disputes. It delves into what girls feel about sexual desire and heterosexual and homosexual feelings. And it suggests ways for you to talk with your daughter about contraception and practicing safe sex.

Your daughter's beginning awareness of her own sexual desire and her knowledge of sex will then become part of her sexual exploration in relationships. Chapter 3, "'He's Hot!' Desire, Sex, and Love," shows girls relating to boys as lovers and friends. Lesbian and bisexual affiliations are part of teen culture. This chapter discusses how to deal with your daughter's sexual identity questions.

While sexuality and body image are both hot topics between mothers and daughters, there are also other areas in which you and she are likely to have differing opinions. Chapter 4, "Girlfriends?", goes into the ways in which you and she may define being female. It offers ways to bridge the gap and learn from one another. You must recognize your teenager's different social context from yours as well as respectfully communicating your individual values. Many positive, nurturing, and empowering ideas for spending time with your daughter in both traditional and nontraditional ways are explored here. Aunts, godmothers, and other adult women are valued friends for your daughter, but her own girlfriends will be the most influential social group for her feminine identity.

While you may have been able to protect your young daughter from exposure to drug use and alcohol consumption, you will both have to deal with it when she reaches adolescence. She may also be threatened by violence, sexual assault, and harassment. Chapter 5, "Party Time: Hip Hop, Beer, and Weed," addresses teenage "partying" and how to handle your daughter's initiation into experimenting with drugs and alcohol. When she wants to go to her first party, you can handle the situation in a positive way for you and her. Knowing that your daughter must negotiate and master this social arena in order to grow up, you can encourage her to take calculated risks instead of foolish or destructive ones as she explores her group's identity.

The risk-taking social environment of high school is not the only stressor for girls who are trying to define themselves. Academic and athletic demands at school and family pressures at home combine to cause anxiety for your daughter. Chapter 6, "Great Expectations: Living Up to It All," uncovers the pressure that teenage girls feel from all sides. It talks about the role that your expectations of her and hers of herself play in her stress, especially when those two collide or overwhelm her. It shows you how to see when that is happening, understand the importance of her social life, and help her get her schoolwork done, fulfill her commitments, and stay grounded. You can teach her the skills of time management and scheduling. By addressing her anxieties, you can help her establish healthy patterns for her future and explore, at least in fantasy, what she wants to do next with her life.

Expectations come from both mothers and fathers in families. Ideally, a girl needs to have the support of both parents in her teens. Chapter 7, "Daddy's Little Girl," takes up the role of her father and how that differs from your maternal role. Her father can be especially helpful in counteracting the sexism that she encounters in the world. He can stay engaged with her without insisting she dull her lights to please him. This chapter suggests ways you can help your daughter understand her father, and your husband or partner understand her. If his views about what she is doing or who she is conflict, it tells you when to mediate between them, when not. Her father's relationship with her and with you will directly influence her relationships with her male peers.

As your daughter leaves her childhood, she gains new emotional and intellectual strengths and practical skills. Chapter 8, "Days of Reckoning: Crossroads and Crises," outlines developmental passages on the way to adulthood for girls and their mothers. At each step, your daughter grows psychologically: her first bra, first period, first boyfriend, first date, first rock concert. Acknowledging these passages will alleviate her anxiety (and your own) and make her path to adulthood more meaningful. Through conversations and fitting celebrations, you prepare her emotionally for each of these firsts in her life. Ritual celebration opens avenues to the soul that you and she will continue to draw on to live happy, fulfilled lives.

While honoring your daughter's teenage initiations, you may feel the need for an initiation of your own. You are more and more free of the moment-to-moment needs that she had as a child. You suddenly (or so it seems, because moving apart takes place over time) have some room to breathe deeply, think, feel, and reflect on childbearing and raising. The next step for you is to move into a new identity that includes being a mother but also reclaims and expands your individuality; it is imperative that you have your own life at this time. Chapter 9, "'Get a Life, Mom!'" challenges you to look at what the next stage of life holds for you now that the emotional, psychological, and time demands of your daughter have diminished. More specifically, what is calling you from within, what desire, wish, or direction wants to be explored, that has had to live only in dreams while you mothered wholeheartedly all these years? It shows you how to find nurturing forms for your own rites of passage.

"Wrapping It Up," chapter 10, concludes with a look at how your relationship with your daughter has matured through these adolescent years in connected, healthy ways. You have both become self-possessed women, at different stages of life.

To understand our daughters is to understand ourselves in a new way. Ask yourself, How can I be wholesome in relation to my child? The secret is that mothers and teenage daughters have a wonderful resource in each other for finding a deeper relationship to the feminine, to their own strength, creativity, and spirit.

Each time you embrace your daughter in all her fullness, the energy of new life renews you, too. If you stay connected, you will have a vital, lasting, and mutually rewarding rapport. By taking our lesson from the original mother-daughter myth of Demeter and Persephone, we can emerge more authentic and vibrant, secure in our relationship to one another, and secure in ourselves.

1 ෴

"*You Don't Understand Anything!*"

ON CONNECTING

No matter how often your daughter turns away from you with the refrain "You don't understand anything!" you must be steadfast in maintaining your relationship with her during her adolescent years. Girls both seek and respond to genuine healthy overtures from their mothers. You need only an openness to yourself and to her to develop the emotional skills you will use to stay connected as she moves through these years. The tools provided in this book will help your relationship grow.

Resolving conflict creatively becomes crucial to a healthy engagement between mothers and daughters. Ask her to put herself in your shoes and do your best to do the same for her. This will help bridge the seeming gulf that opens between you as she enters her teens.

Resolve to adapt and evolve both as her mother and as an individual as she grows and changes. Ask her to adhere to rules based on her safety, health, and integrity, and communicate your values in a loving way, and she will respect them and you. As you slowly hand over the power for making choices to your daughter, you can intervene in all the places where girls may lose ground.

On Your Mark, Get Set . . .

Anticipate changes when your daughter enters seventh or eighth grade or freshman year (and every year after!) in high school. As her body changes, her mental, emotional, and social development will sometimes accelerate, and she will sometimes flounder as her body, mind, and heart try to find a new balance. Sometimes she will regress two steps in order to move forward three. The day after her first class dance in eighth grade, she may burst into tears when you ask her to baby-sit her younger brother. Although she swore she had a wonderful time, the challenge of relating to boys and to her girlfriends in a new way took a toll. Support her need to fall apart and to spend some time alone.

Your task as a mother is to prepare yourself by thinking about these issues before they arise. Inform yourself about the reality of the world that your daughter is growing up in and how different it may be from when you were young. Visit the middle school and high school that she will be attending. Talk with other parents who have daughters in the school. Ask them about problems that have arisen with drugs, alcohol, sex, and sexual harassment. Find teachers who will answer your questions about sexism in the classroom. Get a sense of the atmosphere in which your daughter will spend most of her time for years.

Beginning high school is a momentous occasion—an initiation into a new and frightening stage of life. Every girl I interviewed spoke of freshman and sophomore year as being awkward and painful. If you don't get ready, you may find yourself at war with your daughter from the outset. Fourteen-year-old Leah has intense disgust for her mother, Ruth. "My mother treats me like a baby," Leah said. "I have to lie even to go to a movie with my girlfriends. She thinks I'm going to get in trouble with boys and alcohol because she did." Ruth needs to let go, but she is afraid and trying to correct her past by restricting Leah. Beginning in sixth grade, Ruth refused to let Leah go to the well-chaperoned birthday party dances or to movies with a group of friends because she didn't want Leah out after 10:00 P.M. As a result Leah became more and more excluded from her friends' middle school social activities. By the time Leah was a freshman, she was seething with resentment and determined to find every avenue to escape from her mother's hypervigilance.

Ask Yourself the Hard Questions

In order to mother your daughter well as she moves into middle school and adolescence, you must be willing to confront your memories of your own adolescence. "How did my mother handle this for me? What did I appreciate and what did I detest about those years? What do I want to preserve for my daughter and what do I want to change? What were my parents' expectations? And how did I feel about them?"

To guide your daughter, you must probe even deeper. Think about when you first encountered or experimented with drugs and alcohol and what kinds of problems ensued. Remember your humiliations and your triumphs in high school. Were you a wallflower, the school slut, a jock, or a brain? Who did you go to when you got into trouble? How did all this influence your feelings about being a woman? Keep these questions in mind at each new encounter and try to sort your feelings out from hers. At any given moment, are you feeling sadness, humiliation, or joy for her or for yourself or both?

You also have to explore an area that is deeply personal for each woman. Ask yourself: "What does it mean to me to be a woman?

What has my daughter learned from watching me? Why am I uncomfortable with the way she is dressing (or talking or acting) now? What memories does this bring up for me? What are my values, and have I conveyed them to her in a positive way?" My work with women over the years has shown me that we can ask these difficult questions and be more creative with the answers than we ever thought possible.

If you can recall what your mother did that you hated as an adolescent or the excruciating times when you weren't getting what you needed from her (or anyone else), the times when school was a living hell and you were miserable, you can begin to come up with responses to your daughter based on your own earned wisdom and the reality of her adolescent life today.

Stay Emotionally Available

Learn to tolerate some hostility or withdrawal from your teenage daughter. Some girls are moody. If you react strongly to her moodiness, you may push her deeper into her bad feeling, and you risk alienating her. If you can be matter-of-fact and remain available emotionally, she is likely to work it through on her own sooner, and your relationship with her will be intact. Do encourage her, however, in neutral moments to tell you when she is upset with you and why so that you don't have to wonder about every bad mood. You can always inquire in an open, light way whether or not you have done something to offend her. If she shrugs it off, leave it alone. You have opened the door; she's not ready to come in yet.

Let her go through her changes—one evening screaming that she hates you because you don't trust her when you have said you need to speak with the parents of her new-found friends (strangers to you!) who are driving her to the movies, and the next day cozying up to you and asking you to make her favorite lasagna dinner.

Respond to her overtures even if she is only asking you to drop her at her friend's house or take her to the store. Granting her requests gives you a chance to spend time, often alone, with her and shows her that you care. Similarly, if she invites you to watch a television show or play a game of Scrabble, join her, if you possibly can. Wise mothers know that these are openings for relationship. You often have to take your teenage girl on her terms.

This is not to say that you have to endure her being surly, rude, and demanding while you wait on her. But if she offers positivity, take her up on it. You need also to set limits or boundaries on your own time and energy. If you don't, you will feel resentful that you are gratifying her every whim. But look for the places where you can meet.

"I Want to Meet You Where You Are Now."

Tell your daughter that you want your relationship to grow as she grows. Ask her questions that bring up the dynamics between you: What are you doing that makes her feel uncomfortable at her age or stage? What ways does she think you are still involved with her that are unnecessary, that you could let go of because she can handle those situations herself now? You can make a few suggestions based on her cues, what you have observed in her testy, negative reactions to you. Such reactions are signs of your daughter needing more room in which to feel autonomy, her own authority, so that she can feel good about herself. Young women need to feel less and less dependent and more interdependent.

Noting how your freshman daughter promptly completes her homework, for example, might lead you to ask: Would she like you to not ask her about homework? Would she like you to stop using sweet talk, or her baby names? If you are still using her pet names or treating her as you did when she was younger, she may be embarrassed and begin to avoid you in order to avoid feeling like a baby.

Or perhaps she wants to hear such endearments at bedtime, a time when she is comfortable with more affection. You may be surprised at what she tells you.

Joan took her fourteen-year-old daughter, Samantha, out for ice cream one hot October night at the beginning of freshman year to check in with her. She asked her daughter if there was anything she did, as her mother, that she didn't like. Samantha hedged at first, not wanting to hurt her mother's feelings but, prompted by Joan, blurted out, "I don't like how you talk about me to your friends on the phone or when they come over to dinner. You always exaggerate how great I am and it stresses me out." Although Joan had sensed Samantha's irritation, she had been unaware that she was bragging about her daughter. Joan was stung by the criticism. Still, she was able to bring herself to reply, "You know I'm proud of you. I don't want to put pressure on you at all." Samantha was glad her mother could respond to her feelings; she wouldn't have brought this up without her mother's prompting. But it might have come out in anger with more destructive consequences.

Initiating a conversation with your daughter in which you say, "I want to meet you where you are now" has the effect of catching the wave of her development as it comes, rather than fighting it and being engulfed. You then have an opportunity to take up the issue at hand in a constructive way. You are saying that you understand and are happy that she is growing up and you want to support her change, change appropriately yourself, and maintain your relationship with her.

Pay Attention to Her Cues

As Joan discovered, in the fast pace of family life, it is easy to gloss over small signs of distress. Notice your daughter's fluctuations and respond to them. Look for behavioral and emotional clues: tears, angry outbursts, silence, acting out; behavior that is unusual for her, either regressive (not wanting to stay home alone when she's thirteen, when she loved it at age eleven) or too advanced for her age (wanting to go out with a twenty-five-year-old when she's sixteen). You need to attune yourself to the subtle changes in her.

Your teenage daughter may, however, resist talking to you. Be aware of when she has had enough and begins to withdraw. Let her go. Live your own life until something comes up with her again. Don't expect openness on one day to continue on the next. Try to be available when she seeks your company in any form; otherwise, leave her to practice her budding skills and to make mistakes on her own.

How she feels about friends and social issues deserves considered attention. But after the conversation, let it go. Don't go overboard, get overinvolved, and bring up the issue again later. Wait for her to bring it up again; she will! If she confides in you about a problem with her friend and you want to check back with her on how the situation is going, make a vague, gentle inquiry a week later and see what response you get.

Karen ruefully described her dismay the first time she brought something up that her seventeen-year-old daughter, Miranda, had discussed with her the previous week. In a shocked voice, Miranda demanded, "Who told you that?" Karen replied, "Sweetheart, *you* did." Miranda stalked off, flinging words over her shoulder, "Don't ever do that to me again. You use things I say against me!" In the blitz of teenage social life, Miranda has moved on from the conflict with her friend; it's over for her. Karen, at a loss, waited for a more congenial moment to say to Miranda, "I'm not using it against you; I am just trying to connect. But, if you're more comfortable, I'll wait for you to follow up on things you have told me." Miranda shrugged, but Karen was glad she had clarified her stance. A girl prefers not to be reminded of having confided in you as she is trying to separate, but she still wants to know you are there for intimacy when she needs it. She will fluctuate wildly between closeness and distance.

Take note of your own feelings during this process. Karen was stunned at Miranda's lapse, but she recovered enough to meet the situation in a way that left the door open for Miranda to confide in her again. You may find yourself in tears, missing your daughter as she reacts to you in unpredictable ways and spends more and more time with her friends. If she is your only or last child, you will grieve the loss of your mothering and her childhood, even as you know it's right for her to grow up and move away. Take care of yourself when this happens; find ways to make yourself happy without her. She will be back.

"You Can't Do This to Me!"

Teenagers are mobile in the world. When your daughter says, "You can't do this to me," she is often literally right. She can do anything she pleases when she is out of your sight; the more you try to force her to obey you, the more likely she is to rebel against being treated like a child. On another level, this statement is a plea for you to understand just how difficult her inner and outer stresses are. It could be rephrased, "Please, Mom. Don't get in the way of who I am becoming!" It takes a perceptive mother or father to hear the subliminal message, to talk with her calmly, and to reach a compromise that includes your daughter's need for autonomy and your responsibility for her health and safety.

To have any influence over your daughter, you must value your relationship more than your need to control her. As she changes, you as a parent must gradually give up managing every aspect of her life. At the same time, you must teach her the responsibility for making choices that goes with your yielding authority. The questions are: How can you give up control, yet maintain your influence to keep her safe in a dangerous world? How do you intervene in a way that strengthens your daughter's spirit and character?

Valuing your relationship with her means showing her the same respect and consideration that you expect from her. Your fairness and her honesty are more important than any preconceived ideas of how a fifteen-year-old *ought* to behave. She will hear you if you present your values and point out the risks she faces in each situation, in an atmosphere of loving concern, but only if you are willing to listen to her brief on the subject. This ongoing conversation with your daughter is about attunement to her as well as about drawing the line and being the parent.

A positive relationship, however, does not mean relationship without conflict. Thrashing out your different views and feelings is essential, but screaming tantrums and shouting matches as an ongoing mode of communication are destructive. How you handle the conflict that arises between you is your choice. If your parents used shouting and dictatorial punishment as the response to difficulties in your family, you will have a more difficult time managing conflict sensibly than if you had positive models for handling the inevitable ups and downs of life.

Whatever your personal example was, if your daughter has a highly emotional temperament and expresses herself through tantrums, it is your task as a mother or father to teach her how to handle her emotions in a better way. If she is escalating out of control, calling you names, and telling you to "fuck off," you must stop addressing the issue at hand and set sane limits. Mothers and fathers need to be able to say: "I know you're angry at me for not letting you go to the rave with your friends. I am willing to listen to your reasons for wanting to go and to your feelings. But when you call me names and use abusive language, I don't feel like talking to you. If you can change your behavior, we'll continue talking; otherwise we'll have to stop until you've cooled off." Taking charge in this way makes your limits clear to her, gives her a chance to take another tack or calm down, and shows her that you can tolerate her anger, all of which will make her feel better about herself.

A girl who is able to express the range of her emotions in her family without loss of love will be able to withstand the conflicting and chaotic emotional influence of her peers. Every interaction with your daughter is layered with meanings. She is trying to be independent without rejecting you, define who she is, find her own values, and learn to stand up for herself with you and others. In these struggles, she is fighting to resolve her identity. As a parent, you must handle the conflict in such a way as to positively influence your daughter's process and, at the same time, build up her character and your relationship.

Never withhold love. No matter what she has done or what line you have to draw, maintain a position of love and caring. Even when you are angry, your love should be apparent. Conflict arises largely during transitional times when she is exploring new territory and you and she together must make the appropriate adjustments. Remember, as she changes, you have to change too.

Meltdown Time

You and your daughter have to accept that everything cannot be wonderful all the time. Nor will it be terrible all the time. Your daughter will agonize during high school and sometimes make foolish choices. She will sulk, have angry outbursts, and retreat. And you and your husband will no doubt lie awake at night with worry, fret about the dangers, and scream in frustration at your daughter ignoring you or acting out.

Even with all your best efforts to respond to her distress, anger, or withdrawal, there will be times when your tempers flare and you will both erupt. Sometimes anger explodes when, despite repeated attempts to establish basic house rules, she insists on defying your agreements. Other times her frustration with being unduly restricted will push things over the edge.

When communication breaks down, give yourself and your daughter some time to cool off before you attempt to set up a time in which to renegotiate. Do not hesitate to apologize to your daughter; remember, she feels as devastated as you do. Apologizing for losing control or hurting her feelings does not mean that you have changed your mind about her unacceptable behavior or that you will renege on the limit you are trying to set. Your regret and sitting down to work it through shows her that mistakes can be made by anyone, and that it is still possible to pick up the pieces and move on to constructive problem solving. We need to help girls learn how to solve problems and show them our willingness to correct mistakes. This is critical for teenage girls who are being pressured from all sides to be perfect. You also convey the message that you will not give up on her!

The most important thing to do is to reconnect with her after these scenes. Keep the relationship door open. While you won't budge on a fair limit or consequence you set for her, write a note saying something like, "I'm sorry I lost my temper. I love you and look forward to your swim meet on Friday." Leave it on her pillow or bedside table to find when you are at work.

If in your fury you grounded her for a month because she was ten minutes late for her curfew three times in a row, acknowledge your unfairness when you feel calmer and reduce her grounding to perhaps one night. Consider also whether ten minutes is worth the furor. She will appreciate your willingness to admit that you were out of control. Teenagers never cooperate with unfair rules or limit setting for long; they fight you to the end, and you lose not only the peace of your household but also any possibility of a viable relationship.

At heart, your daughter will accept a fair consequence, even if she tells you that it "ruins her life." When you ground her or take away a privilege as a result of her having broken certain agreed-upon rules, she may rage, cry, and slam doors. But often, once she knows that you won't change your mind and that you are remaining friendly, she may be relieved (although she won't acknowledge that to you).

Girls often appreciate having their parents say "no" in appropriate ways when things get out of control; ridicule from their peers is so cruel and pervasive that they are pushed into testing limits beyond their own true wishes. Having your daughter take a break from her peer group at home in a nonhostile environment—even if she continues to feel resentful for a while—will give her a chance to reflect and reorient herself. She can unwind, think about school and friends, and settle down.

"No One Else Has a Curfew!"

Arguments between high school girls and their parents all sound the same. The struggle over a curfew is ubiquitous. One night around nine o'clock, Ellen's fifteen-year-old daughter, Kate, rushed into the family room and said breathlessly to her mother, "Mom! I'm going over to Abigail's house and maybe I'll spend the night." Ellen asked, "What are you girls planning to do tonight?" "We don't know yet," Kate said evasively. "Maybe we'll go out, maybe not." Ellen responded, "I want you home by midnight, Kate, and, by the way, who's driving?" "Mom," Kate moaned, exasperated, "That was my curfew last year. No one else I know has a curfew; why do I have to have one?"

How is Ellen going to handle this confusing exchange? She knows Kate is avoiding telling her the whole truth. She also knows that she is in for a big fight because Kate has a social agenda and is determined to do what she wants. Ellen, a savvy mother, is wondering how much she wants to push for a curfew without forcing Kate into a blatant lie. Interrupted in the middle of both reading to her four-year-old son and saying good-bye to her husband, Jim, and twelve-year-old daughter, Alta, as they leave the house for Alta's basketball game, she also can't give Kate her undivided attention.

Ellen quickly reviews the situation in her mind, and realizes that it is a weekend night and that Kate is caught up on her homework. While she doesn't want Kate going to parties and has discussed that limit with her before, she wants to honor Kate's need to have her freedom extended. Ellen says, "All right, then, tonight you can go by Abigail's rules and spend the night there." Ellen comes over and gives her mom a big hug. "Thanks, Mom. You're the greatest," she says, beaming.

Ellen had learned to be more flexible with rules by the time Kate was a sophomore. She had realized that by prohibiting Kate from going to parties, she had eliminated the possibility of Kate calling home to get a ride or asking for help if she got into trouble. In order to call, Kate would have had to admit that she had defied her parents.

Kate, now an accomplished seventeen-year-old, talked about her feelings of insecurity on entering her freshman year. "I thought I'd never be cool, never make it in high school if I didn't go to parties. I was different from most of my friends because my mom wanted to talk to the parents and have the phone number where the party was being held. Mostly the parents weren't there and I didn't have the number. The way it works, you don't even know where the parties are until you're out late at night calling around. So I ended up having to sneak out to go to the parties. I'd stay at a girlfriend's house where the parents didn't pay as much attention to the kids. Parties seemed like the real thing. Now I'm totally bored with them." Teenagers who want to go to parties find a way.

Kate would have liked this scenario to have gone differently. She said that she understands why her parents objected to her going to parties. "Sometimes I'd end up having to take a ride with older guys who were drunk or walking home in the middle of the night through the city because whoever said they'd take me home left the party without telling me." Kate said it would have been better if her parents had let her go and agreed on a time when she would call them to pick her up. She said, "That would have worked as long as they picked me up outside the party or down the road."

Even if you have checked out the situation with the parents of your daughter's new girlfriend, you have to accept that by age fourteen you cannot prevent her from climbing out a window, having unprotected sex, or trying beer or marijuana, if she chooses to do so. You can use the issue of going to parties as leverage to ask her how she feels about smoking, drinking, or sexuality and hope to get an honest answer. Girls who have a good relationship with their mothers will not be happy lying to them. The psychological challenge for a girl is to create her own autonomy while moving toward more understanding with her mother.

"You Don't Trust Me."

Early on, you will realize that you have no real control over the teenage environment with which your daughter must learn to cope. You will not know all her new friends, and she will resist your calling the parents in these families. Any such intervention will threaten her sense of security in the high school social scene; she wants to be seen as independent, not as a baby needing parental supervision. "You don't trust me" is an often effective defensive maneuver on the part of a teenager. If it makes you pause, consider that your daughter is also wondering whether she trusts herself. Give her accusation some thought before you try to answer. It's tricky business to sort out what kind of trust she is asking for from what kind you are willing to give, partially because the context changes all the time.

Often you trust her but you don't trust the situation she may find herself in without parental supervision. When Kate asked to stay at her friend's she was implicitly asking for her mother to trust her to make her own decision about what time to get home. Ellen understood the unspoken request and honored it. If Kate had been younger, Ellen would have called her friend's parents to be sure they were home.

If you feel you should call, especially as a condition of her spending the night with a new friend or going to a party, explain to your daughter that it is your concern that is operating, not distrust; you care about her and are responsible for her well-being. Negotiate with her instead of legislating what you want her to do. This conversation usually entails some time and a lot of strong emotions, and she still won't agree with you. It is often a conflict about her autonomy that first comes up when a young woman enters high school; this will continue until the time you choose to completely let go and let her lead her own social life without any direction from you.

"I Hate School."

"I hate school; it's dumb, boring, and irrelevant. I'd rather be working. I'm never going to do anything with this in my life." Monica, an energetic, artistically inclined girl, was floundering without any direction. Mary, her mother, managed a jewelry store; her father, Chuck, was an independent contractor. Both worked long hours to earn a living for Monica and her younger siblings. Initially, they rolled their eyes at Monica's complaints and dismissed them as "growing pains." When her litany wore them down, they gave unsolicited advice. Mary said, "You should get more involved. When I was in high school, I was a pom-pom girl. I loved it and it helped me find classes more interesting." Her pragmatic father told her, "You'll never get a decent job these days without a college education." As Monica became more and more despondent and angry, her parents became more and more frustrated with her.

Monica and her parents are not connecting. Neither Mary nor Chuck is listening; they are not attuning themselves to Monica's frame of mind and her problems. They are asserting their own experiences without asking her about her reality, inner and outer. Yet they are both concerned and worried about Monica. Mary is remembering her own awkwardness as a teenager and how much fun she had cheering the football team on. Chuck is anxious about Monica's future; he is less tuned in to her distress.

If your daughter is hanging out downtown instead of going to the soccer game or, worse yet, instead of going to her classes, you have to ask her what is going on with her from her point of view. Are her class demands overwhelming, or is it her social life that is a disaster? Girls who hate school are usually having trouble because they haven't learned to communicate their needs. They got by or did well until high school, when the struggle between academics and social life becomes central.

Listen to her, ally yourself with her dilemma, join with her emotionally. Don't begin to try to fix the problem until you have listened. Approach her gently: "I feel badly that you hate school so much. I remember how difficult it was to make friends and to feel comfortable with who I was in high school. What is it that is hard for you? I want to hear even if I can't do anything about it."

Chuck agreed that Mary would try to talk to Monica because she had more compassion for her daughter's suffering. Mary made frequent overtures to Monica over several days before Monica began to respond. Mary was surprised to hear her say, "I detest the girls in my class. They are so-o-o superficial; all they talk about is clothes, boys, and parties. I don't want to deal with that shit; it's boring." Monica is telling it like it is in high school, with everyone jockeying to be cool. But she is also stuck, feeling helpless to meet the task of finding the right social outlet. She has withdrawn from the field, given up on her studies and on making friends, and given up on herself. Monica dropped out to hang with the skaters on the street who have no use for school. She definitely needs guidance and support from her parents to help find a subject, a creative outlet, or a sport that she cares about so that she can begin to feel more capable and alive. That will give her a ready-made group within which to develop her emotional skills.

It is nearly impossible for you to solve your child's social problems. You have to stay in the background. But you can encourage her to seek out one girl with whom she has something in common to befriend. One alliance at school will change everything for her. Mary's initial plan of action, however, was the best one—to listen nonjudgmentally. Monica got it off her chest and now knew there was at least one person who understood what was going on with her; she felt less alone.

Listen and Learn

The first step in any confrontation with your daughter is to stop and listen. Truly listening takes time and concentration. Actually hearing her side of the story is a learned skill. Girls have an intense need for focused parental attention.

Eighteen-year-old Danielle, motivated toward academic excellence and struggling with perfectionism, thinks that parents have to go out of their way to ask their daughters how they are feeling. "Just listen. There is only so much that a girl can go to friends with because they are all going through the same things. My mother and I go out to lunch together now and talk about feelings. My father is there for family time, all of us together. With him, I talk more about politics, history assignments, or religion."

More socially oriented Kate, for whom a flexible curfew is important, presents another side to mother-daughter interaction. "I think a mother should let her daughter decide when to talk, when not. I hate it when my mom tries to get things out of me when I'm not in the mood; it's our biggest problem. A daughter knows when she needs to talk to her mom." Both Danielle's and Kate's comments express a part of the picture. You must know your daughter's moods and respect them.

Listening to your daughter involves opening your mind and heart to her and to what she is experiencing. Notice the nuances. Try to listen without interrupting or pulling rank: "I'm your mother (or father) and you have to do what I say." Listen without prompting or second-guessing. Give your daughter as much time as she needs.

When she is finished, you can respond honestly. Express your concerns and your values in as straightforward a manner as possible. You must be willing to elaborate on your reasons for your concerns and to listen to your daughter's responses, as well as enumerating consequences. Adolescent girls still need parenting.

If you have listened respectfully to your daughter, she is more likely to listen to you while you present your observations and worries. In a group of mothers and daughters at a bookstore, one mother asked me, "What do I do when my teenage daughter talks to me in a rude, offensive way?" A thirteen-year-old girl in the audience immediately raised her hand and said, "I think if parents don't like the way their daughter talks to them, they should look at the way they talk to their children, because sometimes the parents are being rude and offensive, too." You can only ask of your daughter what you are willing to give her.

Ideally, your goal is to help your daughter evaluate the choices she is making and to make decisions based on her knowledge of both the practical and the emotional consequences. But most exchanges with teenagers happen at the very last minute. You will find yourself having more emotionally charged conversations after she has done something unwise, illegal, or impulsive rather than before.

"I Was Afraid to Tell You."

When Georgina's daughter, Connie, complained of headaches in sophomore year and frequently wanted to stay home from school, her mother was concerned. Georgina had always had exacting standards for Connie's grades. Busy with her own job in an insurance company, however, she rarely had time to discuss Connie's classes with her. Georgina started to ask questions, and Connie finally confessed, "I'm failing my science class, and I was afraid to tell you." In a flash, Georgina remembered feeling the same fear with her father, who rapped her on the head with his knuckles when she couldn't figure out a math problem. She winced with the pain of realizing that she had terrorized her daughter in a more subtle way by demanding perfect report cards.

Dismayed, Georgina told Connie that she was sorry she had been acting like a taskmaster about her school performance, leaving Connie to harbor her failure, instead of asking for help. Georgina said, "What do you think the problem is with science? What can we do to make school a more positive experience for you? Would it help if I went to talk to your counselor?" Connie said she simply didn't understand the material and she was embarassed to tell the teacher or her friends because she felt "like an idiot."

Georgina had not paid attention to Connie's daily homework, and her high expectations had caused Connie to present a smiling front about school in order to avoid her mother's criticism. Both you and your husband have to look at your participation in order to stay connected to your daughter. Georgina realized that she had been too busy and too rigid to inquire nonjudgmentally about Connie's progress as she went along. This had left Connie sinking deeper and deeper into failure. They had a conference with the teacher and worked out a study program for Connie to follow that included weekly visits to the teacher's office. Georgina also made herself available to quiz Connie in preparation for tests. Georgina changed her message to, "I want you to feel good about yourself, not get good grades for me. You need to pass this class to graduate. Let's help you meet that goal."

You often need to evaluate a situation and then let some time elapse between the initial venting of a problem and offering new suggestions. When you feel that your daughter is receptive, propose some realistic alternatives that will help her change her view of herself. Encourage her to take small steps in a direction that will restore or enhance her sense of self-worth. Trying something new or different will help her achieve a sense of mastery in the situation.

"When I Was Your Age . . ."

As Karen discovered, you constantly have to recalibrate your relationship with your daughter. One Saturday morning, she found herself standing in the doorway of Miranda's bedroom, berating her half-asleep daughter, "Miranda, when I was your age, I had to stay home all day Saturday and help my mom clean house. I can't believe you think that you can sleep until noon and then go out to play basketball with your friends. You're lazy and self-centered." Furious in response, Miranda swore at her mother and pulled the covers over her head, saying, "You don't care about me or about my basketball practice. All you care about is your stupid house being clean. You don't even know who I am."

Karen snapped because she resented her daughter's resistance to doing her laundry and keeping her room in order. Furthermore, Karen says that Miranda always finds a way to wiggle out of contributing to the family. Miranda, on the other hand, felt that her personal activities weren't valued by her mother. She associated doing chores with her mother nagging at her. The issue of running a household masked the deep distress of both women and threatened their relationship.

Beneath her aggravation, Karen's memories of her adolescence were simmering. "When I was sixteen, I had no option but to be responsible!" On Saturdays she cleaned bathrooms, scrubbed floors, and dusted furniture; on weekdays, she did the dishes after dinner. Feeling self-pity and sadness for how much work she was required to do, her response is, "It wasn't fair! And here's my spoiled daughter who gets away with doing almost nothing!" Part of her, too, is genuinely worried that her daughter is not learning the skills that she needs to be autonomous and self-reliant. Finally, she feels guilty because she is the one who indulged her daughter by not demanding that she pitch in when she was younger.

Her daughter is also feeling a little guilty because she knows she is taking advantage of her mother. She can't cop to it, so she gets defensive. She is thinking, "You just don't understand. It was different then than it is now. And I have to spend time with my friends." Miranda's accusation that her mother doesn't "know" her is a distracting ploy but also reveals a deeper injury that Karen needs to hear. Clearly, Miranda feels unseen by her mother in ways that are important to her.

Miranda, like most sixteen-year-olds, does not yet have the presence of mind or emotional maturity to take the matter in hand and make things right with her mother. Karen has to recognize her own unproductive reactivity, count to ten, and take a breath. She has to get in touch with the complexity of what is going on before she can talk to her daughter. Leaving the room for a short while, she regained her composure, then returned to sit down gently on Miranda's bed. "This is really difficult for me, honey. I know you aren't responsible for the way I grew up. But I do need you to help out; I'm tired when I come home from work, and you need to do your share. You've got to meet me halfway."

Name calling and getting on your high horse will get you nowhere. You have to listen to each other's feelings and point of view. Karen heard Miranda's unformulated message, "We have different priorities, Mom. My friends are the most important thing in my life." After listening to her mother's side, Miranda reluctantly admitted that the family value of reciprocity had something in it for her, too. After she and her mother worked out a schedule for when she could do her chores, without being asked, Karen turned her attention to Miranda's grievance. She said, "I want you to know that I do appreciate your commitment to basketball. How can I participate more in your athletics and show you how much I care?" Miranda asked her mother to come to the games more often. "It really means a lot to me to see you in the stands!"

If you, like Karen, treat your daughter like a guest and wait until she is sixteen to give her personal and household duties, you are in for an uphill battle to teach her that the world does not revolve around her. But you can still do it, if you are persistent. The biggest obstacle will be your own temptation to do the chores for her because it's easier than putting up with her resistance. She will try every trick to regain the favored position of being waited on, by ignoring her chores until the last minute before she has to leave the house, or insisting that she has homework, or making other excuses. Be fair and consistent with setting up times and standards for her to follow. Eventually, she will begin to feel pride in her own competence and capacity to participate in collaborating with you. Even if she is learning the skills, she may continue to fight with you or sulk about chores as long as she is at home. But when she's away at college, you may get a phone call from her in which she says, "Oh, by the way, Mom! I'm the only one who cleans our dorm room. Can you believe it?"

"Why Are You Hanging Out with That Girl?"

In Connie's junior year, with science class behind her, she and Georgina hit another impasse. Connie brought a new girlfriend home from school one night. When Connie introduced Jackie to her mother, Jackie barely acknowledged Georgina's smiling welcome. Then Georgina overheard the girls talking in the kitchen where they were getting a snack. Their conversation was punctuated with liberal use of the f-word and covert references to anticipated "partying" on the weekend. Later, after Jackie had gone home, Georgina found soda spilled on the floor in the family room, half-eaten bags of chips on the sofa, and gum stuck on the glass coffee table.

Georgina was outraged, and exploded at Connie, "Why are you spending time with a girl like this? She's obviously a bad influence on you. If she hasn't been taught manners, what kind of family does she come from? And what else is she up to?" Connie recoiled and stalked out of the room, but paused briefly to shout back at her mother, "You don't know anything about her, Mom. You're so mean. You don't understand anything!" On the surface, Georgina feels offended and disrespected because Connie is thwarting their house rules. Connie feels hurt and put on the defensive having to defend her new friend.

Beneath her righteousness, Georgina's gut feelings are fear and loss of control. She blows up the other girl's behavior into a character assassination: "Everything that I've taught Connie about being respectful of others and their property is going to go down the tubes. If this girl is that ignorant of how to behave, she must be into drugs and who knows what else." Georgina's catastrophic thinking deserves Connie's withdrawal and rejection of her mother. She is exactly right when she says to her mother, "You don't know anything!" Another teenage girl might have the presence of mind to say, "Mom, you are overreacting!" If her mother could respond rationally, they could begin to have a constructive conversation. But in most cases a good girl, like Connie, who wants to please and knows her mother's inflexibility, will be too hurt, confused, or afraid to confront her mother in this way. And, in the heat of the moment, most mothers would not be able to hear the truth.

Georgina hit a nerve by attacking Connie's friend. To criticize your daughter's friends is to face a closed door. Friends are the imperative in girls' high school lives. Teenagers use foul language to talk to each other. Obscenities set teenagers off from the civilized majority of adults. If required to by their parents, they are capable of restricting their expression, but for Georgina to blame her daughter's new friend and ignore Connie's vocabulary shows a woman who has blinded herself to reality. Georgina needed to realize that the work of setting standards for her daughter has been done; she doesn't have to worry that Connie is going to throw it all out.

After Georgina cooled off, she went to her daughter with an apology. "I'm sorry I overreacted to your friend. Will you forgive me? I'm sure she has qualities that you like and I don't know about. If you feel like sharing them with me, I'd like to hear." With her daughter's consent, Georgina went on to engage with Connie about the issues that bothered her. "I was shocked when I heard you using that kind of language. In my day that was completely unacceptable; but I'd like to understand what it's about for you and your friends."

Finally, Georgina moved to asking for Connie's cooperation about the house. "I know I have a compulsive streak about keeping the house perfect. I'll try to be more tolerant if you will agree to take responsibility for cleaning up after your friends and telling them about house rules." With this approach, Georgina demonstrates respect for Connie's judgment in choosing this friend. She shows she doesn't have all the answers. And she tries to work out an arrangement about house rules that takes into account both their perspectives.

"Try to See My Side"

One hot summer night, Angela's high-spirited, seventeen-year-old daughter, Elizabeth, told her mother that she was walking over to visit her grandmother who lived down the block. Suddenly, Angela realized that Elizabeth had been gone an unusually long time. Angela strolled over to her mother's house and discovered that Elizabeth had not been there at all. On the way back, she saw Elizabeth and her friends coming out of the park, heading home. Angela walked back, working herself into a simmering fury. She realized that instead of going to her grandmother's, Elizabeth had gone to the park to smoke dope.

Angela, a civilized professor of English literature at the local junior college, said, "I was so angry that she had broken our trust. I wanted to throttle her and embarrass her in front of her friends. But I restrained myself. As I was stewing, I remembered how often I had done the same thing as a teenager, defied my parents' trust and their rules. Strangely, those memories calmed me; I understood where she was coming from."

Later, after Elizabeth's friends left, Angela sat down to talk with her. "You told me that you were going to your grandmother's house, and I heard that you were never there. I saw you coming from the park, where I suspect you were smoking dope. I know how hard it is to not do what your friends are doing, but look at the position it puts me in, if I am not able to trust what you say. My trust in you is shaken by this." Elizabeth said, "Mom, I'm really sorry I broke your trust. I almost never smoke dope and I hardly ever lie to you. How can we work this out?" Angela said, "For starters, don't tell me you're going one place, then go somewhere else."

This was a situation in which the talk between mother and daughter was enough to reestablish their connection. Angela did not give Elizabeth a consequence for her deceit or for smoking marijuana; she knew that her daughter was genuinely contrite. She understood that if she forbade her daughter to ever smoke marijuana again, she had no way to enforce it. Because she and Elizabeth were close, Angela did not worry that her daughter was destructively involved with drugs. They had had many conversations about drug use. Elizabeth did well in school, socialized with friends, and cooperated within the family.

She was also the editor of the school yearbook. Angela was aware that Elizabeth was involved in some experimentation with drugs and alcohol. Angela managed this confrontation beautifully, because she knew her daughter well and she looked at the whole picture. She both engaged Elizabeth about lying and gave her room to have her peer life in an honest way. Elizabeth was affected by her mother's feeling of betrayal and concern; Angela was affected by Elizabeth's regret and desire to reestablish trust with her. They each felt encouraged and closer for the experience of meeting in this way.

"You Lied to Me!"

Lying for teenagers represents the split between the "I" she hopes you will preserve and the "I" she is with her friends. She wants you to continue seeing her as a "sweet young thing" both because she thinks it makes you happy to see her that way and because she doesn't want to give up that identity too quickly or dramatically herself. Yet she needs her own place. The more whole she can be with you without losing her privacy, the more alive she (and you) will feel, and the stronger your relationship will be.

It's critical that you do not get hung up on the refrain, "You lied to me!" as the only issue at hand. You will drive your daughter away from you. What kind of lie was it? And why is she lying? No matter how old she is, rather than simply getting angry at her, find out and accept that she has lied to you. Then you will have an opportunity to turn things around with her and get your relationship on a new footing.

Don't Just React: Act

To act instead of just reacting to your adolescent daughter means to take the initiative. Look for ways to spend time with your daughter in high school. When she is a freshman and sophomore, volunteer to drive whenever she and her friends need a ride, even if it's inconvenient. Once she or her friends get their driver's licenses, you will see much less of her. Being available in the in-between times in her life maximizes your chance to provide guidance, nurturing, or help when she seeks it or to intervene when you see the necessity.

Do something constructive for your relationship at each stage by making time alone with her, a time when you can invite her to share thoughts and experiences. Up to and perhaps including middle school, opportunities for such intimate moments may happen naturally. But when she enters high school, you will probably have to schedule a breakfast or dinner alone or take a walk together.

Try to have a few minutes in the day with her when you both share an event in a non-loaded way, just to keep in touch. Studious Danielle said, "In my freshman and sophomore years, my mother would come in and sit on my bed to say good night. She'd ask how my day went; I got to complain, sometimes about her, and tell her the good things that had happened. I really liked it because I had her all to myself away from my two younger sisters and my father. My little sister was having major emotional problems, so my mother had to spend a long time each night with her. But no matter how tired she was, she always came to talk to me afterward. She listened to me and told me how important I was to my sister; she taught me how much influence I can have on others." For her college application, Danielle wrote about this bedtime ritual with her mother. She felt these conversations profoundly influenced her life.

Show and Tell

Demonstrate your love for and acceptance of your daughter as a person separate from her behavior. When both of you are truly listening to each other, tell her that she can come to you at any time. You know that she will make mistakes, but you prefer to hear about what's going on rather than that she lie to you. Make up and forgive her for transgressions as soon as you can.

Show her, as well as tell her, that you will be there for her when she has a problem, that you will pick her up at any time of day or night if she gets into an uncomfortable situation. Tell her it doesn't have to be an emergency; she should be able to ask for help when she feels she needs it. If you are called in the middle of the night to pick her up and she is reluctant to talk on the drive home, do not ask for an explanation immediately, however much you'd like to have it. Bring up the incident the next day and discuss it with her.

Offer positive events such as a family meal as a reason for her staying home one night so that you don't get into a negative cycle of demanding she be home to do the chores she thinks she hates to do. Give her a choice of times. Say, for instance, "We'd like to have a family breakfast or dinner this weekend. Which day would be good for you?" Create a nice atmosphere for the meal even if she sulks at the beginning. Some families begin the weekend with a family dinner every Friday, after which the teenagers are free to go out.

Your feelings of concern are evident when you have just the right meal waiting for her after a particularly grueling cross-country meet, when you bring her a new CD by her favorite rock musician, or when you tell her about a movie you think she would enjoy. These are not the only ways to communicate love to your daughter. When you notice that she is unhappy and uncommunicative, put a little bunch of wildflowers in a vase on her dresser for her to find, with or without a note. Don't pressure her to talk to you about what's bothering her; let the flower arrangement, gift, or note speak for itself. Tracking down a book she needs from the public library is just as important as having a heart-to-heart talk with her about a girlfriend who's being mean to her or a guy she likes who doesn't seem to know she's alive.

If you're out shopping and see a blouse or skirt that you think is her style, buy it and take it home for her to try on with the attitude,

"Maybe this will work, maybe not. If not, you can take it back and look for something that you like better." Don't be invested in the outcome; it's the gesture that counts. If she storms into the house after school, flushed and hot, rushes to her room, and slams the door without a word, wait five minutes, then bring her a cold drink. You could ask her if she wants to talk, but if she indicates that she'd rather be alone, put down her drink and go on your way.

Another wonderful way of staying connected to your daughter is by sharing reading material with her. Whether you read biographies, mystery stories, or magazine articles, pass along those you think might interest her. Reading the same stories can become ground for future discussions or can simply be shared knowledge that makes you feel closer to each other. Books with women protagonists provide role modeling and provocative material for discussion. Sharon read to her daughter, Rebecca, at bedtime throughout grammar school and shared books with her in middle school. Seventeen-year-old Rebecca said, "Last year, I read *Promiscuities* by Naomi Wolf and gave it to my mom to read. It made me feel better about myself, my sexual feelings and explorations. I think every teenage girl should read it." Sharing this book with her mother was a way for Rebecca to communicate some intense feelings and experiences that would have been too private for her to put into words herself.

Don't Give Up on Her

If communication with your daughter really breaks down, take her out of her environment for a few hours, a day, a weekend. A long walk, a drive, or a visit to the beach or mountains may help her shed her attitudes for a while. Hang in there—remember, you love her and she loves you.

Some parents give up when their daughters begin to move away. Their attitude is, "Well, if that's the way she wants it; if that's the way she acts, I'll just go about my own business and leave her to find out the hard way." Cindy, tense and forlorn, said, "As soon as I started standing up to my mom as a freshman, she got in my face and said, 'O.K., if you want to argue with me about everything, you can just walk home from school and make your own dinner while I work late.' " Abandoned by her mother, Cindy had to tough out high school on her own. She said, "I really missed her being there, but I couldn't just accept everything she said anymore. I had to live my own life. I started talking to my Spanish teacher, who took pity on me. I don't know what I would have done without her. She suggested I try to get my mom to see a counselor with me, but my mom refused. She thought it was a waste of money." Unfortunately, this mother couldn't hold the strong maternal center her daughter needed as she separated.

A punitive, fatalistic, or passive approach can lead to your daughter feeling abandoned at the very time she needs you in more complicated ways than she did as a child. Rise to the occasion. Vilifying adolescence will only alienate you from her more. As one girl said to me: "Why do adults always talk about adolescence as if it were a disease?" Your insights and relational skills will help you negotiate this critical passage without losing yourself or losing touch with your daughters.

Girls develop their strengths through experimentation. They are sometimes impulsive, misguided, and irresponsible. They learn by making mistakes and learning from them. Don't let your anxiety about your daughter getting it right stand in her way. If she is to develop, she cannot remain the same girl she was in middle school or grammar school. Her childhood self will sustain her if you can tolerate her erratic self-exploration as she goes back and forth on every issue every day, week, or month with each new situation.

As her mother you need to be the constant factor offering love and support while she tests herself. You will not always be able to "measure" your daughter's development; she will not always make the "right" decisions that lead to these positive goals. But she must investigate every arena. It is important for you as a parent to let her find her way and not to overreact and try to talk her out of or into making the mature choice, even from your well-meaning point of view.

Remember, your daughter is confused and changing. She may quickly and adamantly adopt the worldview offered by her peers: that a teenager has the right to call the shots and make her own decisions about social life and risk taking. After all, she may think, this is where the fun is, and this is how I will be popular. Our task is to stay in close touch with our daughters as we give them the freedom and privacy to have their own lives within the world they belong to.

You as parents must change too, but you at least have been adolescents before. Your challenge is to listen, empathize, support, and solve problems. Whenever you connect with your daughter, you are showing her how to connect with others. As you express to her the feelings and anxieties that often accompany a decision—for example, to sleep with someone—you will give her the language to identify her own hesitations and fears when facing that decision. If you communicate well, she will learn both to honor her own needs and to seek healthy intimacy with others.

Let her take risks and test herself. Let her spend the time she needs in the underworld. Then let her return home. Your understanding will insure that she will not feel so stifled, insecure, or unloved that she has to find relief or seek love and attention by acting out in self-destructive ways. The way she chooses to handle stress and conflict during her adolescence will be a pattern for the means she will use as an adult. It is best if she learns to confront the knotty issues and analyze what is really going on rather than avoid them through excessive drinking and drug use. She will take these lessons and depend on them for the rest of her life.

2 ♋

$\mathcal{B}$ody *Language*

FOOD, PIERCINGS, AND CLOTHES

"$\mathcal{M}$y mom doesn't want to take any responsibility for her effect on my feelings about my body." Danielle's lament reveals her strong desire for her mother, Marguerite, to recognize the deep connection between them about body image. Do not underestimate the power of your attitude toward your own body and hers on your teenage daughter. Liking her body and having a healthy appreciation for her physical needs are the basis for self-confidence in a girl. In order to like her body, however, your daughter will probably have to fight the cultural ideal of a model-thin shape. Both Danielle and Marguerite are medium-boned, normal-sized women. Like all normal women, they too feel the effect of the skeletal societal images. Although women of all ages are now aware of this problem, eating disorders are still rampant.

"It's My Body"

It is a challenge for a teenage girl to stay connected to her body-based knowledge, to her instincts. *Listening* to what her body tells her about her appetite, sexual desire, and impulse to move is at odds with what the media and her friends are telling her. She hears the message everywhere: "Deprive yourself of food and exercise to burn fat with the goal of being thin." No commercials and few friends say, "Listen to what your body wants." Yet claiming her body is the center of your daughter's selfhood; out of that core comes her judgment about experimenting and risk taking. If she hates her body, she will be careless with it. Promiscuous sexuality, drinking alcohol to excess, smoking marijuana every day, or trying "hard" drugs may become her way of acting out that hatred.

Andrea, a high school dance teacher with a strong, muscular body, said, "Everyone thinks there are two categories of girls—those who have eating disorders and those who don't. But my guess is that 90 percent of girls are obsessing about eating and not feeling good about their bodies. They use a system of reward and punishment for eating. They say to themselves, 'If I exercise it off, if I run ten miles or go to dance class, I can eat this.' They are always asking themselves, 'How many calories did I burn?'"

Kate, who plans to major in drama and has a healthy body image and a normal weight, said of her dance friends, "In ballet and gymnastics, the girls are always comparing the perfect body. In the dance world, the body image thing is connected to a superior attitude. Dancers try to separate themselves from 'the others,' those who have anorexia or bulimia. They say, 'You don't understand, it's part of the dance world. I need to lose five pounds.' It's so weird."

Andrea is vehemently trying to change this attitude in her modern dance program. She points out and rejects standard cultural messages that associate beauty with weight loss; for example, she asks students to eschew such comments as, "You look good; have you lost weight?" Instead, she encourages them to focus on how they feel when they move, emphasizing strength, flexibility, and competence. She teaches body types in her class—endomorph, ectomorph, mesomorph—and dance history, which shows the change in body shape fashion and dance style over the years. Andrea also leads a body awareness group on campus, where girls can talk confidentially about family and peer assaults on their comfort with their bodies.

Mirror, Mirror on the Wall

In the fairy tale *Snow White,* the wicked stepmother's question about beauty to the mirror can be rephrased for girls and their mothers: "Mirror, mirror, on the wall, who's the thinnest of us all?" Cultural pressure about weight is unrelenting for women. We have been indoctrinated from birth with the thin ideal from our mothers, fathers, girlfriends, aunts, and cousins. Television, movies, and the fashion industry use hype about weight loss to cash in on women's misery. The envious stepmother is each girl's self-destructive shadow. Our daughters turn their own envy and sense of helplessness against themselves in the face of an impossible ideal.

At puberty a girl is trying to take ownership of her body, to separate her self-worth from her weight and her looks. Andrea said, "I see many girls using dance as a vehicle for claiming themselves. But at midlife, a girl's mother may also be redefining herself and doing it with a tuck or liposuction. If she is having plastic surgery, her daughter is going to assess her own looks in terms of needing correction. If her mother is dieting, she is going to look at her own body critically."

The mirror can be a valuable tool for girls. At the moment the earth opened and Hades seized her, Persephone was leaning down, entranced by the beauty of a lovely flower. She was looking at her own loveliness. Standing alone in front of a mirror locked in the bathroom or her bedroom, a girl undergoing transformation searches for the truth of who she is in her reflection as she prepares to meet a confusing outer world. With a dance teacher like Andrea, she finds her truth in the mirror instead of losing it.

Face Your Own Demons

Face your feelings about your own body as an adult woman. Are you constantly on a diet? Do you bemoan (to her) not being the size 2 you were before you had children? Did your mother push you to eat at meals, then turn around and say, "You would look better if you lost five pounds, darling"? Perhaps, without knowing it, you have become the envious stepmother by reinforcing the cultural stereotype for the daughter you love. Your unconscious competitiveness can show itself in many ways. Bonnie tried on her senior prom dress a month after she got it; it was a little snug on her. Her mother, Gayle, then tried it on to show her daughter how much better it fit her.

Bonnie was devastated. "I couldn't believe she did that; I was dying inside. And when I burst into tears, she just looked at me like I was crazy and said, 'Oh, don't be so sensitive, Bonnie. You've just been eating too much, and you have to learn to control yourself if you want to look good in your clothes.'" Girls have critical "shadow" detectors; Bonnie knew her mother was being competitive with her, but Gayle turned away and refused to acknowledge it. Bonnie felt betrayed.

Gayle may have imagined she was just joining in the fun by comparing the dress on their different bodies. She remembered such repartee with her teenage girlfriends: she had always been the envied one with the slim figure. But Gayle had never owned up to hurting the other girls when she tried on their clothes. Secretly, she had gloried in the adulation she had received for having the naturally "perfect" body. These were shadow issues she had ignored. Defending herself against a fear of growing older, she regressed to her adolescence and disregarded her daughter's feelings. In order to regain Bonnie's trust she had to take up her own "shadow" and be authentic. Sadly, many loving mothers do not ever get the picture. They continue to fight unconsciously for a place as the "thin queens" in covert, destructive ways with their daughters and friends.

You are your daughter's original mirror for the way she feels about her body. You may unthinkingly contribute to her feeling bad about herself and distort her self-image. Never criticize your daughter's size or shape. Geri recounted a shameful occasion for her when her family was out to dinner at a restaurant. As she reached for another piece of bread, her mother, Pam, teasingly slapped her hand. "You've had enough," she said coyly to her daughter. Geri felt wounded but didn't let on that she was hurt. Instead, the incident added to her fear of becoming fat.

On the surface, Pam was only aware of a feeling of camaraderie with Geri, summed up as, "We girls have to watch our weight." She doesn't realize that she has bought into the self-destructive thin image and is subtly forcing her daughter to accept it. The darker side of her message is, "If I have to suffer and keep my weight down, so do you."

Think about the priority you are modeling about meals. One girl who struggled with feelings of inferiority about her body was looking forward to Thanksgiving, to being off from school, relaxing, and enjoying her family and the feast. Before the meal was served, her mother and the other women started talking about having to go for a hike to burn off calories in order to be able to eat. The problem for the young woman wasn't that they included a hike in the day but their emphasis on controlling their weight. "This is just like school," she thought, as her spirits sank and her depressing thoughts about her body welled up. The day was spoiled for her.

Fathers, too, can hit sensitive areas in girls' feelings about food. Jade's family was health conscious but not weight conscious. "I managed to ignore the message that was going on all around me until junior year, because I had a group of friends who weren't crazed about their weight. But it's everywhere, so it finally came in." In spring of Jade's junior year, she and her parents were on a trip, looking over colleges for her. They went out to dinner at a fancy restaurant. Jade said, "My mom and I were going to share a dessert. She went off to the ladies' room and my father said to me, 'Are you sure you should be getting dessert?' I got so mad. I just blew up. I said 'That's so rude! I'm not speaking to you anymore.' And I didn't talk to him for the rest of the trip."

Although it was the first time she remembers her father referring to her weight, Jade was furious and hurt. "I was mad and I knew he was wrong, but I also thought, Why aren't I enough the way I am?" Jade wanted him to embrace who she is, not try to edit her. In his defense, she says, "I know my father is trying to equip me for a world that is tough and competitive. But his way isn't the way to do it." Instead of chipping away at his daughter in the name of priming her for success, Jade's father had to work on changing his ingrained attitude toward women's bodies. It was not a comment he would imagine making to his son.

No Blame

If you feel pangs of doubt or remorse about your own conduct in similar situations, don't despair. Blaming yourself will not help; it's not your fault. You are not alone; most women were brought up trying to lose weight and looking for success in achieving thinness. Becoming aware of your attitude and the way it leaks out and poisons your daughter is an amazing first step. Instead of being unconsciously competitive, you can use your awareness to help counteract the cultural message for her and for yourself.

In middle school or high school, when she talks about being uncomfortable with gaining weight, do not placate her with a quick, pat answer like "You're fine." Sit down, listen, and respond in a thoughtful manner. Examine your feelings and thoughts before you say anything to her; you must be honest with yourself to come up with a helpful response. Girls need positive messages and influence from mothers and fathers.

"I'm Not Hungry, Mom."

You need to separate the struggles that you had about food from hers. Jill realized one morning that for the past couple of weeks her sixteen-year-old daughter, Eleanor, had been rushing out the door to her car pool without sitting down to her usual breakfast of toast and juice. Feeling a little worried, she watched what Eleanor ate after school and at dinnertime. She noticed that her daughter was pushing her food around on the plate at meals instead of eating, and avoiding contact with the whole family. She seemed preoccupied and edgy.

Jill's worry was exacerbated by the fact that she had had problems with eating when she was in her late teens and early twenties. Jill was always trying to lose ten pounds, thinking she would fit in and be more accepted by other kids. She remembered obsessing about food and sometimes fasting for days to fit into a slinky dress for a special date. Jill had lived into accepting her body in her mid-twenties, and her adolescent self-loathing had faded to a sad memory. She had been careful with Eleanor to emphasize health with food, instead of weight. As she watched her daughter reject food, however, her old bad feelings came back to her. Jill's fear that Eleanor was enduring similar self-torture was almost unbearable to her mother.

Although not eating is one possible signal of your daughter having difficulty with her body image, don't jump to conclusions. You know her well enough to know that she is bothered because her usual eating patterns are disrupted, but she could have lost her appetite for many reasons. Balance your parental concern with the understanding that she is in the throes of change in many areas while she is forming an identity.

Jill found some time alone with Eleanor (not during the morning rush or in the midst of her doing homework at night) to sit down and talk. She told her she'd noticed her skipping meals and avoiding chatting. Jill gently asked, "What's going on with you, honey? I can tell there is something up." Jill did not interpret Eleanor's behavior, nor did she blame her for being out of sorts. Eleanor said with a mixture of embarrassment, excitement, and distress, "Oh, Mom. There's this guy I've liked for so long; now I think he's interested in me." Jill was immensely relieved and switched gears to remembering how important and unsettling a relationship with a new boy could be. She said, "Do you want to talk about it? Or would you like me to make you something special to eat?" Eleanor said, "I'll have some hot chocolate, if you'll make it for me, but I don't want to talk about the guy right now." Feeling thankful, Jill went off to prepare Eleanor's drink.

If your daughter's response to your inquiry about her seemingly not eating is a dismissive, "Oh, Mom, there's nothing wrong, don't worry," or a rejecting, "I don't want to talk about it," persist a little to see if you can break through her veneer. Back off if she is firm in her rejection, but quietly continue to observe her eating and bring it up again if you continue to see patterns that concern you. Tell her that in order for you not to worry she must talk to you about what is going on with her. If she is vomiting, losing weight rapidly, or becoming depressed or anxious, do not condemn her for her behavior. Express your love and support and get professional help right away.

"You Are Keeping Me in Prison!"

Stay tuned in to what she is needing from you and what she is struggling with internally. Consider her change in eating patterns a clue. Ask her what she is feeling and thinking. Fourteen-year-old Marla tearfully told her mother that her parents were too strict with her. "You have no idea how important it is for me to be out with my friends on weekends. Nobody, absolutely nobody, I know has to be home on a weekend night by eleven o'clock or is restricted to one night out a weekend. I cannot have any social life with those rules."

Peggy was astonished that Marla was so upset that she had virtually stopped eating; their family had always gone to bed early because both Peggy and her husband, Steve, were early risers. She asked Marla, "But what can you possibly do in this small town after eleven o'clock?" Marla said, "We just hang out together, Mom. And most of the time kids don't even go out until ten. I'm really going to die or do something drastic if I can't be with my friends."

Peggy was moved by Marla's distress and said she would think about it, talk to Steve, and decide on a plan. After she conferred with her husband, she called a few friends who had older teenagers to ask their opinions. Every one of them told her: "Teenage social life is nightlife after ten o'clock. You have to compromise if you want your daughter to have friends. Otherwise she will be isolated or start lying to you." Peggy and Steve agreed to a midnight curfew for Marla's freshman year, on the condition that she wake one of them up when she came in to let them know she was home. She could also go out both nights if it didn't interfere with her homework. If Marla showed she could keep her agreement with them, her parents would renegotiate for a later time each year. Marla was overjoyed to have the freedom to be with her friends. She no longer had to control her eating to feel empowered. Through expressing herself to her mother and having her need met, she both gained autonomy and strengthened their bond.

"I Feel Fat."

When something goes wrong in a girl's life that she feels she cannot change, she often tends to find fault with her body, usually criticizing herself for being fat. "I feel fat" is a common refrain for girls, code for "I don't like who I am" or "I hate myself." Danielle said, "The most important thing my mom ever said to me about my body image struggle was, 'Danielle, this is displaced anxiety. When you are stressed out at school, either academically or socially, you worry about your weight.' I really think that's true." Danielle had to deal not only with her own distress in this area but with her younger sister's battle for life with anorexia. "Because it was a near-death experience for my sister, I feel I'm immature to have any feelings about myself."

When Persephone was in the underworld, she refused to eat. Near death, away from her beloved mother, she was homesick. But, the myth says, she still had hope in her heart. Anorexic girls are disconnected from themselves and their mothers. Girls who refuse to eat need to be called back from their isolated secret world to their bodies. They have gotten lost in the shadowy underworld of self-starvation. Their hope is that someone will find them.

Many girls also become obsessed with hatred for a single physical characteristic, for example, "My nose is too big." The extremes of this self-loathing are self-destructive behaviors, but the milder phases of body rejection, such as dieting, a preoccupation with how much she eats, or how many calories she is burning, are more common. It is wise to be cautious about addressing this issue; it is so loaded for girls.

As her mother you can help build a sympathetic relationship in which she is able to express the underlying issues that are troubling her, and then help her gain some control in the areas that are giving her difficulty. Sometimes just airing the difficulties in a safe situation can relieve a girl and take the pressure off her feeling that the only thing she can control is her body.

Danielle said, "My most explosive issue with my mother is my body image and food issues. She says, 'What can I do?' I just want her to listen. I want to tell her what is going on in my head, how I see all these ultra-skinny girls at school and it really bothers me that I'm built bigger. At home she and my dad are always talking about eating better to lose weight, and it all just sort of jams together in my mind. Talking to her about it at least helps to get it out of my head." Be available to listen. But just because she is struggling with her body image does not mean she wants to talk about it all the time. Be attentive to her cues.

Never, Ever Tell Your Daughter She Needs to Lose Weight

You are the model for your daughter's feminine identity. You can choose what you model. Girls are unanimous in their view that mothers can set an example for their daughters by not obsessing about thinness.

Kate had a clear directive for parents to avoid exacerbating their daughters' difficulties with body image. "Moms and dads always need to support their girls and never, ever say, 'You need to lose weight.' Some of my friends have moms who tell them that, and then they'll say, 'Well, my mom's right, you know.' And I think, Oh, you make me sick." Parents should always deliver the message, "I love you the way you are." You have to mean what you say, or your daughter will see through your false attempts to make her feel better. And she will hear all the places that you slip up with your true feeling that she ought to be thinner.

If she confides in you that she dislikes her body, communicate your own battle or coming to terms with yours. Remember what a confusing time it was. "Who am I?" often phrased as "Who likes me?" is a common question. When will my body stop changing, and what will it be like when it does? Talk to her about how you coped.

If you are on a constant diet, use your awareness of your daughter's environment to help you change. Ally with her. Do something about it for yourself and for her. Stop talking about weight and focus on nutritious foods, health, and well-being. Stop weighing yourself and sign up for a few sessions of Feldenkrais or Alexander techniques of postural integration where you will learn to trust your inner perception of your body. Get wise to the media and its manipulation of your feelings about yourself. Shift your focus to pampering your body. Whether it be long, luxurious bubble baths or taking a nap one afternoon on the weekend, you will be paying attention to your body in a valuing instead of critical way.

Examine what you want to change in your life, and ask her what she wants to change in hers. Redirect your own energy as you help your daughter redirect hers. Emphasize the activities that you do well, and encourage her to name those that she enjoys and excels at. Pride and confidence in work, sports, or play changes your perception of your body. Your body doesn't change, only your attitude toward it. Talk to her about blazing trails as a goal, setting new standards for other girls and women by shedding the old refrain, "If only I were thin, everything would be all right." If both you and your daughter are trapped in a negative obsession about your bodies, find a counselor who works with mothers and daughters on these issues. Or encourage her to speak to a counselor at school or ask her if she would like to go to a private therapist. You and she will feel empowered if you take action to break the cycle.

"How Many Calories Did I Burn?"

The demeaning of women's bodies the way they *are* goes on in insidious ways every moment of every day. In school cafeterias, boys and girls often make negative comments about what girls are eating. Even the servers behind the counter sometimes banter with girls, "You're going to eat all that?" or "That much food for a little girl like you?" One high school had an awareness day when students took a pledge: "I will not comment on other people's food choices."

Unfortunately, even if the kids are not talking about it, they are thinking about it.

Eighteen-year-old Rae said, "When a group of my girlfriends went to Baja on spring break, the skinny girls were all standing in front of the mirror saying, 'I'm too fat.' It makes someone like me who's a normal size feel bad. I think, if they're fat, what am I? But I am healthy. I dance a lot." Rae, well-adjusted, an excellent student, and a successful actress, still feels insecure around the self-distortions of her friends. The "thin" problem is contagious and contaminating. It is imperative, therefore, for a girl to be able to retreat to a mother who has a different outlook.

High school girls who travel and do community service are confronted with formidable culture shock when they return to the disturbed atmosphere that swirls around eating in most American middle-class high schools. Kaylie came back to her junior year after a summer spent in a poverty-stricken village in Ecuador with the Amigos program. "There are so many girls with eating disorders at my school; one of my friends got bulimic this summer. Girls don't eat or they talk about eating only bagels or about working out three times a day to burn calories; they're worried all the time. Someone gave us an African dance workout in one of our classes. A lot of girls missed the experience of what they were doing because all they are thinking about is burning calories. Girls are so competitive."

Jolted by her girlfriends' self-starvation, Kaylie described how she had been hungry all summer in the Ecuadorean village because there was never enough food. "My host family and all the people were incredible, generous, warm, and friendly. They shared everything with me. But when I visited even poorer families, the little kids would always say, 'I'm hungry, I'm hungry.' I didn't know what to do; I wanted to feed them every day. I couldn't, though I tried to give them crackers and cookies from the little store. I wanted to be able to help, but it was so impossible." When Kaylie came home, she was overjoyed to have an abundance of food to eat again. It was deeply troubling for her to see her friends in this narcissistic and self-destructive spiral.

You can hear the contagion and competition for who can eat the least in these comments: "My friends are all thin." Everyone talks about eating: "I ate so much today" or "I'll be a good girl and not eat that" or "I haven't eaten much today and I'm so tired" or "I'm too tired to eat, I'm going to bed instead." You cannot change what your daughter is exposed to at school. But if you are self-aware, you can offer her an environment at home that goes against the cultural pressures and provides some relief.

"Maybe You'd Like to Stay Home Today"

As her body develops, your daughter will have to grow into it, whatever its shape, become familiar with her menstrual rhythm, and learn how to take care of herself during her period. Weight gain is normal in early adolescence; after several years, girls' bodies settle into the shape their genes determine for them. Nutrition and exercise will affect your daughter's body.

Your daughter needs to know the foods to eat and those to avoid in order to minimize PMS, or premenstrual syndrome, and how to treat cramping with mild exercise or a hot water bottle, or finding what works for her. Tapping into her cycle also includes her learning the value of taking a break from the pressures of school or routine activities either while menstruating or when feeling overwhelmed by the demands of school or her friends. She needs to learn to listen to her body.

Dissatisfaction with her weight may be closely related to your daughter's menstruation. If she is feeling bloated and grouchy, and is having cramps but is not changing her schedule in any way to address these discomforts, she may be depriving herself of food in a misguided attempt to take care of herself. Suggest that she take a day off to lounge around, soak in a hot tub, read, and write in her journal.

Offer to rub her neck and shoulders or to find her a simple herbal remedy for her cramps.

Give her permission to nurture herself in special ways during this time of the month. Let her take time out from her usual school schedule to do something she loves. Going to an art exhibit or visiting the beach will help her attune herself. Letting go of the customary demands will have a cumulative effect and contribute to her vitality the rest of the month. She needs to use the time to renew herself physically and psychically, instead of getting strung out and either eating too much or not eating at all. If you are still menstruating, show her that you take care of yourself in these ways during your period. If you tend to menstruate at the same time, play hooky together.

Body in Motion

Instead of commenting on her size or weight, encourage your daughter to move in a healthy way. Physical activity promotes body awareness and emotional balance. Whether she walks, dances, or plays soccer or basketball, she will feel better all the time. Regular exercise has been shown to be one of the strongest indicators of physical self-confidence and emotional self-esteem in women. Emphasize fitness and healthy moderation, instead of the calorie-burning mentality that girls focus on. A stable exercise program with regular nutritious meals will be a supportive substratum for her demanding life.

Kate said, "It's better for a mom to point out unhealthy habits that a girl is into, like not getting enough exercise or not eating right. I'm not into sports, but I love to rollerblade. If my mother sees me being grumpy, she will suggest that I put on my skates and go out. I always feel better afterward and can concentrate on my homework or shrug off what's bugging me about my friends." A new ideal of beauty and sex appeal has emerged as girls and women work out and develop their muscles.

Again, your example as her mother is important for her. Kate's mother, Ellen, sees a pattern in her daughter that she recognizes in herself. "I have to walk or hike at least once a week or my mood disintegrates." If your daughter sees you doing regular exercise and eating healthy meals, she will be more likely to do the same. If you are always counting how many minutes you did the Stairmaster as a measure for whether or not you can eat dessert, you will reinforce the climate that she endures at school.

Food is fuel and nurturance; exercise raises your natural endorphins and promotes strength. Both should be built into a healthy way of life. Mothers often promote their daughters' participation in sports or dance but neglect their own fitness. With her busy courtroom schedule, Maureen, a lawyer, had never found time to exercise. When her daughter, Jamie, was in eighth grade and joined a soccer team, Maureen saw her rapidly developing daughter begin to grow in self-confidence. Maureen arranged her schedule so she could go to the games. She saw Jamie—usually awkward and shy, with her arms wrapped around her body in an attempt to hide—running from the field to greet her, cheeks flushed, head held high, and arms outstretched.

Maureen, meanwhile, was battling early menopausal symptoms—headaches, hot flashes, and exacerbated premenstrual syndrome. Her gynecologist had prescribed exercise as a first step. But Maureen let it slip in the face of her professional and family commitments with Jamie and her younger son, Kevin. Her husband, Tim, never missed a day of running because he had established a regimen before he married from which he had never deviated. Like many women, Maureen had trouble taking time for herself.

When Jamie entered high school, she was unsure about whether to continue playing soccer because she wasn't one of the best players. Seeing how Jamie had thrived since joining the team, Maureen encouraged her to persist just for fitness and fun. Maureen had been mulling over her own upbringing, when most girls didn't play sports. She felt robbed of something essential that had continued to affect her health as a woman. Jamie's indecision tipped the scale for Maureen. She resolved to go in to work an hour later each morning in order to walk. Maureen told Jamie her new plan and said, "I'll support you doing soccer and help you plan your time to get your homework done if you'll help me stick to my resolution to walk every day." Making this agreement struck a deep chord in both Maureen and Jamie; it was a reciprocal energy builder. They would compare notes every few days about how they were doing. Maureen related to her daughter and dramatically improved her own health at the same time.

"I've Got to Do It for the Team, Mom."

If your daughter is involved in competitive sports, you need to be in touch with her about the coaching she is receiving. Monitor whether she is determining her body's limits or whether her coach is legislating them. Be alert to the eating habits the coach is advocating for his athletes. Coaches can encourage team spirit, promote girls' active, assertive use of their bodies, and support a cooperative drive.

Coaches can also negatively influence girls by reinforcing their obsession with weight. Toni, a tall, talented athlete, said, "When I played basketball, I was the starting point guard. Suddenly, in senior year my coach said, 'You're too heavy, you're not running fast enough.' He kept me a half-hour after practice to do laps to get me to lose weight. I got so discouraged that I eventually quit." This is a common scenario and one that you want to keep close tabs on with your daughter.

Research has shown that girls perform better on an all-girls' sports team (boys perform better on a coed team), where female bonding encourages each member to do her best for the sake of the group. She doesn't have to worry about what the boys on the team think of her. But some girls prefer coed teams. Each girl is different, so treat your daughter as an individual and let her choose her sport or activity.

When your daughter becomes physically active and feels the rewards, she will never turn back. Not only will she improve her mental and physical performance, but she will also feel more confident in her body and its wishes. If she listens to her body's needs, she will avoid the never-ending diet that so many women still pursue well into adulthood.

Body Decor

A girl's body often becomes a canvas for self-expression in middle school and high school. She will paint, draw, and pierce her skin, and dye her hair. As she does so, she designs herself. Self-decorating design is healthy, playful experimentation, but it can also move into self-injury that is destructive to your daughter. Use your wits and your instinct to know when it is a good thing and when it is not.

Fourteen-year-old Tammy said, "I'm into doing henna tattoos for a $55 fee at birthday parties and at kids' clothes and toy stores. I love it! Now I'm redecorating my room Indian style. My parents won't let me get my ears pierced until I'm sixteen. But I don't feel bad because there are trade-offs; my friend Delia has pierced ears but can't have henna tattoos because her dad doesn't like them." Tammy, secure in her relationship with her mother and father, is being an entrepreneur with her favorite body decoration. Her mother, Jean, supports this outlet for self-design. Jean had pierced ears, but "I found it more trouble than I thought it was worth." Her husband balks at the permanent process of ear piercing because he feels it's a sign of girls growing up too fast. At sixteen, Tammy will be able to make her own decision.

Piercing as body adornment has undergone a radical evolution since the fifties. Some parents still associate the image of girls with pierced ears with being called a hussy or a whore. In the nineties, multiple ear piercings are commonplace. The controversy now centers around tattoos and body piercings, especially of the nose, tongue, nipple, and belly button. With all this hardware on her body considered normal, you are likely to have some serious debates with your daughter about the extremes to which she wants to go in permanently decorating her body.

Self-Mutilation

Body decoration that serves to express a girl's personality must be distinguished from self-mutilation. When a girl's self-image becomes distorted, she becomes a mirror for what she thinks others expect of her. Feeling empty and unworthy, she disconnects from her true self. Many girls are cutting their bodies with razors and knives in order to see their blood and release feelings of frustration and to affirm their own aliveness. Girls who cut and hurt themselves are disturbed. They are often quiet perfectionists who injure their bodies because they feel ugly, ashamed, or isolated. They are expressing bottled-up suffering that has no other outlet. In the moment of cutting into their flesh, they relieve their inner pain by inflicting outer pain. The relief is only temporary because the self-loathing is still there. Girls need education and consciousness-raising about their bodies. If they are comparing themselves to movie stars and fashion models, they must learn to discriminate between media illusion and real life; real bodies aren't airbrushed.

Corinne, a therapist who works with adolescent girls, said, "I give girls journals so they can write down their thoughts and feelings, reflect on themselves, rather than it all being a soupy mess in their heads and their hearts. Instead of impulsively acting out—drinking, doing drugs, cutting—they can tap into an inner world. Writing is a self-soothing activity."

Fifteen-year-old Sheila had been cutting herself with razor blades and burning her arms and legs with lighted cigarettes for several years. She was a delicate, wraithlike girl with fair skin and a soft voice. Her mother, Fran, worked full-time and was consumed with controlling the chaos created by her eighteen-year-old son, Daryl, who robbed grocery stores and stole cars. Her husband had abandoned the family years before. Overwhelmed by this adversity, Fran could barely get through the day and meet the needs of her youngest child, eight-year-old Lynna. Sheila quietly withdrew to the bathroom and her bedroom and took out her feelings of frustration on her body.

When she was fifteen, a teacher noticed the scars on her arms and called Fran to suggest that Sheila see a counselor. Sheila described her cutting to the therapist, and Corinne gave her a journal and asked her to write down her feelings at home. Corinne also made an agreement with Sheila that she would show her any fresh scars each time they met. She did not insist that Sheila stop cutting immediately because she had first to build trust and enable Sheila to substitute naming her pain for acting it out.

Corinne said, "She could have lied to me, but she had no reason to; I was listening to her anguish. She would read from her journal, the naked truth in poetry and prose, and show me the new marks on her skin. Gradually, she cut herself less, felt happier, and finally stopped." Sheila said, "Instead of making myself feel the pain, I could write about how much it hurts. It gave me a whole new life." Through Corinne and her own naming of pain, Sheila was able to make sense of her suffering. She could value missing her mother, missing nurturing, supportive parents, and relieve her lonely burden. Eventually, she could value herself.

If you discover that your daughter is mutilating herself, it is cause for alarm. Do not ignore it; it is definitely a bid for attention and a cry for help. Mutilating is usually a sign of deep disturbance, a serious disorder. She is trapped in a dark, dark underworld. Some girls talk about it as "the way I take myself away," or they say, "It takes my mind off other things." Others say they feel dead: "Seeing my blood makes me feel alive." If your daughter is injuring herself, you will be horrified. Tell her, "This frightens me. What is the message here? What are you trying to tell me?" But do not confront her with an attitude of blame or overwhelm her with your fears and anxiety. Like eating disorders, this is a behavior that needs professional help. If Demeter had not wailed and searched for her daughter, Persephone would have been lost forever. As mothers, we can never give up on our daughters.

While girls cutting and burning their bodies produce a shocking visceral response in us as parents, the sad truth is that it is more socially acceptable than it used to be. It's a form of acting out conflict that has become more common. Perhaps the increase in younger and younger women seeking plastic surgery and the high visibility of those procedures have contributed to the indifference with which girls often regard mutilating their bodies.

The solution for women is to fight the cultural perversion of women's bodies being correctable commodities. We mothers need to honor our bodies the way they are. The Body Shop reminds its clients with posters and postcards, "There are 3 billion women who don't look like supermodels and only 8 who do." We must make our daughters aware of the way in which the media manipulates women in order to make money. Embrace your daughter's body, whatever her type.

"You're Not Going Out Wearing That, Are You?"

Fourteen-year-old Marie came to breakfast one September morning of her freshman year wearing a tank top showing significant cleavage. "You're not going to school wearing that, are you?" her mother, Louise, squawked. Marie said, "Of course! Why not?" Louise responded, "You can't go out with your bra straps showing!" Her daughter hotly retorted, "What do you mean? All the girls dress like this. What's wrong with it?" Her mother exploded, "You don't look like a nice girl!" Hurt and angry, Marie slammed out of the house.

What are this mother and daughter thinking and feeling as they fail to connect here? Louise is remembering her own high school years, when a girl dressed in that revealing a blouse would have been branded a slut. She is so overwhelmed by her angry feelings that she rushes to judgment without asking Marie any questions. Her outrage is based on her own confused teenage struggle with sexuality and peer pressure. She had had no help from her own strict, repressed mother, who had barely mentioned menstruation to her daughter. Deserted, Louise had fumbled through feeling ashamed of her sexual feelings and humiliated by her peers' jeering at her good-girl persona. Confronted with her daughter's sensuality, Louise's painful feelings erupted. In the mix are also Louise's love and protectiveness for Marie, whom she sees as unaware of her seductive appearance. Marie's unconscious confusion about her own past causes her to betray her relationship with her daughter.

Initially, Marie is completely outraged by her mother's outburst. "What's the problem? I've been dressing this way for ages. And it's my body!" As a middle school girl she had been skinny and flat-chested, and Louise had not objected to her wearing a tank top and jeans like the rest of her girlfriends. When she developed and reached high school, Marie said, "I tried to reason with my mother, but she wouldn't even listen to me. She always got so mad! I just didn't get it! Then I started wearing a T-shirt out of the house, stuffed my tank top in my backpack, and changed in the school bathroom. That made me feel bad too, to be hiding something from her, so I stopped wanting to talk to her about other things."

Over time, Louise's lashing out at Marie without taking up the problem in relation to her daughter resulted in both of them feeling alienated. Marie was hurt, her mother felt disrespected. Marie took her mother's reaction as criticism of her appearance—her body and her self-expression. And she really wanted her mother's approval on both counts. She was also bewildered by the vague sexual accusations implied in her mother's fury.

"Let's Talk."

When Louise finally realized that she was sacrificing the close bond she had enjoyed with her daughter, she decided that she herself had to change. She took a hard look at her own feelings and thought about their origins in her adolescent years. Then she made a Saturday afternoon date with Marie to go out to the state park and spend some time together walking. In spite of feeling injured and misunderstood, Marie loved her mother and wanted her understanding; she warily accepted the overture.

Louise waited until they were on the trail and said, "Marie, I know I've made things difficult for you the past few months by nagging you about the way you are dressing. I'm sorry we've become so distant over this, and I want to make things better. I'd like to hear from you how you feel about your choice of clothes." Cautious, yet secretly pleased, Marie said, "I don't know, Mom. It's just OK with me to have my bra showing; we all do it. I guess we just like our bodies. Besides, look at the actresses on TV and the women singers. They all wear tight, low-cut tops." Startled, Louise realized that she had been giving Marie the message that she should be ashamed of her body. Louise went on to ask, "But what about the boys? Aren't you afraid you'll give them the wrong impression?" Marie answered, "The wrong impression about what? All the girls dress this way!"

Marie's emphasis was on joining her friends in their style. Louise heard that bare midriffs and bra straps were the norm. Having sorted out her own feelings, she realized that she had jumped to the conclusion that Marie was making a sexual statement. She told her daughter that she feared that her wearing low-cut tank tops might attract unwanted attention from men. Marie said, "Jeez, Mom, don't you have any faith in me? I know how to behave on the street. You've taught me all that, and we've learned it at school, too." Louise felt a great sense of relief hearing her daughter's genuine response to her fear. It hit her again how prejudicial she had been without ever listening to Marie's side. She thought, "I really have to stop living in another decade if I'm going to help Marie deal with her reality."

Chastened, Louise went on to tell Marie that her own mother had never talked to her about sexuality or becoming a woman; she had been left to fend for herself. Marie sympathized with her mother's loneliness during high school. Louise was surprised at how much it meant to her to have Marie show tenderness for the frightened girl her mother had been. Marie happily opened up, feeling her mother listening in a nonjudgmental way as they continued to talk.

Marie and Louise had an impact on one another, and both felt rejuvenated by the experience. As a result of Louise's reaching out to her daughter, Louise reestablished a warm, connected relationship. Marie wore her tank tops without hiding and felt her mother's admiration and support for her healthy body image. With this fresh look at the situation, Marie playfully began to suggest little changes in the style of clothes Louise wore. Louise was able to relax and accept Marie's input. She began to appreciate her own body, her sensuality and sexuality, in a new way. This all-too-familiar battle over clothes is a chance for mother and daughter to meet over the issue of their essential alikeness, their female bodies.

"Mom, Can I Borrow Your Sweater?"

Marie actually initiated changes in Louise's style. Mother and daughter began to talk and share the ritual of dressing. If you are comfortable with your daughter borrowing some or all of your clothes, this can be a wonderful relationship bond. You need to be careful, however, about boundary issues on both sides.

Establish your rules first. Do you want her to come into your closet and take things without asking? If not, what are your terms? Which things are off limits because they are special to you? What kind of care do you want her to take with your things? Pam, who had subtly implied that her daughter Geri needed to lose weight, let Geri borrow her good work clothes with the instruction to ask first and hang them up after wearing them. When Geri began taking her mother's clothes while Pam was at work and leaving them on her bedroom floor in a heap, Pam found herself screaming at her daughter. This conflict escalated until Pam put a padlock on her bedroom door, which did nothing to mend the rift with Geri. Neither Geri nor her mother realized that her refusal to cooperate mirrored Geri's feeling of being rejected by her mother because her mother criticized her body.

Borrowing each other's clothes does not have to end disastrously. One hopes you will have taught your daughter to respect your property before she is a teenager. If not, don't despair. Begin now. Firmly and calmly tell her what you expect in terms of her borrowing your clothes (or other belongings). If she doesn't follow through, do not lend her an item the next time. Then try again a few weeks later. If you are clear and consistent, she will learn. If she can't cooperate with your guidelines for borrowing, then give up the hassle and move into a different arena in which you can enjoy each other.

Follow your daughter's lead in terms of her boundaries. If she invites you to wear her dress, then she is open to it. But, just as you don't want your closet raided, don't poach on hers. Look at her clothes with her and make a decision about what's appropriate for you to take. Do not compete with her by trying to look like a teenager or comparing your sizes. To feel you being competitive with her about looks is more of the same that she experiences at school. When you and your daughter can happily share clothes, it will expand your wardrobes, but, more importantly, you will have fun together. Sharing ideas and opinions for what to put together, what works and what doesn't, will create a strong bond.

What is it you need to know about yourself in order to reach out over these impasses to connect with your daughter on the other side? Instead of reacting out of fear, we need to ask our daughters how they feel about the clothes they choose to wear, as well as telling them our stories and impressions. For most girls, clothes are a way to represent and define themselves. If your daughter eschews fashion to wear her basketball sweatpants and sweatshirt every day, that makes as much of a statement about who she is as another girl who wears only certain name-brand outfits as her trademark. How did you like to dress in high school and why? What sort of struggles did you and your mother (or father) have about what you chose to wear?

"Clothes Are So Important!"

Your daughter will want to dress like her friends. Yet she will also want to define her own style within the broader range of what's acceptable to her peers. Some of her choices will depend on her allowance for clothes; others will reflect how she feels about herself. Her attitudes toward her clothes will also be influenced by yours. If you have not paid attention to the way you dress, she may either follow your example or go in the opposite direction and become a clothes maven. Ask her how she feels about clothes and talk to her about the way the fashion industry preys on teenagers to make money. Teach her to know good value in buying clothes versus going for name brands to impress her friends. Your limiting her allowance will help her learn how to budget.

Seventeen-year-old Kate said jokingly, "I *hate* clothes; they're so important and so much fun. I'm envious of my friends who have money to shop at Bebe. I've given up shopping at places like that because of my budget. I do more retro, thrift stores, tank tops and jeans. Now when a friend calls and says, 'Ooh, I found it, do you want to hear what I got?' I'm not so interested. I do share clothes, but most of my friends are smaller than I am."

Kate described her mother as "not a very stylish person." She said her mother always looks nice but dresses modestly and simply. "She would never wear a bikini or anything tight, sexy, or showy." As Kate was growing up she looked to her aunts, cousins, and friends as role models for dressing because her mother's clothes "didn't excite" her. Ellen tries gently to curb her daughter's display of her body. "My mother says, 'That shirt is too tight' or 'You need a different bra; your boobs look like they're popping out' or 'Your jeans are too tight.'" To Kate's surprise, her girlfriends' reactions are the opposite. "They're always saying, 'You have such a good body, you should show it off more.'" Kate says "I really think I'm in the middle between the two extremes, and that I always will be." Kate is mature enough to acknowledge that her mother has influenced her in spite of her adopting her peers' values.

Girls have to worry what guys think and what other girls think about the way they dress. Kate continued, "Guys are into clothes, too—both their own and what girls wear. A guy will say to me, 'That's really cute, but I don't know about that shirt ...' and I'll say, 'Hey, do you want to dress me or buy my wardrobe?'" While this exchange is a form of flirtation, boys have also been affected by the advertising geared toward teenagers. The difference for boys is that when they are just going to "hang with the guys," they don't bother to shave, shower, or think about what to wear. Girls, on the other hand, care about their girlfriends' appraisals and sometimes go to great pains to create the image they want to project when going to a friend's house to watch a movie.

Even those girls who decide not to pay attention to how they look admit that they feel better when they take some care with their clothes. Seventeen-year-old Rebecca, with her artistic flair, is a thrift store fanatic. "When I was in eighth grade I was into crazy clothes: I'd go to the flea market and buy a sequined dress to wear over jeans or a tie-dyed T-shirt. My hair was a different color every week. Then freshman year it changed. Clothes became like a bother; I just started wearing jeans every day. But my friend Sally has lots and lots of clothes. She doesn't really have more money than I do, but she works and spends her money on clothes; I work and have to spend my money on gas for driving my parents' car and meals when I eat out.

"When Sally and I go out, I like to dress. Then I try on her clothes and wear them; she's about the same size, just a little bigger. Sometimes, I think I'd feel better about myself if I dressed every day; when I went out for coffee with my ex-boyfriend recently, I wore a skirt and shoes with a little heel, and I felt more confident and attractive. I felt people looked at me differently." Rebecca's mother, Sharon, dresses very simply, as befits her work as a minister. Rebecca attributes some of her own emphasis on valuing internal qualities over her image to her mother's example.

Play underlies some of the energy that girls use fooling around with their looks. In addition to her henna art, Tammy is "on a fashion designing kick. I love clothes and drawing pictures. I saw the movie *Selena*. Now I'm into power with makeup and designing clothes; I want to have a fashion show." Tammy's bubbling enthusiasm shows how a girl's focus on clothes can take on a creative life of its own. She is equally animated about her schoolwork and competing on the water polo team. Clothes and henna tattoos stimulate her imaginative side. Tammy's mother, Jean, is indifferent to her own clothes, but she encourages Tammy to explore her creativity, whatever form it takes.

Girls are always sharing clothes with each other. You will routinely find sweatshirts, jeans, boxer shorts, and other items that you don't recognize in your laundry hamper. Sometimes they will take up residence for weeks only to disappear one day, returned to their rightful owner. This sharing is part of the bonding that goes on between teenage girls. They are mirroring and validating one another through this exchange. Don't fight it, but do teach your daughter to discriminate about what she chooses to lend. Make her aware if a dress is too special to let out of her hands or that she needs to have her jeans available in her closet. On the other hand, if you are in a department store and you say, "I'll buy you that shirt if you promise not to lend it to anyone," it is likely to vanish. It's best to let her use her own judgment in lending and borrowing relationships with her friends.

Girls often project that the girls at other schools have it better in terms of peer pressure to look a certain way. Kaylie said, "My freshman and sophomore years were really difficult, even though I always got good grades. None of my girlfriends from eighth grade public school came with me to private school. Everyone in private school dresses the same, buying clothes at J. Crew and Gap. In public school it seems they don't care as much about clothes; but maybe it only seems that way to us." Kaylie is right. Public school girls, like Rebecca and Kate, express themselves differently with clothes, but they are equally preoccupied with them.

Girls are always moving back and forth between conformity and nonconformity with their clothes. Young grammar school girls are often eager to look exactly like their friends, but in middle school and especially high school, the loaded question is, "Do I buy from the same stores and look the same? Or do I branch out and do something different and risk it not coming off or being ridiculed?" Your daughter will be walking the tightrope between becoming an individual and relating to her social group.

Expressing herself through clothes, jewelry, makeup, and hair dye is not going to harm your daughter. Such experimentation is worlds away from self-mutilation or self-starvation. Battling her over adornment is not worth power struggles and bad feelings between you. It is better to let her join her peer group in these benign pursuits and save your power for the things that matter.

Respect as many of her choices as you can, even if you don't like them. Instead of trying to prevent her from adopting a certain look, say something like, "I certainly wouldn't choose to dress that way, but I trust that you have good judgment about what's right for you among your friends." If you can join with her in honoring her body with outlandish makeup and clothes, she will love you for it. You will be mirroring who she is, not who you want her to be. With this attitude, there's a better chance of her accepting the limits that are important, although she won't give you credit for your wisdom until she is older.

3

"*He's Hot!*"

DESIRE, SEX,
AND LOVE

"Girls are *totally* open about being interested in sex," seventeen-year-old Erika asserted. Girls' sexual desire is out. Your daughter will soak up many messages from her highly eroticized teenage milieu. Acknowledging her sexual desire is part of developing a healthy body image. It's important that she be educated to responsible sexual behavior and to healthy relationship values at the same time; she will be less likely to be drawn into sexual behavior at too young an age.

Having sex will always mean something different for a girl than for a boy when one act of intercourse has the potential to change her whole life. Although sex has a high profile with teenagers, shameful feelings about menstruation, body image, and sexuality continue to underlie many girls' suffering with their feminine identity.

Talking about sexuality with your daughter should begin as early as she raises sexual questions. In middle school, you could make a special date, take a walk together, go out to lunch, or go shopping in order to bring up this subject and talk about it in depth. A girl may need neutral ground; she doesn't like to feel cornered or trapped in her room or yours.

By the time they enter high school, girls shun questions about personal areas of their lives, especially about sexuality. Your daughter is claiming her sexual energy as she claims her body. Bringing up your concerns or obliquely initiating discussion is most likely to be successful if you are driving to the airport or to visit relatives and are alone in the car. If the current status of your relationship with your daughter is too embattled or you are too uncomfortable to broach the subject of sexuality with her (or if you are a single parent father), enlist a trusted woman friend to connect with your daughter about the pleasure and the risks of exploring sexuality.

There may already be a woman in place with whom she is close, a godmother or aunt or mentor. If her pediatrician is a woman, she would be a natural choice as a resource. If her doctor is a man, ask him for a referral to a woman doctor who supports educating girls about their bodies.

In December of her freshman year, Grace told her mom that she had been invited to a coed sleepover party at her friend Emma's house on New Year's Eve. The kids were each to bring a sleeping bag to crash on the living room floor. Eve, Grace's mother, knew that her daughter had never been in this situation before. She also knew that with the exception of a few movie dates in eighth grade, Grace had never had a boyfriend. Eve was slightly acquainted with Emma and her family from Grace's class; she told Grace that she would call Emma's mother to check to see if the parents were going to be home.

When she and Grace had some time alone, Eve told her daughter she wanted to discuss the party. Eve said, "The condition of you going to Emma's party is that you talk to me about where you are with sexuality." Grace rolled her eyes, squirmed, and blushed, but said

"OK, Mom, what do you want to know?" Her mother asked, "Is there anyone who's going to be there that you are interested in as a boyfriend?" Grace said emphatically, "Absolutely not . . . not at all . . . no one . . . it's just friends." Eve continued, "Are you interested in having oral sex or any sexual relationship now? Do you feel ready for that experience?" Grace said, "No! I'm not ready, and I wish you would stop talking about it." Eve patiently persisted, "I have one last question then—what if a guy you're not interested in came and tried to climb into your sleeping bag?" "I'd jump out!" Grace almost screamed.

Eve saw her daughter's genuine feelings and could see that she was having an impact on Grace. She responded lightly, "Thank you for talking to me . . . I feel all right about you going if Emma's parents will be there. Let me say again, as I have in the past, that when you begin to feel ready to have a sexual relationship, I want you to tell me so that we can go and get you some form of birth control." "OK, Mom. OK," Grace said, exasperated, uncomfortable, yet relieved. It is heartening when your talks with your daughter alleviate your concern because you are assured the risk is low. And despite Grace's discomfort, she now has a valuable piece of information: she knows her mother accepts her sexuality.

Donna was out shopping with her fifteen-year-old daughter, Aline, for a dress to wear to the school's holiday formal. In the department store dressing room, she pulled Aline's long hair back to zip up the dress she was trying on. Donna was startled to see that Aline had a "love bite" on her neck. Unaware that Aline was heavily petting and making out, Donna felt a series of unsettling emotions that included memories of her own early encounters with boys, a sense of loss, of losing her daughter to her increasing independence, and a feeling of protectiveness toward Aline. This was a perfect opportunity for Donna to reach out and talk to her daughter and expand their relationship to include discussing sexuality.

"Mom, I Know All That!"

Bring up the topic of sex with your daughter not only to communicate your values but to discuss birth control and health. You want her to be protected, to take care of herself while exploring her sexuality. When you raise the subjects of safe sex and contraception, you are likely to hear the frustrated and slightly embarrassed refrain: "Mom, I know that already. They taught all that in health class in seventh grade!" She is probably right that she knows the facts. Perhaps she knows some of the newer data better than you do. In that case, you can learn from the conversation too. But it is important for her to close the loop with you.

Your respectful, boundaried relationship with her about sex will have an effect on what she chooses to do with her body. Ask her what kind of experimentation she envisions with boys. Ask her if she's attracted to girls. Even if she has no answers to your questions, they will encourage self-reflection, so she doesn't just find herself alone with a boy with no idea of how far she wants to go. Tell her what you know about sexually transmitted diseases. Share what you think about safe sex and relationships. Having your input will offer her a different perspective than her peers give her and will help her observe and evaluate others' behavior as well as her own.

Your daughter's age determines what you say to her about sexuality. At age fourteen, for instance, you will probably still be saying, "I hope you wait until you are older to have a full-blown sexual relationship, because it carries a lot of emotional responsibility, but *whenever* you think you're ready, I want you to come to me, and we'll set up a doctor's appointment to get you set up with birth control."

Your daughter should see a gynecologist or go to Planned Parenthood before she has sex for the first time. Many girls go on their own to get birth control. Kate said, "Everyone's on the pill because you can get it from Planned Parenthood, but you still need condoms for safe sex. A lot of girls blow off that fact. My best friend says, 'Oh, he's only been with so and so—we don't have to use a condom.' I think she's crazy."

Don't hesitate to talk about sexuality with your daughter in a constructive way. This should not involve direct questions about current relationships but observations and meditations on the various paths relationships take, sexual or otherwise. You can also bounce off movies and television programs, sometimes in a joking way, to express your point of view. Ignoring the subject does not mean that she will stay innocent; quite the contrary, she may become prey to boys' or other girls' pressure if she has not formed some sense of what sexuality means to her.

Toni said, "My mom never talked about sex. At age fifteen I was drunk and pressured into having sex with a guy who never spoke to me again. I didn't gain respect for sexuality and I started sleeping around. I married at twenty-two and I don't want my daughter to go through what I did as a teenager." Alcohol loosens inhibitions and can encourage sex. Be sure your daughter knows how you feel about intimacy, sex, and the effects of alcohol.

"Don't Tell My Mom I'm Being Sexual."

Sexuality can be a powerful source of tension between mothers and daughters. Adolescent girls in counseling say over and over again, "I know there's nothing wrong with being sexual, but please don't tell my mother." It doesn't have to be that way. We, as adult women, are responsible for enabling our daughters to feel good about their sexual desires and for preparing them emotionally and practically to engage in healthy, mature sexual relationships.

Girls' resistance to talking to their mothers is both fear of judgment and a need for privacy. A girl is sometimes afraid her mother will condemn her for being sexual because she is questioning herself, feeling guilty, and attributing those feelings to her mother. Other times, her mother has imparted shameful feelings about sexuality to her daughter.

Early sexual exploration is a precious emotional time; your daughter needs her secrets. Learn to talk with her about your feelings and concerns without invading her privacy. This requires you to be sensitive to her emotional cues. Be available in a way that will encourage her to approach you about these issues. Show your availability by subtly making it known that you expect her to be sexual. If you hear her crying on the phone with her boyfriend, don't say, "I hope you're not crying over some boy!" as one sixteen-year-old's mother did. This kind of comment belittles her feelings. If you want her to come to you with her dilemmas, you have to be empathetic. Be judicious in your reactions to sexual issues that come up with her friends or yours. Your respecting the boundaries she establishes will help her trust you.

When you have an opening, tell her about the attitudes toward sexuality in your generation. If you tell her that girls didn't call boys when you were an adolescent or that your high school years were chaotic for you sexually, you will prevent yourself from unwittingly reinforcing old stereotypes. Ask her what high school is like for her. Girls do call boys; do take the initiative. If you share your experience in a considered way, instead of carelessly espousing old-fashioned notions of gender roles, your daughter will feel more comfortable talking to you.

Discuss the conspiracy of silence around sexuality that made it difficult for you to negotiate this passage. Talk about promiscuity versus sexuality in a contained, safe relationship and the emotional implications of being intimate. Name normal sexual awakening and desire. Ask her what she thinks and feels; each girl is different about what she wishes to share.

The psychological challenge for your daughter is to learn to create intimacy without losing herself. She needs to own her sexual desire and still feel good about herself. Girls are up against the pervasive cultural images and beliefs of the female body as a sexualized object. A deep-rooted attitude splits the "good" (nonsexual) girl from the "bad" (sexual) girl, labeling them the prude and the slut. Adding to these complications, one out of every four girls has been physically or sexually abused. Abused girls are more likely to get depressed and to engage in risky behavior.

When you see signs that your daughter is becoming sexual or when she begins group or one-to-one dating, this is an opportunity for you to communicate with her again, on a more mature level than when she was in grammar school, about your sexual values and your experiences. Examine your feelings before you talk to her, and work through old prejudices you may have.

Remember your own adolescence and coming into woman-hood, painful and difficult as it may have been. What were your first encounters with sexuality? Do you recall your first kiss, petting, oral sex, sexual arousal, intercourse? What did you know about sex, and how did you know it? What do you wish you had known, and why? How did your experience make you feel as a young woman?

The more girls claim their desire and choose how to express it, the more whole and authentic they are. Your task is both to sanction her healthy sexual desires and to help her be responsible for her ac-tions. Remember, this is a learning process for both of you; it won't be done once and for all, and both of you will make mistakes. If you keep your connection open, with a positive, loving attitude toward who she is, she will know that you are there for her to turn to when her friends are not enough, or when problems arise in which an adult needs to be involved.

"What About You, Mom?"

Your daughter's understanding of your sexual history will have an impact on her efforts to form a relationship. Erika, child of an intact, long-term marriage, said, "No one I know wants to get married or have children. We've all pretty much given up on the family structure." Divorce, dysfunctional marriages, and blended families have all taken a tragic toll on girls' optimism. Talk to your daughter about what you have learned from your experience. This does not mean that you should tell her the details of your sexual encounters, any more than she wants to tell you the details of hers. But if she asks questions, answer honestly. Err on the side of saying too much, rather than too little, because sexuality has been kept in the dark for girls. Sexuality is an intimate subject, but it can be treated matter-of-factly.

Assess yourself: Where are you as an adult woman? Are you enjoying an intimate life with your husband? Or has sexuality faded in the press of daily married life with children? Are you a single parent who has not dated in years because you have been too busy working and caring for your children? Or are you a single woman who is dating, savoring her sexuality, and feeling some new, uncomfortable twinges of competitiveness with your teenage daughter?

If you married at seventeen because you got pregnant and wished that your mother had suggested birth control to you as a young girl, tell your daughter that story. Be thoughtful and real with her. Don't let your fear that she will make the same mistake get in the way of your connecting. Angela's daughter Elizabeth found her mother's marriage certificate in a box in the attic when she was twelve years old. After counting back from when her older brother was born, she came to her mother and asked, "Mom, were you pregnant when you got married?" Angela sighed, "Yes. Let's sit down and talk, Elizabeth."

Angela told her daughter that premarital sex had been taboo when she was young. "And there was no birth control, even if I could have dared asked for it. I was four months' pregnant before I told my parents, and I felt such shame. I gave up two scholarships to college because I felt so guilty and humiliated. This is why it's important to me that you take control of your sexual life and fertility. I don't want you to have to abruptly change your life or make deci-sions that you aren't ready to make, the way I did."

Your daughter assumes that she will not make your mistakes, but, like Angela, you will know that one good way to prevent repeating a pattern is for you to be a different mother to her than yours was to you. Your fear of telling her your truths will make her think that you don't understand her; sharing your knowledge will enlarge her per-sonality and let her know that you trust her. You want to make it clear that your experience of adolescence was different than hers but also name ways in which hers may be the same.

Whatever the situation in your intimate life, it will have an effect on your daughter as she is becoming sexual. Whether it has a posi-tive or a negative effect is up to you. If you become conscious of your own situation and how you feel, then you will be able to relate to her about her issues in a healthy way, whatever the circumstances of your married or unmarried life. Your daughter's natural develop-ment will touch on sexual and gender issues that you may not have resolved for yourself. Without self-examination, you are apt to be unconscious and defensive in responding to her needs.

Linda, a responsible single mother, had tried to enforce a mid-night curfew with her daughter, Julie, in her freshman year, but Julie often ignored it. Linda would get angry; Julie would say she was sorry and then come home in the wee hours again. When Linda grounded her, Julie withdrew, slammed the door, and ignored her mother. Linda, an accountant, had taken on more work when Julie was in middle school to save for college tuition. Julie maintained a sullen facade with her mother, and Linda did not pick up on her daughter's cues that she was missing her.

One evening, when Linda was doing the laundry, she found a note from one of Julie's girlfriends in the pocket of Julie's jeans. The note discussed sex and boys in explicit terms and implied that both girls had had oral sex. Linda was shocked and came unglued when

Julie came home from school; she screamed at her and grounded her for six months. Later, when she had calmed down, Linda realized, "I completely lost it because it was instant replay of my own bad behavior with boys in high school." Linda had had no sexual education either at school or from her mother; she ran with a fast crowd, took risks as she explored her sexual desire, and enjoyed the feeling of power it gave her. But she also remembered humiliations as she heedlessly spent nights with young men she barely knew. She married the first man who asked her after a few months of dating him; they divorced soon after Julie was born.

Linda had repressed her own painful feelings, but they surfaced in her reaction to Julie. Although she had observed signs of Julie becoming sexual, Linda hadn't reached out to Julie to connect with her about this passage. Instead of paying attention to Julie on a day-to-day basis, she had been trying to control her daughter's behavior and ignore her own adolescent memories. She admitted that she didn't want Julie to do what she had done because it had made her feel dirty and disgusted with herself.

Linda's first step was to become aware of her own memories and come to terms with them. She also had to confront the excruciatingly painful fact that she was jealous of her daughter having sexual encounters. Linda had been alone for many years and often yearned for a sexual partner. When she had begun to absorb her own feelings, Linda began to repair the damage she had done with her daughter by acknowledging her reactivity. She told Julie where it came from in her. "I regret that I've avoided this subject with you; I guess I just thought if I didn't talk about it, it wouldn't happen until you were older. And I'm truly sorry I've been exploding instead of listening to you. I've realized that I had some sexual encounters in high school that I regret. I think I was trying to protect myself from remembering that pain and protect you from having to go through it. I see that I've done just the opposite." Linda did not tell Julie the particulars of her own high school sexual escapades; she rescinded the unfair consequence she had imposed, began to listen to her daughter, and learned about sexuality within the teenage social context.

The Sexual Milieu

One of the big differences between Linda's high school milieu and Julie's is the instant communication between teenagers. The use of pagers and, in wealthier communities, of cell phones has increased minute-to-minute intimacy. Many girls also have telephones in their rooms. Wherever they are, whomever they are with, they can be beeped by friends. A complicated numerical beeper code allows your teenage daughter to send and receive messages on her pager.

The good news about pagers for parents is that you, too, can reach your daughter at any time of day or night, if you need to. The bad news is that your teenager can end up being sleep deprived if you don't set limits from a young age about turning off the bells on phones and pagers. Communication at any hour is the norm for teenagers.

Teenagers also use e-mail and get on-line to spend time in chat rooms. Flirting with a boy using electronic communication very quickly gets to sex. Twenty years ago, flirting would be "Do you like me?" Now it's "Would you French kiss a guy?" or "How about a blow job?" Media, TV, movies, and magazines have helped create a faster shift in girls from being maidens to becoming sexual.

Girls and boys talk incessantly through electronics or in person about sexual interactions. Discussions about who said what to whom or who is doing what with whom are laden with sexual innuendo and profane language. Girls' conversation is peppered with comments like, "Oh, he'll do!" or "What about him?" or "I want him!" Feelings about one another, family problems, and school are also incessantly under scrutiny. Girls in particular are the conveyors of this feeling-laden processing of life. But boys are increasingly being initiated into the constant back-and-forth.

Your daughter is operating in a mobile and savvy peer group. Classes on sexually transmitted diseases are taught early in middle school along with a curriculum that identifies all variations of sexual behavior. It's important for you as a mother to realize how sophisticated your daughter may be so that you interact with her in an adult manner.

Bisexuality

Many musicians and teen idols are bisexual and model bisexuality for teenagers. In some high schools same-sex contact is treated very lightly. "Kissing other girls is just an option," seventeen-year-old Erika said. The cherished elder daughter of three children, Erika is unassuming and straightforward. "A girl looking at a magazine could see a picture of a really gorgeous female model and say, 'Isn't she hot? I could totally have sex with her. I would totally fuck her.' I would feel comfortable saying something like that." While some of this is affected, some of it is not. Erika went on, "It's not the same for me as being interested in a boy sexually. It's more playful, being attracted to a girl because she's beautiful; it would be fun to kiss her." Psychologically, this kind of sexual play can be about a girl wanting to merge with the feminine beauty she admires. Such play also permits lesbian feelings to come out more easily than they ever did before.

This homosexual freedom exists largely in liberal cities. Cities influence the suburbs. "Liking girls or guys is accepted in my high school, but I know it's not everywhere. Girls like to hang out with gay guys; they feel comfortable with them. I think gay culture is more acceptable now, so straight guys mimic being gay, just for fun." If your daughter expresses a sexual interest in girls, be as matter-of-fact about it as you can. While it may be part of her intense adolescent experimentation, it could be a genuine lesbian calling. Making her feel shame will only exacerbate her conflict and cause her to act out or develop a false self in relation to you. Either way, you will lose her.

Many girls are already exploring sexuality with either boys or girls by their freshman year. Erika, whose passion is creative writing, is comfortable with a range of sexual fantasies, but, in practice, she is more restrained than a lot of her friends. "Nobody I know goes on dates. But every girl wants a great boyfriend. We want the safety of not having guys hit on us; a lot of people have sex when they start high school. The HIV and sex education at school is awesome. They even gave out Ziploc bags of condoms." Heavy petting, kissing, and oral sex are not seen as intimate but as a safe way of being close. This is worrisome, because there are health risks associated with performing oral sex. While kids should be using protection, most don't. Oral sex is considered routine and does not imply loss of virginity. "Only once," Erika said, "I heard a guy say, 'You're not a virgin because you had oral sex.' That was the only time I ever heard of it being a gray area."

Erika needs a relationship to have oral sex. "But oral sex is usually not serious; it depends on the person." Some of Erika's friends lost their virginity in eighth grade; others are still virgins as seniors. "I'm the innocent virginal princess to all my friends. For me, having sex will have to be love. My friends tell me, 'You can't have sex; you have to hold the standard for all of us.'" But in some circles, a girl can have a hard time because she's a virgin. "One of my friends who goes to another school is thinking of having sex with a much older guy that she doesn't even like, just to get it over with. I think, if she has to, she has to, but I tell her, you know, there's *such* a much better way."

The teen language for pairing off with a boy begins with "messing around," which loosely means that a girl and a guy get together at parties, exploring kissing and touching a bit. But, according to Erika, "You haven't labeled anything yet. You could go out with someone the next night." "Being together" means that a girl and a boy are paired off, and "sometimes the guy cares about her flirting with someone else." "Going out" defines a boyfriend–girlfriend relationship: "You have to be good, no cheating."

The stereotype of boys wanting sex and girls resisting them still exists. In a television ad for *Ally McBeal*, a man says, "I can't stop thinking about you. I have to make love to you right now." This ad realistically conveys the ease with which a boy gets an erection and his sense of urgency when aroused. Most girls feeling desire want sex only in the context of a relationship. A study of high school girls and boys involved in sports showed that boys on athletic teams are more sexually active than girls on similar teams. The study concluded, "Boys who feel good about themselves have sex, and girls who feel good about themselves don't." For teenagers having sex means sexual intercourse.

Among most girls, sex implies a relationship, and a relationship implies love. However, Erika said, "For some girls, sex is just sex." One day in chemistry class, for instance, Erika's friend Suzy said to Bobby (her good friend who has a girlfriend), " 'It's been so long [since I had sex]; I'm going to go crazy.' And he said, 'You could get with anyone you wanted.' Suzy says, 'Really? No I couldn't.' Then Bobby says, 'Well, I would go with you.' So at lunchtime, they went to her house and had sex. But nothing changed between them. They're still just friends."

A girl's image counts for a lot. According to Erika, "If a girl had sex with two guys on the weekend and she comes to school wearing a tight short skirt and a tiny tank top with an attitude, she's going to be called a slut. She will lose respect from both guys and girls, even though guys will still want to have sex with her." A boy who comes on to lots of girls doesn't lose the respect of other boys, only of the girls.

Dealing with the old double standard, girls are conflicted about their sexual behavior. They say, "If I have sex with my boyfriend, will I be a slut?" or "Having sex with my boyfriend is OK, but the girls who just have sex for pleasure are sluts." Preppy Briana, still withdrawn at sixteen, said, "Dating is difficult. You're afraid the relationship will stop if you say 'No' or if it gets more physical. Your reputation is on the line; you'll either be called a prude or a slut. You want intimacy. I learned that if I'm under stress or feeling depressed and I turn to a guy it makes it worse, because he just takes advantage of my feeling bad. For a guy it's not the same. He's called a sleaze, but it doesn't change anything. He's still respected."

Initially, Briana speaks to the general experience of her girl peer group. She shifts from the general "you" to the first person "I" when she begins to talk about what she has learned emotionally in relation to boys. She is keenly insightful about the distinction between wanting her feelings met versus wanting a sexual encounter. Girls who are self-conscious about sexual desire say "you" instead of "I" because they don't want to own it. Like Briana, they haven't been given permission to know their desire. Unfortunately, Briana feels that she cannot share these feelings with her mother. Without an adult ally, she talks only to her best friend. Be sure your daughter has a woman in her life to talk to about the difference between romance and sex, love and lust, and making a life with someone.

Emotions are intense for teenagers. One minute it's hatred, the next minute love, the next indifference. Much posturing goes on. Erika said, "It's not uncommon for a girl to go up to a boy she likes and say something like, 'You know you want some of my sex because I want some of yours.'" The high school grapevine is as high amp and high volume as the music teenage girls favor. If a girl has been asked out by a boy, all their friends will know by the next morning, even if she told only her best friend on the phone that night. The details of how he asked her, what he said, and what she said will also be shared with everyone in her circle and his. After that, there will be close monitoring of their interactions by the whole social group. You, on the other hand, will no doubt be outside the loop.

A close friendship between a girl and a boy may lead to sexual negotiations by a third person. Rebecca arranged a relationship between

Morgan and William. Rebecca said, "I was in the middle, I helped them get together, and then helped them break up. They hardly ever talked directly, even though they messed around." A year later, Rebecca broke up with her boyfriend. Three days later, sitting in Spanish class next to William, she wrote him a note saying, "Are you a virgin?" William wrote back, "Yes." What started out as a friendship, an intellectual relationship, became an intensely emotional one.

Rebecca and William "messed around" in the fall of sophomore year. "It was an on-and-off thing. But we missed somehow really getting together." Rebecca went off to be a counselor-in-training at a camp that summer. "When I got back, I thought it was over. We were just friends, but sometimes he wouldn't talk to me. Then I wrote him a fat letter saying, 'I love you, but you treat me like shit.' He would talk to my best friend, Sally, but not to me. Finally we ended up talking and we were going to be friends.

"I matured after camp and I'm a girl, so I'm more mature than he is, anyway; I'm willing to be honest and to take risks. Another guy friend of mine told me, 'William can't deal with you—you're too much for him.' I got invited to a party. When I came in, William saw me and left. I thought, it's cool that I have the power to repulse some-one like that, but it hurts too. I think I need to stop looking for a soul-mate. William was a soulmate." Rebecca's description of the ins and outs of her connection to William shows a lot of self-awareness. Through relationships with boys, she is forming her feminine identity.

Both Erika and Rebecca experience themselves as more skilled at relationships than boys. Erika defines her feminine power as con-centrated—more powerful than a boy's. She is able to relate deeply to both boys and girls. Kaylie, home from her first year at college, has another slant. She feels that guys' focus on sex is a disability. "I think girls are capable of being more focused and concerned with their own goals. Guys like my brother are always thinking about who is the next girl they are going to hook up with. I have my plans for the summer—to get in shape, work at my job, be here, and see my friends. I don't have to let my mind wander to my two-week romance at the end of school. I think girls have had to fight for their identities so they've worked on detaching themselves. Guys have always been on top, so they're still dependent."

Appearances Are Deceptive

Underneath your daughter's cooperative, cheerful exterior, hidden fires may be burning. Your straight-A student could be smoking marijuana every weekend and exploring sexuality without using any protection. Blair, one such star student, agreed to go along to Planned Parenthood and get an AIDS test with her girlfriend, Christine. Christine was worried because she had lost her virginity one night when she was drunk. "That was stupid," Blair said. At the clinic, Blair was stunned to hear that, of the two girls, she was more at risk than Christine, who had had one unprotected encounter. Blair had been having reciprocal oral sex with a guy who had used intravenous drugs and who had had sex with both guys and girls before he met her.

Neither Blair's nor Christine's mother had any clue about what her daughter was doing. Both girls are creative, high-achieving individuals. Your daughter will be taking such risks on her own and addressing them either with or without your knowledge. Angela had talked to Elizabeth about safe sex and birth control options in appropriate ways when Elizabeth entered high school. At the end of her sophomore year, Elizabeth called her mother from Planned Parenthood to ask her a few questions. Angela said, "I felt jolted. I had it in my mind that she would be getting birth control pills down the line, in some nebulous future. And here it was happening. It took me a few minutes of stumbling over my words to move into her reality and support her." The conversation further disturbed Angela because one of the questions was, "Mom, am I a DES baby?" Puzzled, Angela admitted, "Yes, Elizabeth, I did take DES to prevent miscarriage when I was carrying you. Why?" The gynecological exam had revealed some changes in Elizabeth's cervix. It had never crossed Angela's mind that DES could cause her daughter damage. Although it was an upsetting truth for both of them, dealing with it together deepened their relationship. Angela and Elizabeth had many discussions about sexuality, fertility, and motherhood in subsequent years. Your own reproductive history is a key piece of knowledge for your daughter as she begins to explore her sexuality.

Some freshman girls feel comfortable with strict parental guidelines. Tammy, at fourteen, has yet to become interested in boys. "I hear about people playing drinking games, sex stuff with girls younger than me. I'm shocked by it. It makes me feel sad for them that they don't have the self-worth to not do such things. My parents set standards for me. I can group date now as a freshman and sophomore. When I'm sixteen and start driving, I can go on individual dates."

How to Say No

With sexuality at the forefront of girls' awareness, it is not surprising that many young girls don't know where to draw the line. Fourteen-year-olds lose their virginity and then want to pull back. One girl said, "It doesn't feel right to me; it feels bad. There's no pleasure; it's not fun." She wants to know, "How can I stop, become strong and nonsexual for a while?" Girls who begin too early then have to backtrack and learn how to say "no." They may not know any other way to connect to boys except by being physically affectionate. Emotionally and psychologically, it's not healthy for kids to go straight to intercourse too fast.

Heed the warning signs that your daughter is beginning to orient herself to boys instead of to herself. Tina, a multitalented fifteen-

year-old, has only boyfriends, no girlfriends. The connection between her and boys always begins in a sexual way. "Then, after sex,
it's how to go back to being friends." Tina's mother, Faye, is a young,
beautiful woman in her early thirties who is invested in her sexual
persona and attracting men. Tina was molested at an early age by her
stepfather and had to testify against him in court. Faye works full-
time as a clerk to support her daughter. Yet when she inherited a little money, she spent it on liposuction. Tina is following her mother's
example by basing her self-worth on being attractive to boys.

Promiscuity is dangerous and self-degrading. Yvonne was having
unprotected sex with a different boy every week in her freshman
year. Her twenty-eight-year-old mother, Joy, who had Yvonne when
she was fourteen and married her seventeen-year-old boyfriend, was
in complete denial about her daughter. Joy loves Yvonne but was un-
informed about her school social milieu, where Yvonne would cut
class to smoke dope and have sex. Joy refused to think about the fact
that her daughter could follow in her footsteps. When the school
called home to report Yvonne's absences, Joy would reprimand her
daughter for not attending class, but she would not inquire into what
she was doing. Alarmed by Yvonne's scary, impulsive behavior, her
therapist had her write letters and mail them to her about how she
was feeling. Finally, the therapist took a stand and sent Yvonne to
Planned Parenthood for birth control pills in an attempt to save her
from her mother's fate.

These girls were looking for love and security from relationships
with boys. They think, "If I have sex with him, he'll love me." Or, "If
I have sex with him, I love him." Then they get trapped: "If I have
sex with him, I have to stay with him." They struggle with sexual
feelings, described as being "in love." Love means sexual acts. Many
girls don't know how to have one without the other. Be sure your
daughter feels your love and that of her family. Make your home a
secure base for her to come back to as she moves out into her world.

Breaking the Mold

Your daughter needs to develop a center, a sense of being the subject of her own life, not the object of a boy's life. Women and girls have traditionally been taught to be pleasing, sweet, and nice—that is, to nurture others. They have been trained to subdue their own feelings and needs, especially in the interest of men's needs. Fundamentally, our daughters need to learn to nurture and sustain themselves and to follow their own passions, thoughts, and inspirations. Girls and women struggling with relationship demands—boyfriends, husbands, children, parents—need to hear: "Take care of yourself. Figure out what *you* want to do, work in constructive ways to bring it about, and everyone in your life will benefit from your wholeness and self-determination."

"Don't Be Like Me"

Sixteen-year-old Josie is an athlete, a leader, a strong girl who is radiant with self-esteem. But again, her only friends are boys. Josie chooses boys who need to be taken care of; she seems to need someone who's not competing with her. Her father, with whom she lives, showers her with money and things but doesn't have time to be involved in her life. She spends his money on the boys she dates.

Her mother, Meryl, had been an alcoholic, drug-using teen who was now getting clean in her thirties. She didn't want her daughter to end up like her, so she treated Josie with vigilance and suspicion, never letting up on her. Josie hated her mother and finally asked her father to let her see a counselor because she felt powerless. The counselor worked with Meryl to get her to back off, trust Josie, and authorize her to make informed choices for herself. If your daughter asks to see a therapist, support her. Try not to feel that you have failed her because she doesn't want to talk to you. Some girls need an impartial adult outside their family who is not an authority figure or a teacher.

Tina, Yvonne, and Josie all focused their energy on boys. Tina chose boys who were not as alive and talented as she was. Like many girls, she loaned her own vitality to boys. The habit of intelligent, beautiful girls choosing less competent boys is ubiquitous. Yvonne had sex with boys, hoping to find the comfort and attention that she wasn't getting at home. Josie chose wounded boys that she could take care of.

Girls connecting with boys who are not their equals can be partially explained by their mothers' examples of not connecting with healthy, competent men. Girls give another reason: boys are slower to mature, so the field is narrow. Mature freshman and sophomore girls are particularly at a loss for boys to date, because the boys in their classes have yet to catch up. On the other hand, many freshman girls are sexually innocent compared to senior boys, so parents are wary of letting their young girls date upperclassmen.

One therapist suggests, "There seems to be a rescuing complex in girls, part of a maternal urge. I see them saying, 'I have so much energy; let me help you out' or 'I want to be fair, not be a snob.'" Some girls are insecure in spite of their accomplishments and attractiveness. One thirteen-year-old picked up a homeless boy on the street. She had an eating disorder and didn't feel good about herself; the boy put her on a pedestal. Temporarily, this unequal relationship made her feel better about herself.

Some girls get involved with boys who aren't their equals for the excitement. Boys whose attention is more on risk taking with alcohol, drugs, shoplifting, and being on the edge of trouble can be more interesting than those who are taking their lives seriously. Girls want to taste life in all its extremes. For this reason, it's important that your daughter have many opportunities for healthy challenges and risk taking in high school.

Once involved with a boy, a girl will often begin to give up parts of herself to stay with him. As you observe your daughter giving in and doing whatever a boy wants, it will undoubtedly bring up memories and feelings from your own adolescence. Angela said, "I remember sacrificing myself for my boyfriend. Chase wanted to go to the roller derby—I hated it and thought it was disgusting, but I smiled and went. I wish I had said, 'I hate roller derby. I'd rather go to a play.' That would have shown us the truth of our relationship so much sooner. I wouldn't have spent two years trying to please him and being bored. I also remember giving him too many chances. I felt sorry for him because he came from a troubled family. He'd been a foster child." Angela told Elizabeth these stories and gave her permission to stand up for herself instead of following boys around as her mother had done.

"Mom, You Do That with Dad!"

You will face a bigger obstacle in those times when your daughter's struggle to be equal in relation to a boy she likes makes you (and her) aware of the ways in which you are hiding or pretending in relation to your husband or boyfriend. Ask yourself, What am I modeling for her? All relationships require compromise, but if you find that you often defer to a man in your life in ways that compromise your integrity or wholeness, you must look seriously at your behavior in order to help your daughter. Do you speak up when you feel differently than he does? Have you sacrificed your own creativity or friendships with other women in order to be at his beck and call? If you see room for improvement on this score, try to make subtle changes and share your effort with your daughter.

Donna, a single parent, recognized that whenever she and her partner, Richard, were getting ready to go to a party, he would decide that he didn't want to go. "Then I would plead, cajole, and persuade him until he went." When Donna heard fifteen-year-old Aline on the phone with her boyfriend pleading with him to take her to a concert, she recognized her own voice. She went to Aline and said, "I'm sure you've noticed this pattern with Richard and me every time we are about to go out. Well, I'm not going to do it anymore. From now on I'm going to say, 'I can see that you don't want to go, but I do. So I'm going by myself and I'll see you later.'" Aline cheered her mom on. Donna continued, "I also think you've learned some of that from me. Let's both try to help each other take a stand."

If you are involved in unequal relationships with men, seeing your daughter begin to pattern herself after you will be a terrible awakening. Becoming aware and doing something about it will be painful, but it is an opportunity to turn things around for both of you. Toni said, "My friend Jane gets boyfriends who treat her horribly; her stepfather was mean and hit her mom. I think it's important to break the chains from mother to daughter." If you are living with a man who is verbally or physically abusive, or who uses drugs or alcohol, and you repeatedly ask him to leave but do not follow through with action, your daughter gets the message that a woman has to give up her standards, values, and herself in order to stay with a man.

Darlene, a responsible single mother of three, worked full-time in a travel agency. When she dated, she had a penchant for choosing abusive men. Her daughter, Lonnie, came of age and started hanging out on the street. Darlene was a conscientious parent, providing her children with clothing and meals, but she had no spare time for her daughter, and no experience giving guidance or emotional support. Undernurtured, Lonnie had to create herself. She became tough and streetwise and hit rock bottom in terms of self-esteem. She had no idea that she was both attractive and smart. Determined to self-destruct, she became a prostitute. When Darlene realized what was going on, she sought therapy for Lonnie. It took several years for both Darlene and Lonnie to grow together and reestablish a relationship. Just as Darlene's choices had affected Lonnie, Lonnie's acting out allowed Darlene to recognize her own part and to begin to change with her daughter.

Just Friends

The more grounded a girl is in her feminine identity, the healthier her exploration of relationships with boys in high school will be. Adolescent boys and girls often develop deep nonsexual friendships. They talk to each other not only about their fears and joys, successes and failures, but also about everything ranging from algebra homework to a mother's drinking problem and a father's angry outbursts. Feelings about one another, family problems, and uptight teachers are hashed over all the time. Sifting through emotional issues and social conflicts in a mixed group of boys and girls helps your daughter learn to negotiate intimate relationships.

It is not unusual for teenage girls and boys to end up sleeping at the same home on weekend nights. This often has no sexual implications, but, of course, it could. One morning when she woke up, Eve found a note under her bedroom door from sixteen-year-old Grace. The note read, "Dear Mom, It was too crowded at Janet's house for the all-night cast party, so we came here to sleep. Love, Grace." Eve quietly opened her daughter's bedroom door to find Grace and her best friend, Emma, in Grace's bed. Two of their male friends were sound asleep on her floor in sleeping bags. Eve knew that these teenagers were all friends. She let them sleep and gave them breakfast before they went on their way. But later she talked to Grace and suggested that, the next time it happened, Grace have the boys sleep in the den.

Eve felt good about this unexpected happening. She was glad that Grace had felt free to come home instead of being afraid to bring her friends to their house. She was thankful that Grace chose to come home and sleep in her own bed rather than staying out just to prove her autonomy. And Eve was happy to have an opportunity to express some different parameters in a nonloaded way for the next time. She said, "Even if she brings them home again, I feel confident that Grace is exercising good judgment about what is going on."

It will be a different matter for you if you wake one morning, go to your daughter's room, and find her boyfriend in bed with her. Carla said, "I immediately shut the door again, knocked loudly, and told Brigid to send Dan out!" When he left the house, I lectured her for an hour. I completely freaked out. I was so fearful that this was the beginning of her bringing home one guy after another." After Carla calmed down, she and her daughter had a real conversation about boundaries. Carla knew Brigid and her boyfriend were having a sexual relationship, but she had never been confronted with it before. She realized she had never given the matter enough thought.

Suddenly, Carla had to come to grips with many questions. Be prepared for them yourself. Am I comfortable with her bringing her boyfriend to her bedroom instead of having sex in a parked car in an isolated place? Will I be encouraging her promiscuity if I am so accepting? What about me and my husband? What happens to our privacy at home? What about her younger brothers or sisters? What kind of example do I want to set for them? Then again, do I feel comfortable being hypocritical and saying "I know you're sexual, but I don't want to see it"?

This is an exceptionally complicated issue with no easy answer. Teenagers mostly do their sexual explorations away from their families. Cars, parties in homes where parents are absent, and rented motel rooms provide places for teenagers to experiment. How safe are these venues? Whatever this brings up for you, there is only one way to arrive at a fair, considered stance that includes both your acknowledgment that your daughter is a sexual being and your own boundaries and values: respectful conversation with her at the right time.

Rebecca felt held back by her parents' fears the summer after ninth grade, when she first asked them if she could sleep with her boyfriend, Gerard, at his house to celebrate their six-month anniversary. "My parents wouldn't let me. I couldn't understand. Why did it matter if it was day or night? I often spent twelve hours in the daytime there with him. It frustrated me—logically, it made no sense. I had started out honest, so I didn't sneak. I told them, 'You know, I could pretend I'm going to Sally's, but I won't.' I did end up sleeping with him a few times later when there were other people around, at Sally's once and at a party after the winter formal." Rebecca learned from this encounter not to ask for permission, but as a senior she allowed that she thought it had been the right thing for her parents to do. Although she had assured them and herself that she and her boyfriend would not "have sex" (intercourse), she thought that she probably would have lost her virginity that night and regretted it. Rebecca's asking her parents instead of deceiving them reflected not only her solid relationship with them but probably her own doubt about her ability to hold the line.

You will not be able to dictate which friends your adolescent daughter goes out with or which young men she chooses to experiment with sexually. It is wise to accept this fact gracefully. You can certainly tell her how you feel and what concerns you about her dating older guys. But you must rely on your relationship with her and mutual respect in order for her to listen to what you have to say. Simply forbidding her to see older boys will have no impact, because teenagers, for the most part, don't date in the way they used to. Even under the old norms, where a boy came to the house to pick a girl up, she could arrange to meet her boyfriend elsewhere if her parents objected to him. Now your daughter's social life will consist of group activities and pairing off from the group. Only for proms or formals will you hear talk of formal dates, and on those occasions, the girls often meet at one girl's house to dress and have the boys pick them up there.

Teenage girls need to be friends with a lot of boys and girls. In order to hold erotic tension and not act out indiscriminately, they must be able to resist the cultural pressure that it's "cool" to have sex, to not hold onto your virginity. They need to choose. Talk to your daughter about wanting her to have a safe, loving experience of sex. Discuss strategies for getting out of uncomfortable situations. Ask questions like, "If you walk off with a guy, how far do you intend to go?" "What are you seeking?" "What are the consequences of getting what you want sexually?" Even if she doesn't have anything to say in response to your questions, your having asked them will get her thinking about these situations.

When she comes home from school and tentatively confides in you that she is upset about a fight with a guy she likes, ask her about it without demanding details. Listen carefully and encourage her to trust her own instinct about what is going on. Offer some caring advice, but try not to be invested in her heeding it. Such confidences are precious and rare; they must be nurtured. Your loving and respectful response to her about her life will help ensure that she does not turn to sexuality as a substitute for affection and love. If you don't want her to move too fast, you need to be a safe place for her to come for valuing herself as a woman.

Sexual Harassment

If your daughter is being sexually harassed or intimidated, get help! Don't leave her to deal with this on her own. Talk to teachers, school counselors—try to get some class awareness about the way to treat one another. A boy who is pressuring her for sex or a group of boys threatening her for "fun" may be causing distress. An inspiring male teacher may be coming on to her. How can she deal with it? How can you help her? The school is legally required to take your concerns seriously.

Briana said, "I know how to get out of a difficult situation. A guy bought me a drink at a club and I just split. I double date if I'm worried about a guy pressuring me for more sex than I want to give. It's protection to have my friend there. I'm still a virgin, no full-blown sexual experience yet. I'm not ready for it."

There has been no societal protection for maidens in our culture. Almost every woman and girl has a history of sexual harassment, if not sexual abuse. Girls express both desire and fear of handling their sexuality. With the new awareness of girls' issues, there are now self-defense programs for girls and a strong emphasis on girls participating in sports, both of which encourage girls to become physically and emotionally strong. Girls claiming their bodies and owning their own sexuality are also empowering themselves.

Many creative, articulate teenage girls are writing plays and poems that feature their experiences of relationships, sexuality, and problems with body image. Theresa quietly observes her mother's sexuality in her poem "Mommy."

> Just being mommy
> she never wore black
> or sex
> or showed her sweet tummy.
> Maybe it was because of her babies
> stretching her skin
> like cheap miniskirt material—
> it could never reshape.
> Did she think she was ugly? or
> are bikinis only for models?
> She made herself at home
> hidden in daddy's T-shirts . . .
> and I didn't know how to say sex
> because hell was still a bad word.
> She was beautiful in striped flannel oversized
> so I bought her a soft red camisole.

In this crimson thing that matched her lips
and showed off her shoulders
she was shy.
Gently slipped into jeans and her sweatshirt again
and handed the tank top over to me.
Protective of her stretch mark highways,
she continues to giggle at the two-piece bathing suit
she bought last summer.
Being mommy, she hides this
ferocious feminine appeal.
Just being mommy
she'll never wear black.

Eighteen-year-old Sarah, animated and enthusiastic, was bored in English class one day and wrote the first line of her award-winning play *Distraction,* about teenage relationships. Writing the play led Sarah to a deeper understanding of herself. In her freshman year she had an intense, romantic relationship with an older boy. "I lived for him. I was completely in love. He was my purpose. But I learned that I had to discover my own purpose."

Sarah's play dramatizes girls' and boys' erotic feelings—a jumbled mix of desire, fear, rejection, illusion, and reality testings. In these relationships, figuring out love and sex becomes an intense search for the meaning of life.

In one scene, a character named Shannon describes her disgust with herself for trying to give her boyfriend oral sex against her own feeling of revulsion. Shannon says, "He made me afraid of losing him and simultaneously afraid of losing myself." Later, she describes girls' conflict about their sexuality.

Two bodies
I wish I had two bodies

one for you
to play with
and one for me
to protect
I would fling one body away
like I fling my thoughts
(against a concrete wall)
and still have the other in reserve
to guard aginst a sunny day
a day full of other smiles
and other monsters.

Finding their voices, girls are commenting on their own underworld experience in unprecedented ways. Persephone's abduction is a sexual initiation, forced at the beginning, then chosen when she tastes the honey-sweet pomegranate seed. Yet each time she returns from her sojourn with Hades, she flings herself into her mother's arms. Be there to receive your daughter when she resurfaces. She will be changed, fertilized by the seed of sexuality; you must change, too. Your engaging with her about her experience will enhance her and your emotional awareness and depth. It is best if you have been talking to her all along in matter-of-fact ways about sexuality, but it is never too late to begin.

4 ✂

*G*irlfriends?

*Y*our daughter's adolescent search is almost entirely directed at answering the question: "What does it mean to be a woman? What are the underlying values of being female in our culture?" Kate shakes her head, "It's confusing to be a girl. Everyone has their own definition of what being feminine is. We get a lot of mixed messages. For me, the word female is more scientific, it's our biology. With the word feminine, I get a visual image with a feeling—powerful, sweet, and subtle." As she develops her own answers, your daughter must have a secure relationship with you. Spending time with her in her high school years helps you to maintain the core trust you had with her when she was a child, while enlarging your relationship with her as she matures.

If your daughter is grounded in herself, she will not pin her self-worth on boys' attention or views of her. She will continue to form an identity that is uniquely hers, one that will reflect her own feelings, ideas, talents, and activities. She will learn to speak of her own needs in the first person, and to own her thoughts and feelings. She will learn to initiate. Her passions will be vitally important to her.

When a guy she likes wants to take her to a movie at a time that conflicts with another plan, instead of saying "yes" and flaking out of her commitment, she will arrange the movie for another time. Similarly, she does not easily succumb to her girlfriends' pressure when they goad her into doing something against her own judgment.

Women I see in psychotherapy have often lost themselves, lost their centeredness as girls. They suffer and wait perpetually for a man to call, for someone to rescue them, for a career to appear at their doorstep—in other words, for life to come to them. They envy other women for their looks, job opportunities, or relationships. Our adolescent daughters need to be the authors of their own fates.

Green with Envy

Mothers who envy other women often envy their daughters. You may envy your daughter for the freedoms and privileges she enjoys in our culture, freedoms and privileges that were not available for you. You may envy her as the recipient of your conscious mothering because, as a child, you didn't get from your mother what you're giving your daughter now. Even the most self-aware mother can experience resentment. Rewarding as it can be, caring for a child is demanding and relentless. A mother who had children when she was young is sometimes unformed as an individual and feels trapped in her mothering role. An older mother with a career is often pressured by the conflict between her professional demands and her children and has little patience with the conflictual nature of the adolescent years.

Envy of your daughter can poison your relationship and get in the way of your daughter becoming a woman. Adolescent girls are already caught up in the tumultuous cultural change that says girls can do anything. As Kate put it, "I've never felt there was anything I couldn't do with my life, if I wanted to. I've been raised knowing that I will make my own money, not just look for a guy to take care of me. But I think a lot of girls now have pressure the other way to go into a traditionally male career, to be a doctor or a lawyer."

In this atmosphere, the question of what it means to be feminine is often overlooked. Teenage girls are being pushed to challenge themselves on every front. Often when asked about what it means to be a woman, they look puzzled and confused, and revert to a tearful, "I don't know." If you aren't supporting her, she cannot make her way through the intensity of this change.

Envy does not have to be destructive. The feeling can prompt you to become aware of undeveloped potential, unexpressed ambition in yourself. Knowing what's lacking, you can explore your own growth and monitor your conversations with your daughter. If she plays soccer, you can say, "I'm so envious of the opportunities you have to play sports. When I was young, girls played only softball and we didn't even have good coaching. No one took girls in athletics seriously." Go to as many of her games as possible and ask about her practices to show her that you want her to succeed.

At the same time, think about what physical challenge at this stage in your life would make you feel better. While it won't entirely make up for what you missed out on in adolescence, it will improve your health and allow you to let go of the past. Athletics is only one of the many opportunities our daughters have that we did not. Whatever you envy about her life, acknowledge it and ask yourself, "What can I change in *my* life now?" You can't live without loss, but you can use losses to grow, instead of getting stuck and turning them into bitter obsessions that can contaminate your relationships.

What to Do Together

You will definitely have less time with your daughter in high school than in middle school. Increasingly, she is going to have a life that she keeps to herself. What do you do with her to keep the relationship open? These days, traditional mother-daughter activities are often looked at askance by women who may have felt trapped in their mothers' kitchens on holidays while their brothers got to watch the football game with the men. Be careful that you are not repeating your mother's example.

You and your daughter can enjoy doing chores together if you cooperate in making it fun. But don't unthinkingly uphold old gender roles. Eve remembers a critical moment when Grace stormed out of the bathroom, saying, "This isn't fair! I'm sick of having to clean the bathroom on Saturdays and have you look it over and tell me, 'You missed this spot' or 'This isn't clean enough,' while Bart and Doug rake leaves, do the yard, and get to be outside!" Eve, a high school science teacher, was flabbergasted. She considered herself an enlightened woman, yet here she was thoughtlessly reinforcing the split that she had chafed against growing up. When setting up family chores, be sure that you are as equitable with her and her brothers as you expect your employer to be with you.

Self-Nurturing Begins at Home

Show your daughter that you value downtime as well as being active and on the go. Teach her to nurture herself. Declare one weekend day a feminine retreat; choose a day when the rest of the family is out so that you will have the house to yourselves. Turn off the ringer on the phone, curl up with good books, take long, scented baths, do each other's hair or nails. Go back and forth between being alone and being together, talking and being silent. You will be amazed at how rejuvenated you both feel. Such time becomes sacred and gives her permission to turn her attention to her inner life.

"Let's Bake a Cake."

Some mothers and daughters find cooking, sewing, or doing house-work satisfying domestic activities to share. If you love to cook and have cultivated a relationship with your daughter in the kitchen, making meals and discussing food can continue to be a setting for the two of you to meet and talk. If you like to cook or garden and your daughter wants only to play sports, you'll have to find a different arena.

It will be more difficult if you dislike cooking or entertaining, and your daughter urges you to bake cookies and try new recipes with her. Encourage her and join her in whatever way you can. If cooking has always been a burdensome chore to you, teach her what you know, and enjoy her company. If she takes over some of the preparatory work, she will relieve you and you can talk over your day. Kate's fourteen-year-old sister, Alta, loves to cook. Their mother, Ellen, said, "I'm not so good at cooking unless I focus on one dish. Alta and I have a good time making banana bread or a pasta dish. I feel so grateful that she wants to be with me in the kitchen."

You could take a one-day cooking class together where you'll both learn something new. She'll probably quickly surpass your skills and may be inspired to do some of the cooking herself. Preparing food and sharing meals should evoke a positive mood in a family. Remember, her healthy body image (and yours) depends on having a healthy relationship to food.

If the home-decorating shows on TV have caught her eye and she wants to redecorate her room, help her do it. Teenagers like to redesign their rooms as they are defining themselves; they talk about it being "therapeutic." It's a great creative outlet and can be done economically. If you let her do as she wishes, she will probably plaster the walls with posters and memorabilia.

If you loathe homemaking, do not squelch your daughter's impulses toward it. Sonya, a stockbroker, told her daughter, Jody, "I've always hated doing anything domestic. I wanted to get out of what I saw my mother doing. It seemed so boring; it made me feel trapped. I wanted to succeed in a job or career, like my father. And I did. When I'm not at the firm, I'd much rather be outdoors taking a hike in the woods than paying attention to the house. My talent is limited in this realm, but I'll support you in finding books or taking classes if you are interested in cooking or sewing. I'm glad you can feel powerful even doing things that traditionally limited a woman's role." These don't have to be politically charged issues. Inducing your daughter to avoid certain activities because they represent domestic oppression to you does not insure that she will be self-reliant. In fact, it may completely backfire and render her helpless in basic life skills.

If you want to push the boundaries of established gender roles, enlist your teenage daughter to join you in an activity that has traditionally been assigned to men. Taking a class together in basic car maintenance, woodworking, or advanced computer science will extend your skills and hers. Do not confuse what you or she likes to do with being feminine or not. She is a woman, whether she is laying up for a shot on the basketball court or making chocolate chip cookies at home. Support her core by valuing her body, her feelings, and her mind.

Shop, Shop, Shop

Shopping is a passion for many adolescent girls. Our consumer culture has geared itself to this age group, which spends millions of dollars a year. Whatever your daughter's activities in high school, you will find that she needs to buy something every time you turn around. Whether it be folders for school reports, warm-ups for swim team, or a dress for the winter formal, you will frequently either be giving her money to go to the mall with her friends or accompanying her yourself.

Shopping with a teenager in today's mall is a multisensory experience. All name-brand stores play popular teen music ranging from rap to rock to soul at top volume, accompanied by MTV screens, which project continuously over the sales counters. Bombarded by multiple life-sized faces on the screen and resounding lyrics, you almost have to shout to be heard.

After an afternoon making the rounds to her fourteen-year-old daughter's favorite shops, Lois said, "I feel as if I've been on another planet. It takes me a while to come down, and I'm exhausted. I'm always glad when it's over! But Debbie is so used to the music, she doesn't even hear it. I wonder what it does to these kids' hearing? I'd rather give her the money and let her go with her girlfriends." Lois is framing her experience of shopping with her daughter in an alienating way. Lois's life revolves around entertaining with her husband and going to the symphony and the opera. In her well-organized, aesthetically pleasing social life, she feels competent and in charge, but she is uncomfortable in Debbie's intense, unpredictable adolescent world. Avoiding those feelings, Lois pushes her daughter away and misses an opportunity to be closer to her, to join briefly in Debbie's experience.

In the same situation, Cassia is able to be more creative and plan special shopping trips with her sixteen-year-old daughter, Zoe. "Zoe is delighted when I take her shopping. I relax and enter into the spirit of the trip. The noise level in the teen departments can be assaultive, but I ask Zoe questions about the singers we see on the screen or the groups whose music they are playing. I often buy something for myself so Zoe can critique the clothes as I try them on. I do the same for her. We're always tired at the end and like to relax by having dinner out. These are exuberant times for us because we've had fun sharing and giving each other input on what to buy." At other times, Cassia is glad to let Zoe go off with her friends to shop.

Cassia sets limits that ensure the success of a shopping trip with her daughter. "I give Zoe an allowance at the outset of the trip. It's up to her to decide whether to spend half of it on one pair of jeans that she just 'has to have' or to look for bargains and get more pieces. Then we don't have to wrangle over how much things cost." Cassia is an art history professor and has always earned her way. She knows how important it is for a woman to be able to manage her money. Teaching your daughter to budget her money is a critical learning experience. And if she is invested in what she wears, budgeting will hold her interest.

"I'll Race You to the Top."

If your daughter likes to run and you are athletically inclined, try to take a run with her once a week. If she beats you, it will give her a huge surge of self-confidence. She has seen you as the expert in her life, more competent than she is at everything you do. As she masters new skills, she may outstrip you not only athletically but also intellectually. Games provide a good focus for girls to show their mastery and best their mothers. Rejoice in her victories, even though you are the loser. If you win, be a good winner. A girl is often afraid to surpass her mother; she is afraid she will lose her mother's love. Show her that this is not true by conceding gracefully.

Know that your mothering has contributed to her success. This is not to say that you take credit for her accomplishments. Her successes are truly the products of her character, initiative, and talents, but you have provided the environment in which those gifts could grow.

Walking, hiking, rollerblading, or doing any sport can be stimulating and companionable. Go to the gym to work out together. Take up bicycling. Roslyn and her seventeen-year-old daughter, Daria, drove to a national park to take a four-hour bike ride in the mountains. Daria was in great physical shape, Roslyn in fair shape, and they reached a compromise speed that was satisfying to both of them. The old railroad grade was deserted and beautiful in the midst of trees and streams.

While the outgoing trip was without incident, in the late afternoon, coming back down, Roslyn suddenly fell when her bike slid on some loose dirt. Her leg was injured as it got trapped beneath the bike in the skid. Both women were stunned; Roslyn was in pain and could not move. "You'll have to go for help, Daria," her mother said. Daria made her mother as comfortable as she could and left at high speed. "I was so scared because my mom was all alone. It was getting dark, and there weren't any other people on the trail. I didn't know if she was going to be OK; her leg was all bloody and bruised. I didn't know how badly she was hurt." Daria succeeded in finding the park rangers, who took over and got Roslyn out to a medical facility for treatment. Daria said, "I never knew how I would be in an emergency, and I found out that I was good. I kept my head, even though I was scared to death." Roslyn had not worried; she felt sure Daria was up to the task. This experience deepened their trust and brought them closer.

Working Moms

If you are a working mother, you can find ways to stay close to your daughter. Rebecca, an oustanding student, is creatively immersed in her peer culture, and she uses her own judgment as she experiments with alcohol, drugs, and sexuality. She decides how much of her experience to share with her parents. Rebecca said, "After I got my driver's license, I drove my younger brother to and from school, worked part-time, and did school. I was so busy, I never saw my family." Her mother, Sharon, a minister at a community church, and her father, Matthew, an engineering consultant, are both energetic professionals. "My mother and I have been reduced to doing errands and shopping together. Neither of us likes to shop, but we have fun if I need five pairs of shorts for the beach or a dress for the prom. She waits up for me sometimes because she likes to see me; she makes an effort and so do I." Sharon has adapted her way of connecting as her daughter's life changes.

Some mothers and daughters leave each other supportive notes when their schedules have them going in different directions. In fifteen-year-old Jody's household, Sonya has to get up earlier than Jody does to be at her broker's office. Jody's father, Carl, makes breakfast and gets Jody and her older sister off to school. But when Jody has a biology test or a grueling basketball practice that day, she often finds a note from her mother wishing her luck. This has inspired Jody to leave her mother similar notes, when she knows that Sonya has an important meeting coming up or has a project to finish for a client. Writing notes helps them feel more in touch with each other's lives, even in its most mundane aspects. Jody and Sonya also use notes to make dates to have dinner out together or lunch on a weekend when Jody's after-school activities keep her from having dinner with the family.

Pagers are a blessing for a working mother when you need to change a plan about meeting your daughter or picking her up from school. You can page her when you know you have a window of time in which she can call you back. Sometimes, it's nice to beep her just to say, "Hello. I'm thinking of you," especially if you know she's not in class and is free to return the call. Or the two of you can make up a special code to leave messages on the pager. Both writing notes and using a pager are valuable ways to connect with your teenage daughter, suiting her newly independent stage of life.

When I Was Fourteen . . . and Other Stories

Share with your daughter what it was like for you as a teenager. Thinking about your own adolescence will help you recognize the ways in which your upbringing was different. It's often easier to think about what your mother did wrong, and tell yourself, "I don't want to do that to my daughter." Reflect also on what she did right, how you now take after her. Tell your daughter, granddaughter, or niece about your role models growing up.

Storytelling can help your daughter understand you and where you are coming from. It keeps tradition alive and is a wonderful tool for bridging differences between the generations. It gives mothers and grandmothers a chance to describe their upbringing, with its disappointments and its lessons. As older women describe their lives, fears, and good wishes for girls, girls have a chance to reflect. In our myth, Hecate, goddess of the dark moon, and the only witness to Persephone's abduction, recounts the story of what she saw to Demeter. At the end of the tale, Hecate becomes Persephone's companion, lighting the girl's way with her torch, as Persephone moves back and forth between the light and dark worlds. Our daughters need the stories of older women who have suffered to light their way into womanhood.

What Story to Tell, When

Choose the story that you have to tell to help your daughter with the crisis or dilemma that she is dealing with at that moment. If she is asking you questions, answer them. If there is a story you think is relevant to her predicament, ask her if she wants to hear it. Watch her reactions and respond to them with understanding. One spring day, Marlene and her eighteen-year-old daughter, Kitty, were sitting on their porch. Suddenly, Kitty asked, "Mom, have you ever had a relationship with a woman?" Marlene took a deep breath and said, "Yes I have, Kitty. Why do you ask?" Kitty said, "Because I did too, Mom, last year when I was in France. What made you decide to be with men, Mom? How did you decide to remarry?"

"You know, Kitty, I just found that I liked the otherness of men," Marlene replied frankly to Kitty. Kitty said, "My mom had always been open to me asking her questions so I felt all right bringing up something loaded. I felt closer to her after that. I knew I could always trust her to tell me the truth." Marlene felt a pang of doubt about disclosing her secret, but knew she couldn't lie to Kitty. Their relationship was becoming more adult. A few years later, when Kitty was married with a child of her own, she told Marlene, "Mom, that was one of the most powerful things you ever told me. It helped me figure out that I prefer that otherness in men, too."

Mothers are often hesitant to share their personal experience with their daughters. Yet it helps your daughter hear that you had problems, too, that you weren't perfect. Talk to her about what happened to you, what life skills you had, and how you would have liked it to have been different. Communicate in an ongoing way your own deeply held values and your earned wisdom about the discrepancy between ideals and reality.

Know Your Daughter

Your daughter may be shy socially and excel in one talent that requires tremendous dedication. She may be studious and introverted. She may avoid having any kind of social life. She may have her phone ringing off the hook, be good at many activities, given to mischief making, and not a serious student. Choose things to do with your daughter that suit her; ask her how she wants to spend time together. Don't try to force her into doing things that you think are "good" for her.

If you have a common interest and are looking for new stimulation, take an art class or an aerobics class together. Ask her to teach you to do something that she is good at and you are a novice in—for example weightlifting. Volunteer at a soup kitchen for the homeless together. Take karate or kayaking.

If your daughter watches certain television programs, sit and watch them with her now and then. You can learn a lot about her and her world by discussing the shows that you see together. Going to the movies can also be a great way to keep up with her peer culture. The media provide an opportunity for you to make her media savvy by questioning and reacting to commercials and programming.

This is not to say that you simply follow your daughter around doing whatever she wants you to do. Relationships go both ways. But you must make yourself available to her, or you will never see her. Much of the time you spend with your daughter in her teenage years will revolve around her activities. Some mothers make this their first priority. Jean gets up to take Tammy to water polo practice at 5:45 every morning. She returns an hour and a half later to bring her breakfast, dry towels, and clothes. When Tammy has changed and eaten, Jean drives her to the other side of the high school, so she won't be late for her first-period class. Tammy's second practice of the day is from 3:15 to 5:15 P.M., and Jean repeats her shepherding duty. Jean is a constant support person for her only child because, she says, "Tammy will only be fourteen once." Jean works 8:00 A.M. to 4:00 P.M. as a features editor on a local newspaper, in order to optimize her time with her daughter. Tammy relishes her mother's attention. "I don't like breakfast food, so my mom brings leftovers from dinner, like corn beef hash." Tammy's gratitude for her mother's devotion shows itself in her cooperativeness at home and her acceptance of her parents' rules.

If your daughter asks you for a favor and you do it willingly and cheerfully, ask her to reciprocate by doing something with or for you. If she wants you to take her to a weekend sale at a vintage clothes store, request that she accompany you afterward to visit her grandmother in the convalescent home. You need an exchange. As she matures, she will want to give more and you will be able to receive. This is one of the joys of her growing up.

Making It Up to Her (and Yourself)

Looking back at your daughter's childhood, ask yourself, What do I wish I had done differently? Identify a pattern that in retrospect seems

114

unproductive. Adolescence is an opportunity to correct ways in which your relationship went awry. Phyllis was a single-parent nurse who had worked the night shift since her daughter, Lauren, was eight years old. Lauren had learned to set her alarm, make her own breakfast, and walk to the corner to take the bus to school. When Lauren was thirteen and beginning to go through emotional ups and downs, Phyllis decided to push for a day shift with the hospital. Although she had always been on top of getting Lauren's school supplies, clothes, and other necessities, her night schedule had precluded much hands-on mothering of her daughter.

Phyllis had never been properly mothered herself, but she was learning self-nurturing skills in therapy; this led her to change her behavior with Lauren. She was gratified and astonished to see how much doing the breakfast ritual with Lauren in the mornings and driving her to school meant to her daughter. "She comes and gives me big hugs and thanks me for being there. It's made her more open to talking to me. And it makes me feel less lonely, too." Lauren said, "I learned a lot about being independent, but I never felt close to my mother, even though I knew she loved me and was working hard so she could take care of us both. Now, I feel better all day because it started off with us together."

Harriet had a different insight about herself that led her to change her relationship with her teenage daughter. "When Robin was young, I was obsessed with being efficient: vacuuming, folding clothes, cleaning the kitchen, and doing the garden. I was very driven, just like my mother. Robin would ask me to come and play or take her to the park. I would divert her and tell her to go play with her brothers or enlist her to help me. We never did what *she* wanted to do." When Robin was fourteen, Harriet was struck with how consistently she had refused to enter her daughter's life. Robin's father, Bruce, coached Little League baseball for her younger brothers and watched sports with them on television in his free time. Robin was on the periphery of the family.

Harriet told Robin over dinner one night, "Robin, I know you've been giving me signals for a long time that I wasn't meeting you in some way. You've asked me repeatedly why I spend so much time cleaning the house. I've decided you're right, and from now on, we're going to plan one afternoon on the weekend to do something fun together that *you* choose." Once Harriet made time for Robin on Robin's terms, their intimacy grew. Robin said, "It made me feel more special to my mom, that what I thought mattered and that my desire to, say, go to the beach wasn't just a waste of time. It really changed our relationship."

Both Phyllis and Harriet felt strongly that they were happier for the changes they had made on behalf of their daughters. They rediscovered savoring their daughters' company and began to learn from them in ways they hadn't imagined. They both received increased love and support from their daughters as a result of their efforts.

Sometimes, it's right for a mother to do something for her teenage daughter that, under normal circumstances, would belong to a much younger age. If, for instance, there is a sudden death, divorce, or other trauma in the family, your daughter might want to come and sleep with you for some weeks until she has worked it through and she feels secure again. Or she may want to spend time with you in ways that she hasn't done since sixth grade. If you were not able to give her the kind of unconditional, emotional, and physical closeness that she needed at five or six, you can find ways to be more loving with her as a teenager. It won't be the same as if you had been able to do it when she was younger, but it will be enormously helpful to her development nonetheless. You can always turn your relationship around.

Getaway Bonding

If your best attempts at a positive relationship with your daughter continue to escalate her defiance and resentfulness, arrange to take her out of her environment. This can be as simple as going for a long walk or a relaxing drive. Get her out into nature and let her unwind with you as a supportive presence. You don't need to bring up any issues, but you may find her wanting to talk on a beautiful lakeshore or in a green wooded park. Both mothers and fathers can make these kinds of overtures.

Diane felt that she had been too sheltered, dependent on her father and brothers, and then her husband, to take care of anything that went wrong. She knew that her dependence was based on her fear of taking healthy risks, of moving beyond her known safe world of home and family. She wanted to push some boundaries for herself and help her daughter, Maggie, feel more competent. The summer after Maggie's sophomore year, Diane took her on a river rafting trip on the Colorado River. "Shooting the rapids was the most frightening and exhilarating ride I have ever taken," Diane admitted. "I had to do it over and over again and conquer my fear each time. At the end of the two weeks, I felt like a different person." Maggie said, "I was scared, but it was so fun. I loved it. And it was great to see my mom doing something like that. It gave me a whole different picture of her. I realized she was stronger than she looks at home." Taking your daughter on short or long trips with you will give you both a chance to show sides of yourselves that do not come out in everyday life.

When you do something challenging that you've never done before with your daughter, you are both beginners. Toni, a wilderness guide, does team building for girls at a ropes course near a stream in the woods. They alternate silence and camaraderie: listening to the natural world, talking about their perceptions. They emphasize personal empowerment, setting goals, and stepping over comfort lines. "Girls and women learn to use their intuition for direction and safety. I see them becoming stronger," Toni said.

Girltalk

Persephone is dancing in a beautiful meadow with her girlfriends when Hades abducts her. For adolescent girls, Hades represents not only male aggression but also the social upheaval of their high school milieu. When your daughter moves from middle school to freshman year, you should expect her idyllic girlhood friendships to be disrupted. New faces in a new setting are daunting to the most confident girl. Rae, secure and accomplished on her way to drama school, said, "The advice I would give to a freshman girl is not to worry about what people think of you. When I was that age I was always wondering: Am I popular enough? Do the other freshmen like me? What do the seniors think of me? Freshmen need to hear, 'By the end of senior year, you will have good friends.' "

Your teenage daughter wants to make friends, be accepted, test her limits, and explore her new world. Her social life is her priority. It is the laboratory and testing ground for new skills, new adventures. Any social rejection is a source of intense anxiety. Without the support of friends, she will miss out on a crucial learning experience. Through her social context she establishes intrapersonal as well as interpersonal skills. She determines her likes and dislikes about herself and others by monitoring what she feels and thinks in relation to what others feel and think.

Being rejected by peers leads to diminishing self-esteem and can undermine her belief in her ability to master new situations. In its extreme, peer rejection can lead to deviant behaviors and unhealthy risk-taking patterns, like having unprotected sex and substance abuse. A girl may find her own ground if she is brave enough to endure some social disapproval for not going along with unhealthy peer behavior.

It is vital for an adolescent girl to find at least one intimate girlfriend whom she can count on in high school. Studies have shown that girls work more productively and effectively in all-girl settings;

girls cooperate with one another on homework, in team sports, and in the classroom. Girls and women are enlivened by this kind of creative collaboration. But there is often an underlying competition among girls for thinness, beauty, or attention from boys. This can get in the way of their finding friends whom they can trust. Just as girls have radar for their mothers' weak points, they are always scanning for other girls' weaknesses. A girl who has too high an opinion of herself or who has an irritating characteristic will very quickly find other girls avoiding her or putting her down. Even among friends, girls are continually mulling over, describing, and analyzing the personalities of the other girls in the group. Most of this conversation happens on the phone or at overnights with friends.

Through their intense analysis of one another, girls can become more self-aware. Kate remembered an incident with her girlfriend Abigail. Kate was packing to leave for an intensive Spanish language camp after junior year. Abigail was helping Kate decide what to wear the first day of class, to make an impression. Suddenly, Abigail said, "Oh, God, I just realized, you have to walk in with Lisa." Lisa was another friend going to camp, whom Kate described as "drop-dead gorgeous." Kate said, "It doesn't bother me. I'm used to it. I've been best friends with her since preschool." Abigail said, "It would bother *me*. I'd plan it out to walk in with someone uglier than me, so I'd look good." Kate said that at first she was shocked, but also proud of Abigail for being honest. But then later, she found herself wondering if Abigail saw her as the "ugly" one. She hadn't realized her friend was that scheming. "But," she said, "I always want to be with the pretty girls so I'll be seen as pretty, too. And I guess that's scheming, too, but in a different way." Kate was perceptive enough to recognize the shadowy implications of what Abigail was saying and evaluate herself in the same light. It's healthy for girls to reveal their darker sides to each other.

A girl needs to find her own community instead of withdrawing from school and clinging only to you. You can help her. Encourage her to stay in touch with a strong, true sense of self by reinforcing the activities that she loves to do. If she follows her passions in spite of being pulled this way and that by girlfriends or boyfriends, she will stay on course and true to herself.

Your relationship with your daughter is key to her sense of self. Firmly grounded, she will not always put others' needs before her own in order to be liked. You will have to walk the fine line between allowing her to choose friends and being aware of who her friends are and what they are all up to. To understand your daughter and her social context, you need to be observant and neutral. Debbie said, "I don't tell my mom anything about my friends, because she hears one little thing and judges the girl on that." The lesson here is to take what your daughter shares with you as only one reality instead of jumping to conclusions. Her confidences often betray the current state of her friendship, rather than representing a reliable character assessment.

If over time you get clues that suggest her friends are up to no good, then you'll need to intervene. But you can be sure that your daughter is also involved. Don't make the mistake of seeing your daughter as innocent and her friends as the bad influence. Your daughter will take her friends' side and turn away.

The Deadly Triangle

One fall day, when Usha picked up her freshman daughter from high school, Devi burst into tears the instant school was out of sight. When she cautiously asked her what was wrong, Devi told her between sobs that her best friend since fourth grade, whom Usha knew well, was ignoring her at school. Her friend was now hanging out with a third girl who previously had been on the periphery of their group and hadn't returned her phone calls in the evening for the past week.

This is a common scenario during the transitions from grammar school to middle school, middle school to high school, and even high school to college. Although triangles emerge even earlier, in high school such rejection is marked by a higher level of angst. At this age, your daughter will register more levels of meaning in being rejected: she will blame herself for not being good enough in a thousand ways. Girls' desperate insecurity in high school often rules out compassion for the rejected girl. And in high school, "mother love" cannot make up for the loss; once, she could find refuge in you, but now she has to make new friends. You can no longer intervene the way you might have done in primary school; you can only listen to your daughter and offer her your experience. Being able to confide in you will give her the courage to reenter the fray.

When best friends go separate ways, one of them is always hurt. As girls seek to realign themselves in new schools, there is often a lot of meanness and back stabbing. Your daughter will probably be the victim one time, the perpetrator the next. Yet, at the same time, compassion for others can be learned in these excruciating high school intrigues.

When confronted with your daughter's distress, listen and empathize. Then try to explore her feelings about herself in relation to this friend. What might have led up to this alienation? Had she seen it coming? Don't blame her for the break, but help her to look at both sides. Tell her a story about when you found yourself in a similar plight. Share with her how the situation resolved for you. Help her feel secure enough to stand a temporary separation from her friend. While a week is a long time for a teenager, you can offer a longer perspective. If she broadens her social horizons and spends time with other girls, her friend may come around at some point.

If it becomes a permanent rejection, then help her see that, sad as it is, she and her friend may have grown apart. Feel out that possibility with her. If she fears that she has told her friend her whole life story and now the friend has betrayed her by telling other girls her secrets, acknowledge that this makes her feel fragile and vulnerable. Over time, she will be more careful with how much of herself she wants to share. After the initial disappointment, you want her to realize that the rejection is not a reflection of her worth but rather part of the ebb and flow, the good and bad, of relationships. When she is in the position of power, of being the rejecting or demeaning one to another girl, perhaps she will be able to handle the situation in a less hurtful manner.

Outright rejection is not as common as a girl being gradually pushed away, ostracized, and forced out of a group. Walking away and looking for friendship elsewhere is not as easy as it sounds. Your daughter may be so crushed that she withdraws instead of making overtures to other girls. Support her in taking time to recover. Meanwhile, encourage her to find activities or arenas in which she will naturally meet new friends.

Delia was Tammy's best friend all through grammar school. "When we carpooled to preschool, we hated each other and were always fighting. Delia had chicken pox when she was six years old, and, for some reason, I sympathized with her. My mom and I brought her flowers; we became great friends even though we didn't go to the same school. I was very athletic; Delia wasn't. In eighth grade other differences showed up. Delia got into acting, singing, and drama. Now she's into wild cast parties and older guys. She listens to rap music and is very critical of her appearance, much more than I am.

"I know people from my swimming and water polo teams, and I listen to alternative and swing music. Delia and I aren't comfortable together anymore. We've gone separate ways for now. My mom told me that this is what happens—it happened to her and her best friend." Jean, Tammy's mother, described how she and her best friend, who now have lengthy phone calls several times a week, drifted apart for years in high school. Jean became editor of the school newspaper, while her best friend dropped out and got into the drug scene. Jean said, "We still called each other *sisters,* but we lived different lives. I think we were ashamed of each other." Shame is a strong factor in girls distancing themselves from other girls. Whether wanting to be seen for who they are or trying to ally themselves with the popular group, they often cruelly reject a girl whom they see as a liability.

Jean and her friend reconnected in college when their values leveled out and their old closeness reemerged. "We were in each other's weddings and our babies were born five weeks apart. We can't imagine life without each other."

You are a role model for your daughter's relationships with her girlfriends. Who are your good women friends? What are your relationships with them like? Ellen, Kate's mother, has a group of women friends from high school who meet for lunch or dinner a few times a year. Last year, the eight of them went on a four-day cruise together. Ellen, a self-contained librarian, said, "I had a great time, once I got all the logistics arranged to leave. With three children, ages seventeen, fourteen, and five, it was really complicated to organize everything so I could leave. But my kids loved it that I was going away. They like seeing that my women friends have a place in my life."

Tribal Mentality

Belonging to a group is the key to high school life. Eighteen-year-old Danielle said, "My best friends were a year or two older than me. As a senior, I had problems when I was forced to be with my own class. It was difficult at first until I found friends." Danielle's dilemma came about because in the first months of freshman year, she had been part of a group of girls in her own class. One Friday in December, they were all going to a girl's home to get dressed together for the winter formal. "I was waiting after school in front of the library for one of them to pick me up. They forgot me, not on purpose. A group of sophomore and junior girls were milling around and, amazingly, said,

'Why don't you come along with us?' That was that; I joined their group. After they graduated, when I was a senior, I came back to the original group of friends who had forgotten to pick me up." Forming friendships can be whimsical or circumstantial, or your daughter can find true soulmates. But most of her social energy will go into dissecting, strengthening, and maintaining those relationships.

Erika faced a problem when she found herself unhappy with her group of girlfriends. They were into partying, which she quickly found boring. Their conversation centered on who was cool, cars, money, and popularity. "There was nothing there for me." Although she didn't want to hang out with them and have lunch with them at school, she felt trapped. "I didn't know how to change groups. I was too insecure and afraid to go through a period of time without friends. Finally, I changed schools; it was the right move! In my new school, the kids have varied backgrounds; there's not so much sameness. Now I have a new group of friends, and I still see my old ones sometimes. It's the best of both worlds. It's not easy to make new friends once you're in a group." From her eighteen-year-old vantage point, Erika also said that all girls talk about other girls' being superficial and silly. "So who are these *other girls?*"

When a girl steps outside her normal environment, she may learn new lessons about friendship. After her junior-summer Amigos trip to Ecuador, Kaylie said, "Usually with my friends, if I'm annoyed, I don't say anything. I just get frustrated inside and I keep my thoughts to myself. But after two weeks in Ecuador, my partner, Midori, and I had to start processing, and we got closer. We spent so much time in our room working, planning what we were going to do in the village. I just started blurting out whatever was on my mind because I had to—we both did. And I really liked it. We both opened to our feelings. And that was strange, because we would never have been friends if we hadn't been put together like that."

When to Ask for Help

If your daughter is being continually scapegoated, you must intervene and seek help for her. Being singled out to ignore or cruelly
tease can quickly become harassment. If she seems to be in a downward spiral of depression or despair, be sure there are options that do
not compromise her developing independence. One option is to
seek counseling. If she has learned that she needs to do things "on
my own" or "tough it out," she may be in over her head before you
are aware of it. If you disparage counseling, she will feel embarrassed
to seek it or to share her distress with you.

Most high schools have on-site counselors to help students who
are having trouble. If your daughter's high school does not have a
counselor, and you see that she is sinking emotionally, find a clinic or
an individual counselor who treats adolescent girls. She needs an ad-
vocate, someone on her side to help her survive this rough time.

You and Her Friends

Friendships with other girls are crucial for your daughter's development, and she will value these friendships in much the same way you
do yours. You can foster her friendships by making your home a wel-
coming place for her girlfriends; if she asks you to make dinner for
them, enjoy it. Bask in the presence of girls' exuberance. Be careful
of the boundaries when your daughter's friends are visiting. She
won't want you competing for their attention. Maggie told her
mother, "I don't like it when you chat with my friends when they
come over. It feels like you're grilling them, putting them on the
spot." Diane was surprised and a little hurt; she was doing her best to
be friendly. But she was able to say, "Sorry, Maggie. You'll have to tell
me what the rules are, because I really don't have a clue." Maggie
sensed that her mother was offended and said, "Sorry, Mom, I didn't

mean to hurt your feelings. But thanks for listening. I really appreciated that you made spaghetti for us and talked to us in the kitchen, but I just don't want you to come in my room to chat." Diane suddenly realized that she had felt elated at being included because she was still haunted by her experience of feeling left out as an adolescent. And after their river rafting trip, she and Maggie had been closer. You can't redo your own adolescence by becoming one of the girls with your daughter and her friends. But you can heal some of your wounds by using what you learned to mother your daughter as she has to run this gauntlet.

If your daughter is willing, invite one of her close friends to join the two of you for a play, a concert, or a bike ride. Look for ways to spend time doing activities with other women and girls—for example, volunteering at school or church to do a special project, baking for a holiday sale, or driving a carpool for the girls' swim team. You could organize a mother-daughter book club. Discussing plots and characters gives you an opportunity to examine many life issues together. Your reading books about girls' development also shows her you care, and she may even pick them up herself. Jade said, "My mother reads all the books about girls and parenting and does the work. She doesn't always get it right, but she tries. I appreciate that." As your daughter spends less and less time with the family, you will have to find the spaces where she will allow you to participate in her world just a little.

You will more often be supporting your daughter going off with her girlfriends by themselves. Encourage their interests and enjoyment of each other. Being the accommodating driver for movies and community service jobs, and even picking them up from parties will earn you your daughter's goodwill. You are mostly a spectator in between events in these situations, but you will stay connected.

Use her girlfriend milieu, too, as the measure for some of her behavior that you may question. For example, if she comes downstairs wearing a slip one morning for going to school, you may feel more comfortable if you know that she and five friends have decided to make a statement together. If she is fourteen, you will question her judgment more than if she is eighteen. It's prudent to get to know a few of her girlfriends' mothers well enough to check with them now and then about what is going on with your daughter. Even though your teenager will object to such parental collaboration, it can be crucial.

Miscommunication

Try as you might, you and your daughter will sometimes miss. Jade said, "Sometimes my mother thinks she knows what is going on with me and she doesn't. But she *does* listen to what I say. When I talk about becoming a doctor and treating the homeless, she doesn't put me down. She had her "save the world" phase and came out of it. I don't know whether she thinks I'll get over it someday, but if she does, she keeps it to herself."

Danielle said, "My mother will reach out to me and say something wrong, something that just sets me off. Once when I was complaining about getting so many telephone calls, she said, 'Why do they want to call you?' She didn't mean it the way it sounded. She meant, 'What's going on?' But I had a big reaction. I want her to understand all the time." It irritates girls when their mothers do not approach them in exactly the right way.

In these missed communications your daughter is showing her confusion at being caught in an internal conflict. Part of her still wants to be your little girl and have you perfectly understand everything about her. The other part wants to be the more independent young woman that she is becoming. If she complains that her friend is bad-mouthing her to other girls and you respond with empathy— "Oh, honey, I'm so sorry she's being mean to you"—the other side comes up in her and says, "Oh, Mom, you don't get it. I can take it. This happens all the time." But if you respond by telling her to just tough it out because "such is life," it's likely that she'll be hurt because you showed no sympathy and say sarcastically, "Thanks a lot!" Remember that teenagers are highly sensitive, so that even innocent remarks can be (sometimes willfully) misconstrued. The delicacy of their feelings should never be underestimated.

When you miss connecting with your daughter in such moments, all you can do is try not to take it personally. You are doing the best you can. Give her some time before you continue the conversation. Know yourself well enough to remember your own inner conflict about wanting comfort but needing autonomy, and sometimes just wanting to fight to let off steam. You have to accept that you simply can't get this right all the time.

With a strong base in her identity as a girl in relation to you, her mother, and ways to touch back in with you routinely to remind her of your shared love and values, both of you will have an easier time with her intense social life at school. While parties and experimentation will have their draw, she will be less likely to lose herself in that scene if she is close to you.

As mothers we need to balance our daughters' developing independence with their need for us during adolescence and young adulthood. While she may want to do something challenging with you one day, like climb a mountain and feel the exhilaration of conquering the peak, the next day she may want to sit on your lap and rock back and forth as if she were a child again. If she screams at you one minute, she may be asking for milk and cookies the next. She needs you to be able to adapt to those different needs. Honor her (and your) capacity to be both self-sufficient and vulnerable, and she will be able to form friendships with other girls and women in which she can express herself fully, see herself mirrored, and grow.

5 ᔧ

Party Time

HIP-HOP, BEER,
AND WEED

The teen party scene is a mass of contradictions. As Rebecca said, "Even though we had all this education that makes the harder drugs like heroin and cocaine sound scary, marijuana and alcohol are so available. You see your friends do it and you see they're not getting really messed up, so you think maybe it's OK to try it." Our daughters and their friends are the most informed generation to date about addiction, and they are also the youngest to dabble in substance abuse. This paradox is confusing for kids and parents alike. As her mother, you know that your daughter trying one drink or drug may lead to her trying another; that both are bad for her health immediately and long-term; and that girls who are under the influence are more likely to become victims of sexual predation. You also know that experimenting with her friends will be appealing; like Persephone, she will be drawn to the unknown. Negotiating between the reality of her peer group and your concern for her health and safety can be complex and disturbing.

Entering this culture creates tremendous anxiety for girls. If some of your daughter's friends are going to the same high school, she may feel more secure than if she branches out by herself. But, as we have seen, in the new environment she won't be able to count on even her best friends. Briana described herself as a freshman. "I wasn't open-minded. There were all these different people and personalities. I was hearing a lot about doing drugs and alcohol. I withdrew, clinging on to the people I knew best; I wasn't quick to introduce myself to new kids." Briana's predicament is one that many girls face. Protected through eighth grade, she was frightened and intrigued by the shadowy world at the edge of the school community.

If your daughter is the oldest or only child in your family, you may have been able to shield her from exposure to the teen culture through middle school. But if she has gone to summer camp with older children or has an older sibling, she will likely have been offered a cigarette or some other substance to try by the time she enters high school. The value of sheltering your daughter from these experiences is that she maintains a core sense of her own value that helps her when she enters middle school.

By this time, you cannot simply legislate your parental authority without understanding the pressures she is feeling to join in with the so-called popular crowd—often those girls and boys who are experimenting with a lot of negative risk-taking behavior. In Briana's middle school, parental values were strictly reinforced, so such pressure did not exist. This made freshman year all the more overwhelming.

Girls in middle school may be personally satisfied with risk taking in the form of a more challenging piano or cello piece, taking up a new sport, or going to malls and movies with their girlfriends. But making friends in high school entails a whole new order of risks. A girl immediately begins sharing and comparing with others her age what she has "done" or "tried" that is respected in the teenage world. A girl who has not kissed a boy, been drunk, or tried marijuana at a party by the time she enters high school may feel she is "behind" the other girls she meets.

Risk taking is the fulcrum around which girls and boys develop their identities in the middle school and teenage years. At school, positive risk taking can include academic or sports activities that challenge girls to push beyond what they believe are their physical limits. Theater and dance also provide healthy outlets. Camping and rock climbing on weekends stretch young people who spend week-days behind a desk in a classroom. In the current teenage milieu, sooner or later, a young woman will have to make choices about experimenting with cigarette smoking, drugs, and alcohol as part of her initiation into teenage culture.

Briana did not feel close enough to her mother, Carolyn, to turn to her for support in her freshman year. Carolyn, a loving mother, had a long-term stable marriage, and her life revolved around her husband, son, and daughter. She was a hands-on mother, driving to and from school and doing volunteer work. But her daughter's temperament was a difficult match with hers; Briana was moody, introverted, and sarcastic. Carolyn was extroverted and even-tempered, and she naturally gravitated toward her younger child, her son, who was more like her. Over time, conflict between Briana and both her parents intensified.

If you feel that you and your daughter are temperamentally mismatched, you will have to try much harder to understand her. Stay rooted in your love for her, ask her a lot of questions about herself as you go along, and you will reap the benefits of a complex relationship built on acknowledging your differences.

Family Values

Think about your adolescence and compare it to your daughter's. What was your cultural milieu? What was your family's socio-economic base? What were your parents' values? How do their values differ from those you are trying to instill in your children? You may have been in psychotherapy, which has given you a different perspective on your identity as a woman and on family life than your own mother had. In Carolyn's middle-class family, her motivation had been to earn a scholarship for her college education. Cultured and sophisticated, she was now raising her children in an upper-middle-class home where money was a given.

Carolyn valiantly tried to assert her original values of hard work and responsibility for her children, but it was an uphill battle when her daughter had a car and a credit card of her own by age sixteen. Briana felt misunderstood and put upon by her mother. Her untamed mood swings stirred up constant trouble in the family; her father continually erupted at her, and Carolyn found herself in the middle, mediating conflict.

With the family in emotional chaos, Briana withdrew from her mother and fended for herself. Having money at her disposal, she could do as she liked. Money brings opportunities, but it also breeds entitlement in teenagers already inflated with the freedoms of their peer culture.

How were you raised, and how is your upbringing meshing with the way you are raising your daughter? Nothing will have prepared you for the wildness of adolescent group life today. And when she is going through these years, you will find yourself reliving all the worst moments of your own adolescence. Even an enlightened mother who has an intimate relationship with her daughter can be reduced to tears by her and her friends.

Kay had agreed to drive her fifteen-year-old daughter, Jessica, and three friends to an out-of-town Sarah McLachlan concert. All the girls idolized the singer-songwriter. The trip was a generous gift of Kay's time, because it entailed staying overnight in a motel. Kay had envisioned the three-hour trip as a time to get to know Jessica's friends a little better and to enjoy her own daughter's company. When they got under way, Kay tried to initiate conversation in an upbeat way by asking the girls nonloaded questions; she got monosyllabic answers or two-line sentences in response. The girls politely refused to engage with her. Kay knew it was her presence that silenced them; if they had been alone, they would have been chattering nonstop.

Half an hour into the journey, Kay felt herself slowly begin to disintegrate. "I felt left out, shunned, and ignored, just like in my high school years. Suddenly, I was fifteen again. It was all I could do to keep from crying; I felt terrible, demoralized. Finally, I let Jessica turn on the radio to her favorite station, and the lyrics filled the car for the next two hours. By the time we arrived, I felt so wrung out from my bad feelings that I couldn't wait to be alone. I dropped them at the concert and went back to the motel by myself."

Kay picked the girls up at 1:00 A.M., and they were a little more talkative among themselves, but the next morning's return trip was a repeat of the previous day. "I was devastated," Kay said. Jessica felt badly for her mother but didn't know how to intervene. At home, when they finally talked, Kay appreciated her daughter's sympathy but realized that she had to take care of her own adolescent feelings and not make Jessica feel guilty. Kay was able to be honest and say it had been hard for her, and that next time she would invite a woman friend to join them so that she, too, would have company. Jessica was greatly relieved that her mother didn't blame her and her friends. "I think if she had her friend along it would be easier, instead of the girls thinking she was trying to be one of us."

Kay said, "I don't know why I didn't think about it in advance. It's usually like this when I pick Jessica and her friends up from school; when Jessica is alone, it's different. But I thought since I was doing them all such a big favor, they would open up to me. I was so wrong. They thanked me, but I got no interaction with them out of it." Kay reflected on the fact that not only had she had no intimacy with her mother in high school, but her mother had not spent any time with her friends. Her parents' adult world and her teenage world had been completely separate. There had never been an expectation that the two worlds should connect. Kay did feel close to her daughter, and she wanted to bridge the gap in such situations without intruding on the girls' privacy.

Living to Music

Teenage girls and boys live their lives to music. As eighteen-year-old Natalie said, "We eat, sleep, study, cry, laugh, and converse while listening to music. Music is always blasting from the car stereo as we leave the school gates, one part defiance, another part celebration at being let free. Music fuels our parties. When parents or police turn off the music, the party is over. At night when we go out, it is a constant search to find the perfect song to play on the way to the party, at the party, and on the way back. Finding the perfect song makes a transitory moment turn into a lifelong memory."

Your daughter will be listening to her music not only in the car but in her bedroom, bathroom, and (if you allow it) all over the house. Teen pop that includes alternative, rock, and hip hop now dominate the music and movie industry. Music is unifying teenagers of every ethnicity. Sixties and seventies bands have also made a big comeback. Teenagers have claimed Bob Dylan, Creedence Clearwater Revival, the Rolling Stones, and the Grateful Dead for their own. Here is one place where parents who came of age in the sixties and seventies can join their daughters. Still, there remain the graphic lyrics and profanity in teen pop.

Rebecca said, "In eighth grade, music defined the two popular groups. My group listened to the radio station that played alternative music; the other group listened to rap and r&b. I listen to the lyrics more than most kids because I'm a verbal person, but I don't put a heavy emphasis on meaning."

Meaning, image, and musicality have blended to create female musicians who have become arresting role models for our daughters. When Sarah McLachlan founded the Lilith Fair, a women's music festival that included other stars like Natalie Merchant, Missy Elliot, Liz Phair, Paula Cole, and Lauryn Hill, she made visible the growing power of women in teenage girls' lives. Our daughters see themselves reflected in these musicians' stories of their own struggles with exploitation by a male-dominated industry where issues of body image and sexualization are at the forefront. When Missy Elliot, the queen of hip-hop, talks about being cast in a bad-girl role against Sarah McLachlan, the good girl, girls can relate. Natalie Merchant is known for her awareness of the pain of victimized people, the socially oppressed underclass. All these onstage, out-there young women have taken charge of their lives and write songs about their complicated feelings, their children (sometimes born out of wedlock), boyfriends, girlfriends, drugs, sex, and parents.

These women bring to rock a focus on the same relationship, gender, and social issues that our daughters are processing every day. Another musician, Ani diFranco, for instance, objects to the Lilith Fair, to the idea of women singing together, because she thinks it perpetuates a Women in Rock separatist media mythos. Liz Phair, on the contrary, feels like it's "a blessed event." Phair said she hates her work because she's always surrounded by men and never feels she has peers. "I'm so excited to be around other women who do what I do. Imagine a man in an entirely female workplace, from the boss down.

He'd be, like, 'Periods—whatever!' I appreciate team playing and I can never feel *team* with a bunch of men. I just can't—it's my personality. I can love them and share with them, but I don't feel unselfconscious with them. Because I never particularly understand what men are thinking without having to translate." Merchant's response to Ani diFranco's stand is, "I think there are much more important things to protest than a group of women singing on a certain day together. Don't waste your breath. Talk about Pakistan blowing up nuclear bombs underground. Talk about the millions of children in this country who are not immunized against diseases that people have suffered with for countless generations." Listening to the music and lyrics of these women, your daughter is defining herself, her power, and her vulnerabilities.

"Let's Party!"

If your daughter has an older sibling or friends who are juniors or seniors, she knows that by age fifteen or sixteen, at a minimum, beer is present at most parties. Older teenagers either have fake IDs or tap a likely looking adult (usually male) on his way into a liquor store to ask him to buy beer for them; they sometimes offer the stranger money for his trouble. In every school, there are those who sell marijuana. Some of them grow the plant, others buy it by the pound from an older dealer higher up in the chain of command. Some high school dealers smoke weed every day and support their habit by selling it off in ounces.

Parents who supply beer or marijuana to their underage teenagers or let them have parties where beer is consumed have the attitude, "It's better to have them drinking and smoking at home than out on the streets." Girls whose parents smoke marijuana often know where their parents keep their stash and help themselves. Parents often don't complain, because they don't want to admit to using. Natalie, who occasionally smokes marijuana, said, "I think it's horrible when parents give weed to their kids. Weed demotivates you; parents are supposed to motivate their kids. If a parent does that, the kid won't learn how bad it is." Teenagers sometimes steal hard liquor from their parents' cabinets because they're bored or broke or no one is home.

Don't fool yourself. If you and your husband or partner use any illegal substance, your daughter will know. Girls don't miss anything. If you are trying to hide your habit, your daughter will not respect you for lying to her. If you talk to her about your use, you will at least be honest. Either way, you are giving her permission to experiment with drugs and to break the law. Know the choice you are making and the consequences of your actions.

Most parents still try to control the illegal use of alcohol and substances by their high school students. And most high schools have a code that spells out the consequences of being caught under the influence or in possession of drugs or alcohol on campus. School functions like dances and athletic games are monitored to keep them substance free. School-sponsored awareness programs on alcohol and drug abuse emphasize making choices and using good judgment.

Both teenagers and parents are bewildered by the contradictions inherent in this environment. Our daughters (and sons) are virtually all living at the edge of the law throughout their teen years. Girls lead double lives, doing one thing at school or at home, another in cars, on the street, or in houses that become available when parents are absent. As a mother, how much do you need to know in order to feel comfortable about your daughter? And how much do you want to leave to her discretion? Rebecca describes the classic suburban scene of driving around to look for friends and parties. "Sometimes we follow each other and have coffee or go to the pool hall. If we find out about a party, we go there. After a short time, it's usually, 'Oh, this sucks, let's leave.' Then we repeat the driving around until somebody gets tired and we go crash at someone's house."

Many girls who think that going to parties is the way to be cool as a freshman are burned out on the scene by the time they are juniors. Rebecca said, "I'm not into random parties anymore. It's boring." Seventeen-year-old Kate agreed, "It gets to be a big effort—where's the party tonight? It no longer excites me. I'd rather go out to dinner, rent a movie, or go to a café." Looking for parties, drinking beer, and trying marijuana are avenues for getting together with boys, as well as a rite of passage in high school. Girls are curious, looking for excitement and a feeling of belonging.

Drinking is routine at cast parties and post-dance parties. Kate talked about the after-prom party her junior year. "When I went home the next morning, my friend asked me to get rid of a bag of beer and vodka bottles. I forgot that I put them in the trunk of my mom's car; I had been drinking and hadn't had much sleep, so I went straight to bed. I woke up and realized my mom had taken her car to go do errands. I freaked out! But when she came home, she just put them in the recycling bucket and asked me whether we had stayed at my girlfriend's house when we were drinking. I said, 'Yes.' She said that's what she cared about, that we were not driving, that we were safe. She was cool about it."

Ellen had known in advance that the after-prom party would include drinking and that there was no way to prevent it. By Kate's junior year she is a parent who understands both sides of the story. When she talks with her daughter about drugs and alcohol, she emphasizes safety and moderation and monitors Kate's life in other areas for signs that things are getting out of hand. She is reassured by Kate's responsibility, communicativeness, consistently good grades, and her active involvement with drama.

Although Ellen didn't chastise Kate on prom night, there have been other occasions when Kate was impulsive and unwise, and her mother strongly intervened. Kate said, "I was house-sitting at the neighbor's across the street and decided I wanted to have a few people over, maybe do a little drinking, nothing big. Then I thought it would be cool to invite my little sister, Alta, who had just finished eighth grade, and let her have a few drinks. I wanted her to experience it safely with us instead of what happened to me. My father overheard her on the phone telling one of her friends, and my parents flipped; they felt I had betrayed their trust and my responsibility to our neighbors. After that, they wouldn't let me spend the night across the street. I was really upset—I thought it impeded me doing my job. Looking back, I can see it was fair, but I was really upset. My mom thought my sister had done drugs and alcohol, which wasn't true; it was all my idea." This incident caused Ellen and her husband, Jim, to question both Kate's judgment about her sister and Kate's use of alcohol. Both Ellen and Jim had alcoholism in their families. They took this opportunity to talk to Kate about their worries.

If you have a history of alcoholism or drug addiction in your family, your daughter may have inherited a genetic predisposition for addiction. It's important that you let her know about this possibility as she approaches adolescence. Kate has taken that information to heart and watches her intake carefully. Girls metabolize alcohol differently than boys. Smaller amounts have a stronger effect on girls' systems. Alcohol and drug use inhibit growth in teenagers. Talk openly with your daughter about the pros and cons of using.

Truth or Consequences

You can never completely relax your vigilance with your teenage daughter, because her judgment will be erratic. She can be consistently responsible and level-headed, and then unpredictably hazard a risk that endangers her life. Questioning Kate's plan for her younger sister taught her to think about consequences before she acts next time. It's good to keep your fingers on the pulse of your daughter's experimentation. Kate said, "Sometimes my mom asks me, 'Have you ever tried such and such a drink or drug?' That's OK with me. My parents are big on honesty."

Emphasize honesty before the fact as well as after the fact. Fourteen-year-old Zoe told her mother she wanted to spend the night at her girlfriend's house, where her older brother was having a party. Her mother, Cassia, knew there would be beer at the party and asked Zoe if she would promise not to drink alcohol. Zoe said, "I don't want to do that. I want you to trust me to use my own judgment and take care of myself. It's really important to me, Mom."

Zoe did well in school, was active in sports, and had a good group of girlfriends. She had always shown excellent judgment in the past. Cassia decided to go along with Zoe's request because she knew her daughter and realized that she was reaching for a new level of autonomy. But Cassia extracted a promise that Zoe would not leave the party. She also cautioned Zoe to drink beer slowly and assess its effect before she drank more.

The next day when Cassia picked her up, Zoe thanked her mother for trusting her, and for "being so cool." She said she had fun, drank some beer, and had no problems—she had been initiated into high school life.

There were other times when Cassia had to set a limit with Zoe, mature as she knew her to be. Cassia felt, for instance, that Zoe was too young as a freshman to go to the junior-senior prom. There was a real possibility that she might be invited. Cassia simply said, "It's not going to happen, even if you are asked." Zoe objected, sulked, and pouted but resigned herself. Luckily, word got around through her friend's older brother that Zoe wasn't available to go, and guys didn't put her on the spot by asking her.

Zoe's first encounter with drinking beer was a normal, balanced way for it to happen. Cassia knew where her daughter was that night and with whom; she trusted Zoe not to leave the family's home. It was still a risk, and it was hard for Cassia to let her go.

While Cassia would have preferred that Zoe wait until she was older, she recognized that her daughter was more mature for her age than she herself had been at fourteen. Cassia had not drunk beer with her friends until she was sixteen, a junior in high school. She remembered feeling it was her business, not her parents', that she had had no compunction about drinking without their knowledge. She was more savvy about Zoe's world than her mother and father had been about hers; she knew what parties were about. Cassia was shrewd enough to know that if she forbade Zoe trying it, Zoe would have to resort to lying to her. And she preferred the trust she gained by bowing to the inevitable in a considered, related way. The result of her handling it in this way would resonate throughout Zoe's high school years.

It's Against the Law

Possession of alcohol is against the law for minors, defined as under the age of twenty-one. Drug possession, use, and selling are against the law at any age. While this is the official position, enforcement of the law may be different. Rebecca said, "You have to bring your own beer or alcohol to parties. There are places in the big city who will sell to minors. Most kids have fake IDs to get them into clubs, too." In some communities, the discrepancy between the law and the ease with which teenagers procure alcohol and marijuana has resulted in leniency toward teenagers by police.

When the police respond to a complaint about a loud party, a couple of officers come and break up the party. They generally do not bother to check for substance abuse or illegal possession unless things are grossly out of hand. Unfortunately, this gives some teenagers an erroneous sense that they are "outside the law." If you try to impress the illegality of underage drinking on your daughter, you are likely to hear, "Mom, the police don't care." This entitled attitude leads some girls and boys to take greater risks with no heed of possible consequences. If nothing happens to your daughter the first time, either at home or in the community, it is an encouragement to continue or to push the envelope further. In other communities, a minor caught with just one unopened bottle of alcohol can lose her driver's license, have to pay steep fines, attend counseling, and become entangled with the legal system.

Most girls are healthy and manage to steer a moderate course with experimentation, if their parents are paying attention and walk the line between intervening and permitting their daughters to use their own judgment, as both Ellen and Cassia did. Those teenagers who take the highest risks are usually disturbed, insecure, or alienated from their families. Their parents are either too rigid and restrictive or too permissive; or they are indifferent toward what their daughters do. These are girls who drive drunk, push other kids to drink more, and seek greater and greater thrills. Seventeen-year-old Rae said, "What I've seen is when parents are controlling, their kids act out, go to extremes, and get in trouble."

At frustrating moments with your daughter, letting her do whatever she wants to do or clamping down on her and laying down the law will seem like attractive options. It is emotionally grueling to withstand the back-and-forth struggle with her that allows you to stay connected. Alternating closeness and rejection may wear you down or overwhelm you. You will have to sacrifice moments or days of peace to engage in conflict that seems unnecessary. Understand that it is necessary for your daughter's development. She is defining herself and her boundaries and establishing a pattern not only for other close relationships in her life but for her future relationship with you.

Many mothers don't realize that the self-sufficiency of teenagers is often limited to their being able to move around in the world at will. Judgment, emotional maturity, and a sense of respect for authority are still at an immature stage. Don't make the mistake of seeing your tall, voluptuous seventeen-year-old daughter as an adult who no longer needs your guidance. She is neither a child nor an adult.

"Let's Make a Deal."

As you negotiate the central issue of her comings and goings in high school, make agreements with your daughter that mirror social contracts in the wider world. Consequences of breaking the rules should fit the rule broken and should have the aim of teaching her the repercussions of antisocial behavior; they should not have the aim of being punitive. We need to respect our children's developing individuality and autonomy, and that respect includes knowing that they will test limits and make mistakes. Think about the limits that are most important to you, those that have to do with her emotional and physical safety. Try to be supportive, not intrusive.

Establish fair rules. Know where your daughter is going and with whom. Know how she is getting home and when, or arrange a check-in time for her to call if she can't say exactly when she'll be back. Have a curfew that fits each year of high school and an appropriate allowance. If she is spending money on beer or marijuana, you will notice if you are keeping track of her monetary income and outflow. With her father, you need to lay out the rules and get her to agree to their basic fairness and common sense.

Once rules or guidelines are established, you have to be flexible, too, and be ready to change them as they rapidly become outmoded. If you ground your seventeen-year-old daughter for a weekend because she failed to call you one night at the appointed time, you can bet she'll have to get together with friends Friday night to make a video for her French class. Try to take it with good grace. Give her a curfew for that night and be glad she's home for a "time out" on Saturday.

Kate said, "I think a girl should have rules about checking in, a time set up for calling home, and consequences for failing to follow through." In spite of her occasional defiance of her parents' restrictions, Kate recognizes the need for a safety net, the support system of her family. "My mom would tell me, 'If something isn't OK with you, just call me.' That was a good thing for her to say; I had her to fall back on."

"I Don't Need a Curfew."

Fourteen-year-old Tammy said, "I don't have a curfew now, but I come home by 11:00 P.M." Jean tells the whole story: "We try to accommodate Tammy. Her father has always been rigid about her spending the night at other homes or going to homes of people we don't know well. Although he usually lets me set limits, we keep a tight rein on her. When she was younger, I would pick her up at midnight at overnight parties and take her back at six in the morning for breakfast." Jean understands and shares her husband's concern about overnights, but, recognizing that Tammy found that rule unfair, Jean was willing to give up sleep to ensure that her daughter felt included. Jean remembers her own mother's love and flexibility with her. "She would write me an excuse if I didn't feel like going to school. I never had a curfew." Jean is using her own experience of herself and her mother as a model for her relationship with her daughter.

Kate said, "All parents have different opinions about curfews. Kids are always saying, 'So and so gets to be out later than I do.'" If you don't create safe conditions for discussing such loaded topics, you won't stay close to your daughter. Briana, who felt so insecure as a freshman, quickly moved into the party scene as a junior. "Getting my driver's license changed a lot in my family. I became more separate from my parents, closer to my friends. I can't let my parents know about drinking and sex; my mother pretends she's OK with it, but she uses it against me in later arguments. I want my mother to not ask questions, not pester me." Instead of having to worry about the consequences of being late for a curfew, Briana thinks it would be better for her to have a rule about getting home safely. "I think they should trust me."

Something has gone awry in this family situation. Briana is defining "trust" as unlimited freedom and no familial obligation. Carolyn cannot trust her daughter without connecting with her, and Briana refuses to talk to her mother because she doesn't feel her mother respects and understands her. They are trapped in a vicious cycle.

Rebecca defines trust as her parents' giving her the benefit of the doubt so she can make her own decisions. She is willing to cooperate in order to earn that privilege. Before she got her license, she said, "I used to ask my parents, 'How late are you willing to pick me up?' In ninth and tenth grade my curfew was 12:30. Now that I drive it's 2:00 A.M., but most of my friends don't have curfews. If I don't want to be home by that time, I just tell my parents that I'm spending the night with my best friend, so that they don't expect me. But if I decide to come home at 4:00 A.M., I can still do that and just say I changed my mind. The best thing is that my parents have always trusted me."

Rebecca takes care of her autonomy and keeps her mother, Sharon, from worrying about her. She appreciates her parents letting her run her own life even if she doesn't tell them the whole truth or maneuvers around the rules. Sharon's faith in her is based on Rebecca's outstanding academic performance, her prolific artistic production, and strong community service contributions. Furthermore, Rebecca's cheerful attitude toward baby-sitting her ten-year-old twin brothers and doing her household chores attests to her reliability. Sharon respects Rebecca's privacy so does not push her daughter to tell her the absolute truth. It is enough for Sharon that her daughter behaves responsibly, that she is pursuing her high school work with vigor, and that she is independently pursuing an active social life. She can see that her daughter is happy and healthy.

In tenth grade, when Grace started asking for a later curfew than 1:00 P.M. on weekends, Eve resisted. Then she noticed that Grace began to say she was spending the night at her friend Emma's house. Eve was quick to intuit the connection and decided to grant a later curfew because she preferred that her daughter feel comfortable coming home. She also wanted Grace home at 2:00 A.M., rather than wandering around later with friends who had no curfew. Eve already had in place a practice of Grace calling to check in by eleven o'clock to tell her where she was and if any plans had changed. Grace was allowed one overnight per weekend.

Teenagers usually leave for the evening without knowing how the plans for the night are going to develop. Your daughter may think she is coming home and decide to spend the night out, or vice versa. She may change her mind about staying at one friend's and stay with another. When Grace was going to spend the night out, Eve also had an agreement with her that she call to tell her mother at whose home she was staying. It is critical to know where your daughter is sleeping! Eve realized that Grace could lie when she called, but Grace said, "I wanted to tell the truth. My mom only wanted to know where I was; it's not like she grilled me when I called. Why would I lie? I was glad she cared." Grace felt she had enough privacy. As Grace got older, her curfew got more liberal, but the practice of calling to say where she was persisted.

Eighteen-year-old Rae said, "I never had a curfew. My mom didn't have to know where I was all the time, but she did want to know where I was spending the night. I think moms ought to let a girl mess up on her own, give her room to screw up and learn after that. I stay busy. I don't have time to drink and smoke weed that much, but I do sometimes."

Having People Over

Usually word of a party, coded as "having people over," begins to spread at school on Fridays. Most parties happen at homes where parents are absent for the weekend or gone on an extended trip. Many parents leave their teenagers or a nominal house-sitter in charge. Either way, that house becomes open to an influx. Once on the road, driving around, your daughter may be party hopping and socializing with teens from many schools. With cell phones in many cars and pagers clipped on most jeans, the party scene extends far beyond the immediate school community.

No matter how much you trust her, you would be wise not to leave your teenager in charge of your home. Even if she is discreet about who she asks over or tells her friends not to spread the word, the teenage grapevine rapidly telegraphs news across city and county lines. It is not unusual to have a hundred teens converge when ten were originally invited. Rebecca said, "I have been at parties from different schools where someone comes up and says, 'This is my friend's house and she only wants people she knows here. You have to leave.'" Rebecca says that's fine with her and she and her friends do leave.

But roaming groups of teenagers are not always that compliant, especially if they have been drinking. A carload of teenage boys who have been party hopping and drinking beer is lucky to contain a sober driver, who, however, may not be able to keep his buddies under control. Your daughter can prevent neither crashers nor property damage and theft in your home. You may also be legally liable if you are absent from home when one of her friends gets injured on your property.

Fights between boys from different schools are also common at parties. And teenagers will never call the police until a situation is very far gone. Natalie said, "Our junior year, some girls were drinking so much they were throwing up at every party. My friend Alyssa was one of them. She's weak and dependent because her parents try to control everything she thinks, so she does these dumb things. I would just help her, take care of her. After she threw up, she usually felt better. You don't call the police for something like that."

Call 911

Girls do pass out from alcohol poisoning and end up in the emergency room on weekends. When her friends couldn't revive sixteen-year-old Janice at a party one Saturday night, they called 911, and she was taken to the hospital unconscious. Her mother, Molly, fearfully rushed to the hospital; her father was out of town. Molly came from an alcoholic family and was terrified to think that her daughter might be falling into that pattern. Shocked by her daughter's behavior, she sat by Janice's side while her daughter was revived.

Molly was preoccupied with marital problems and the care of two younger children. Janice's father, who traveled a lot on business, was an absent parent. Janice said, "I didn't feel it mattered what happened to me. I didn't think I was that important to anyone, even my mother." Girls who drink to excess often feel worthless and have a need for attention. Molly hadn't realized Janice was feeling so alone.

Molly immediately sought a therapist for Janice and herself to work on their relationship. "I realized I hadn't been paying attention to Janice. I had given up trying to talk to her; she seemed so closed off, so adult." Molly wanted to connect with her daughter, but she had to face some hard realities first. Molly's judgmental attitude toward girls that Janice tried to befriend had sabotaged Janice's social skills. From middle school on, she had allowed Janice to call the shots about watching TV or going out on weeknights, even when her teachers talked about the difficulties Janice was having in school. Whenever her mother tried to intervene in her life and set limits, Janice resorted to, "Well, I'm going to kill myself then." Molly had refused to take this seriously and had given up on relating to her daughter.

Overwhelmed with her own marital friction and the hands-on care of the younger children, Molly had not taken the time to sit down with Janice, champion her, and talk about her study skills or the way she was feeling about her grades dropping. Janice had compensated for her feelings of failure by becoming more social. As she went mindlessly from party to party, feeling abandoned, isolated, and insecure, Janice became more and more unsafe with alcohol. When her boyfriend rejected her, it was the last straw. Without girlfriend support she couldn't hope to make it through.

After painfully listening to Janice's downward spiral of despair for many hours, Molly pulled herself together and found tutoring for Janice in some classes, helped her with others, and began to negotiate straightforward limits with her daughter in her social life. Janice said, "At first, I hated having to go to therapy with my mom. I was embarrassed about being taken to the emergency room, and I wanted to forget all about it. Plus, I didn't think my mom really cared, just that she wanted me to stop causing her so much trouble. But then when I could see that she was trying hard to change, too, and that she was sorry if she was too busy to talk to me, and she made time to do something for me later, I started feeling better. I didn't feel so alone; I could count on her. It was a relief." Your daughter wants to feel you are with her.

Molly encouraged Janice to take up track, which she had loved in middle school. Janice needed something of her own that gave her the possibility of connecting with other girls. Molly also realized that she was missing out by not having women friends in her life. "I cringe to think how competitive I've been with women all my life. I can see how it's hurting me as well as Janice. My catty criticism of other women is automatic; it just comes out. I feel ashamed realizing

149

that I've always done it to make myself feel better." Molly and Janice both had to learn the skills that would allow them to relate to other women; they began in their work with each other.

Designated Drivers

For your daughter's safety, emphasize designated drivers when she is going out at night. A designated driver is a teenager who agrees not to drink or use a drug so he or she can drive safely. It's a matter of life and death, whether she is going to parties or just hanging out with a group of other kids. Kate said, "We're good about designated drivers in my crowd, but I want to start Safe Rides at my school the way they have them at other high schools."

Safe Rides is a student-run service in which two students wear school pagers and agree to answer distress calls from other students who are at risk for not getting home safely. Safe Rides volunteers pick up the student and drive him or her home. The teenagers on call receive double community service hours for being available overnight. The system works well, although local junior college students and those from other high schools sometimes horn in on the service. Also, teens under the influence of alcohol or drugs can be belligerent and nasty; drivers need to be specially trained to handle problems when they arise.

Soliciting a designated driver within her group is the first line of a safe, rational night out. Safe Rides is a fallback when the driver doesn't hold up his or her end of the bargain. Rebecca said, "Most of my friends are really, really good about designated drivers, but there are a couple of guys who will have two beers, then drive. Everyone says to them, 'Don't be stupid. Why do you do it?' I know one guy who is really smart, who gets straight As, a 4.0, and is athletic, who drives drunk. He just doesn't want to see it." This boy and others like him are willing to take extreme risks. They often think they are exceptions; they like to show off and to prove they are invincible or manly. Some girls also like the attention they get when they drive after drinking.

Rave On

Florence has a terrific relationship with her seventeen-year-old niece, Jennifer, with whom she has lunch once a month. One afternoon, Jennifer told her aunt that she had been going to raves, illicit parties for teenagers that feature the drug Ecstasy. Ecstasy is a short-acting drug that inhibits sleep and produces a euphoric sense of communion with other people. Jennifer told her aunt, "You have this great feeling of love for everyone around you. You make lifelong friends dancing together all night." Raves start after 11:00 P.M. and go until dawn; they usually take place in industrial parts of a city and are advertised by word of mouth and with flyers. Teenagers intoxicated by the drug hold each other and exchange bracelets of colored beads. Sweating copiously as they dance, they drink water to keep moving. The music spun by a deejay is chosen to mimic the heartbeat, a fluttery, quick, repetitive beat that enhances the effect of the Ecstasy.

Most kids buy their own Ecstasy and take it with them. Although there are dealers at the dances, the purity of their product is suspect; it may have been cut with speed or something even more deadly. Jennifer said, "One night the Ecstasy was cut with heroin and kids collapsed, overdosed, and had to be rushed to the hospital. I was so scared." She said to her aunt, "I'm worried about staying safe at these events. I like the music and all, but I don't want to get messed up. How can I go and stay safe?"

Florence knew that Jennifer's parents were not aware that their daughter was going to raves. "I can't tell my mom that I go because she'll worry. She and my dad are so anxious about work and making enough money, and it would panic them." Florence thought her sister and brother-in-law were wonderful parents, but she knew

Jennifer was right. Florence, too, was alarmed and concerned. But she was grateful that Jennifer was talking to her about it and felt her niece would heed her counsel.

Together, they came up with several precautions that made Florence feel better about Jennifer's experimentation. Jennifer had known a driver to fall asleep at the wheel coming home, because he had been using and dancing all night long. At Florence's suggestion, she decided to take a thermos of coffee and snacks to share before they left the rave in the morning. Jennifer had the idea of talking to the driver nonstop to make sure he stayed awake. Florence tried to engage her niece in thinking about the variations throughout the night in her (and her friends') altered states in order to determine when it was safe to leave. She asked Jennifer about her motives for going to these events. Jennifer seemed caught up in a group of kids who liked to try different drugs and especially loved the thrill of going from her small town to a big city and meeting other kids from all over.

Jennifer's reluctance to tell her parents includes a mix of feelings: wanting to take care of them; her own anxiety about the dangerous risk she is taking; and wanting to individuate, needing her privacy. The only reassuring element is that she has an ongoing open relationship with Florence, a perceptive, sensible adult woman. Be sure your daughter has these kind of resources in her life.

Florence is uneasy and sometimes "petrified" about keeping this information from her sister. Thus far, she has chosen to honor Jennifer's confidence because she knows she can't stop her niece if she's determined to go, and she doesn't want Jennifer to shut off communicating with her. Florence has assessed her niece's potential for self-damage. She has seen Jennifer experiment with marijuana and LSD yet keep her life together. If, through their relationship, Florence senses Jennifer is in danger, she will tell her niece that they have to bring in her parents. Jennifer is also moving toward telling her mother; she doesn't like keeping her heavy secret. Florence hopes that her niece will grow tired of the rave scene as she has other experiments.

Some parents assume that because their daughter is studious and level-headed, she won't be tempted to take risks or experiment with drugs or unprotected sexuality. This may not necessarily be true, but if you don't communicate with her on an ongoing basis, you will not *know* and will not be able to prepare her and guide her appropriately. Furthermore, this kind of assumption can create a gulf between you that will be harder and harder to bridge as she grows older.

"I Don't Know How That Got There."

Layla, a high school senior, had borrowed her mother's car for the holiday dance at her school. Her parents had given her the liberty of no curfew for this special occasion. Her friend Penny came home with her to spend the night. The next morning, while her daughter and her friend slept, Rose left to go grocery shopping. When she opened the glove compartment to get her sunglasses, she found a marijuana pipe lying there. Rose was stunned and upset. What did this mean about her seemingly ultra-responsible daughter? She nervously waited for the girls to wake up and for Penny to go home. Then she brought the pipe to her daughter and held it out, saying, "What's going on, Layla?" Layla looked at her mother and said disingenuously, "Where did you find that?" "In the glove compartment," her mother said. "Ummm," said Layla, "I don't know how that got there." Rose was torn between wanting to believe her daughter and knowing that Layla had to be lying. She was also exasperated at being confronted with a problem of this magnitude in the midst of the day's other demands: her younger daughter was calling her to help her pack for an overnight where she was due in half an hour; she herself wanted to squeeze in a walk before dressing for a much-needed dinner out with her husband. But Rose took a deep breath, told her younger daughter she would have to wait, plunged in, and leveled with Layla.

"Layla," Rose said, "I know that isn't true. So let's talk about you and your friends smoking marijuana." Layla gulped. She didn't want to disappoint her mother by letting her in on her partying, but she also felt an odd sense of relief that her mother had found the pipe. "OK, it belongs to my friend. I'm not going to tell you who. We do smoke dope once in a while on special occasions, but I don't do it that often. You don't have to worry about it, Mom."

Rose said, "Of course I'm worried about it, and I'm going to throw the pipe away because I don't support you or your friends doing this, but I know how responsible you are and I just have to trust you to use your own judgment. I want to reiterate that marijuana is addictive, saps your initiative, and can lead to trying harder drugs. I also feel badly that you would spend your allowance on something destructive like pot." "Mom," Layla said, "I earn my money and I don't spend much of it on pot. You know I always do my chores and my homework. Do you think I would be getting such good grades if I were smoking pot all the time?"

When you find evidence that your daughter is smoking cigarettes, marijuana, or cigars or drinking alcohol, do not ignore it. Bring it up with her and talk about both your positions. Your willingness to connect with her about her experimentation shows her you care and helps the voice of reason in her develop.

Rose's considered response to her daughter prompted Layla to ask, "Did you ever try drugs when you were in high school, Mom?" Rose answered, "Not until my senior year, when suddenly marijuana began to appear at parties. I didn't really get into it, though; it made me sleepy. I didn't like it that much. I did drink beer with my friends that year, though. That was before anyone talked about alcoholism or knew that smoking caused cancer or the dangers of drugs. The hippie culture was just emerging. And science hadn't caught up with the use of mind-altering substances." Layla said, "I feel like my mom can relate; she'll understand even if she doesn't like it." You can't hide your shadow from your daughter. If you talk about your own adolescence, you can go into her world, speak her language a bit, and pull her out a little.

Date Rape

Rose was legitimately worried about her daughter getting into dangerous situations with boys sexually, especially if she was drinking alcohol or smoking marijuana. Many teenage girls are pressured into having sex or raped when under the influence. Layla was well aware of this problem; she had heard many stories from her girlfriends. She responded to her mother's concern by telling her that she had given a lot of thought to her own sexual wishes, to self-protection, and that she knew how to take care of herself. Like many girls, she chose to go out in a group, asked a friend to watch out for her, and assessed a situation for safety before she allowed herself to relax. This conversation somewhat alleviated Rose's worries; she was reassured that Layla had a plan for dealing with problems and appreciated her sharing her thoughts and feelings. This is the best you can hope for as your teenage daughter responds to the wider world that is calling to her.

Layla feels a girl does have a responsibility when she drinks too much and lets a guy pressure her into sex. "But it's different from being raped because you passed out. You shouldn't have been drinking that much, but you never said yes."

Girls, like adults, often use alcohol to act out hurt or aggressive feelings. One of Tammy's friends broke up with her boyfriend and got very drunk. As your daughter moves through the emotional highs and lows of her social life, be sure she has many healthy ways to express her feelings that don't wreak havoc on her body. Screaming and crying have a place in the spectrum of expressing pain. So does shooting baskets or hitting a ball over and over against a wall.

The Nonpartying Crowd

Your daughter may be one of the girls who does not get involved with drugs or alcohol during high school. Fourteen-year-old Tammy said, "I've had sips of alcohol—beer, champagne, and wine at home—and I don't like the taste." Danielle went all through high school without knowing about that side of teen life. "I only got an inkling of the party scene this summer after my senior year. It's been explosive with my parents because I suddenly started staying out late. They didn't know that I was drinking at parties; they just didn't want me driving late at night. In my family it was as if drugs and alcohol didn't exist. My father once had a problem with it so my parents just shut it out of our experience. Their emphasis was on academics. I worked really hard—I could have enjoyed more. Somehow, I was always in the crowd that didn't party. Now that I got a taste of it being fun, I hope I don't go overboard with it in college."

The longer your daughter waits to experiment with drugs and alcohol, the better. But, just as with sexuality, be sure you're talking to her about these issues. Once she gets to college, she will be on her own and completely at the mercy of peer influence.

"I Don't Understand How This Happened."

If you and your daughter drift apart, you can still retrieve the relationship with hard work and dedication. Linda gradually became aware of her daughter Julie's alcohol abuse. In Julie's freshman year, over a several-month period from October through February, she couldn't get Julie out of bed in the morning, smelled alcohol on her breath at odd hours, heard her slurred speech late at night when she got home on weekends, and finally found a bottle of vodka hidden in her room. Julie had an excuse for everything: "I'm tired from studying so hard"; "It's just mouthwash, Mom"; "I was just joking"; "It's not a big deal." Linda was frustrated with Julie's avoidant and sometimes angry responses. But she also felt guilty. "I kept thinking, How have I failed?" The last straw was the school calling to report that Julie was cutting classes. Linda realized she had to face the truth.

Tearfully, Linda said, "I cried and cried thinking about my adorable, curly-haired, affectionate little girl who loved to spend time with me until sixth grade. Whether we were making dinner, or doing errands, or going to the movies, we always had fun." When Julie entered the local public middle school, she slowly began to change, but freshman year she suddenly exploded. Every intervention Linda made—from talking things out to grounding Julie—had been met with defiance and led to further alienation between them. Linda said, "I don't understand how this happened to us."

In seventh grade Julie had been abruptly faced with a culture in which alcohol and marijuana were available and watching MTV was standard procedure. Coming from a small, protected grammar school, this permissive environment was a shock to Julie—and Linda. Linda, however, had thought Julie was doing well because her daughter hadn't complained and went about her studies normally. Yet Linda admitted that when she had begun to work longer hours, hoping, as a single parent, to make more money for their increasing expenses, she had allowed Julie to come home alone to an empty house. At the time, Julie had been agreeable to the plan. Linda had drastically underestimated the impact on Julie of losing her normal after-school ritual of seeing her mom, sharing a snack, and having her mother available to help with her homework.

Linda had noted that Julie had become more secretive, but chalked it up to adolescent withdrawal and hadn't taken it up with her daughter. Their relationship had become more and more perfunctory and superficial. When Julie lost the familiar intimacy of after school with her mother, she ignored her distress, wanting to support Linda, who she knew worked hard on her behalf. Her feelings of loneliness made her susceptible to making friends with whomever paid her attention. Without her mother's guidance, she fell in with a group of young people who were also unsupervised after school.

Julie was careful to be home before her mother got there. She still loved and respected her mother, but at the same time she felt abandoned. When she began to try smoking a cigarette or having a stolen drink at someone's house, she just wanted to fit in. Since her mother didn't notice, she convinced herself that it didn't matter, "I thought my mom didn't care and that she wouldn't understand, if she knew."

Although Julie wanted to be accepted by her peers, she also still wanted her mother's help. At bottom, she did not want to be out on a limb experimenting on her own. Sometimes a girl's adolescent bid for increasing autonomy may seem to be a form of rejection, or just a natural development, yet her deeper self will always need an ongoing relationship with you.

Julie's father lived in another state with his new wife and two younger children. When Julie visited at a holiday or for a few weeks in the summer, she was just one of the kids. She never had individual time with her father. Linda tried to talk to her ex-husband about Julie's difficulties but he dismissed her concerns.

Linda was a loving, well-intentioned mother, but, caught up in the pressure of earning a living for herself and her child, she had missed Julie's cues. Linda recalled, "When I first began to stay later at the office, Julie would give me a ring after school to check in and chat for a few minutes about her day. I really looked forward to hearing from her because I missed picking her up from school." When the calls gradually tapered off, Linda, busy with the demands of many clients, relegated the change to Julie's growing independence

PARTY TIME

and suppressed her own pang of regret. If Linda had paid attention to her feeling of loss and had mentioned to Julie, perhaps over breakfast one morning, that she missed their exchange, she would have had an opportunity to connect with her. Instead, Julie read her mother's omission as not caring and withdrew a little further.

Use your own feelings to gauge your relationship with your daughter. If you are missing her, it's possible that she is missing you, too. If you sense something is wrong, there probably is. And if there isn't, your inquiry will let her know you care and allay your anxiety if she tells you otherwise. Trust your instincts; she will learn to trust hers.

"Why Are You Doing This to Me?"

If you see your daughter's acting-out behavior as an attack on you, you are too identified with your daughter. Even when she says it's about you, it's really not. As she is pushing away, she may be punitive, and demeaning, to convince herself that she doesn't need you. She will make you feel as if it's your fault, but it is about her defining herself. She may betray you by doing bad things, just as a two-year-old told "no" will have a tantrum.

If you can separate and see it as her problem, you can have compassion for her predicament. A mother often seeks therapy for herself when she reaches an impasse in which she cannot tell where she leaves off and her daughter begins. Such a mother needs to separate.

If your daughter is involved in substance abuse, she is probably doing it out of her own confusion. Her conflicts set her autonomy and peer acceptance against her loyalty to you or the family's values. You will not be able to see clearly and give her the guidance she needs if you take her behavior as a personal attack on you.

Although the rift between Briana and her parents is long-term and serious, she hopes that some day it will be different. "I think my relationship with my mother can't advance at this point. Maybe when

159

I go to college and get away from my parents I'll be able to appreciate them more." Your daughter wants connection, but unless you meet her halfway, you are doomed to be alienated during these years.

Look at the Whole Picture

Don't let the party scene estrange you from your daughter. Keep a balanced view of her overall life and behavior, instead of focusing on the things she does that let you down. Your basic attitude should be, "I love you and respect you, even if I don't agree with some of your behavior." Find qualities to laud in her that you feel are valuable and worthwhile, actions that make you proud of her. Be specific with your praise. Say "I'm proud of you for sticking with soccer this season and doing the training, even though you didn't get to play that much" or "I'm impressed with the way you handled that situation with your friends. You were very tactful." Let her know when you think that she has used good judgment, even as you acknowledge her experimentation and risk taking.

Ask yourself and her, or a professional, if need be, "What can I do that I am not doing?" Find a balance between discipline and understanding with her. Stay in conversation about the issues. When you have satisfied yourself that you are doing all you can do, then say a prayer, and let her make her own way.

6 ✑

*G*reat Expectations

LIVING UP TO IT ALL

ena lamented, "I believe parents should be the safe place for their daughters, not the place to teach them about the hard realities of life. We are already being subjected to those realities every day." Zena is a star soccer player who struggles to find her place socially at school because she is half black, half white. Her two groups of friends at school are divided along ethnic lines and don't mix. While there is also some unspoken racial tension between her parents, they agree on their plans for their daughter: "You must prepare yourself for a prestigious profession." Because her parents dismiss Zena's talent at soccer as frivolous, she does not confide in them about her strenuous practices, her social unease, or the stress their expectations put on her.

Your teenage daughter is living in a whirlpool of fluctuating challenges: body changes, sexual awakening, intense relationships with girls and boys, and negotiating a teen culture rife with drugs and alcohol. Academics, sports, and parental expectations exacerbate her turmoil within and without. The traditional pressure on girls to betray their core selves in order to be accepted has now been compounded by the pressure on them to prove that they are *not* losing themselves. How can you provide the home base, the place of rest for your daughter in the midst of all these demands?

Social Disaster

Your daughter's ever-changing social life will be one of her biggest stressors in high school. Rochelle's daughter Susan was a remarkable pianist, the orchestral star of her eighth-grade class musical. Susan entered freshman year anticipating playing an active part in the theater arts community. From the first day of school, however, the girls she had known in grammar school went different ways, and Susan found herself alone and increasingly isolated. "I was devastated. My best friend moved into the popular crowd and was going to parties. I wasn't comfortable with that scene, but I was too anxious to make new friends." On many days after school, Rochelle heard her crying in her room, but Susan refused to talk when her mother came to the door. "Leave me alone! I'm fine. Don't bother me!" were frequent retorts.

Although Susan continued her piano lessons, she practiced less often and was depressed and irritable with her family and frustrated with her schoolwork. The crowning blow came when she suddenly began having panic attacks, which prevented her from trying out for the school orchestra or jazz ensemble. After six weeks, Rochelle felt she had to intervene despite Susan's protests. One evening after dinner she went to her daughter's room and sat on the bed. "I can see that things are too difficult for you to bear all by yourself, Susan. I'm so sorry. You must talk to someone. If you don't want to talk to me, I'm going to set up an appointment for you with a counselor. You shouldn't have to suffer this alone." Susan bristled, "I don't want to see any counselor; I'm not sick. There's nothing to talk about!"

Rochelle persisted, "Susan, I love you, and I'm going to sit here until we get further on this issue than that." Although it took some time, Susan finally broke down in tears and despair and poured out her misery to her mother.

After Susan's sobbing abated, Rochelle said, "I think I understand how you feel, because I had a similar disappointment when I was a teenager." Rochelle told Susan that she had been a good student and a debate champion in high school. But the summer before her senior year, she had lost her best friend when her friend's family moved. Her other, less intimate, friends were either working or traveling with their families. Rochelle said, "I felt so alone. All I could do was read and take long walks by myself. My parents were too busy to notice that I felt bad. I went back to school and I was afraid to get up in front of the class, much less debate. I had to withdraw from the team. I have never felt so humiliated."

Susan sympathized with her mother; she felt heard and understood. Her mother had not dismissed her suffering, nor had she sunk into suffering with her. Hearing her mother's story gave Susan hope—if her mother had survived humiliation, then she might get through her own feelings of failure. Over the next months, Rochelle also reiterated to Susan, "I know this will change. You will find friends. You have so many gifts, and you are a wonderful person. The older you get, the more you will be recognized for who you are." When you talk to your daughter this way, you reduce her stress and renew your bond of trust. Your openness gives her a wider perspective than the narrow intensity of the moment.

Redefine the Problem

The next step after acknowledging your daughter's feelings in any situation is to help her redefine the problem. Rochelle, for instance, helped Susan consider what other activity she might be able to do while her anxiety about performing subsided; Susan decided to concentrate on dance for the rest of the year. Rochelle also encouraged her to call two of her grammar school girlfriends who had gone to other high schools to try to renew her friendship with them. One of the two was responsive to Susan's overtures, and the two girls began to spend time together on weekends. If you respect your daughter and relate to her problems in this way, she will not shut down.

Grades, Grades, Grades

Girls find academics an intensely stressful arena. Zena moaned, "We have classes all day, and then come home and have to deal with homework. Sometimes, I just can't handle it anymore." Schoolwork seems to be a way for you and your daughter to measure her success. High-achieving girls, however, are often the ones who are hurting. Jade said that when she entered high school, she was mortified to find that her middle school reputation had preceded her. "I was known as the 4.0 or the 1550 on the PSAT; I hated that. It just put more pressure on me to achieve, and I already put enough pressure on myself." Another young woman felt she was slotted as "the tennis champ." Girls want to acknowledge their shadowy, not-so-perfect sides as well as their competencies. They are mastering new skills, but they are also exploring their vulnerabilities, unprotected by parents for the first time.

Danielle, another high achiever, said that freshman year she was stunned at the high school social and academic challenges. "I was in a slower math group in primary school. I worked much harder in freshman year and found that I was good at math." But Danielle discovered that the high stress levels took a toll. "It's a terrible flaw in me. Both schoolwork and the intense friendship situation got in the way of me being happy. I would manifest it physically: I would lose my period for months at a time."

Danielle described getting edgy with her family; she could keep it together at school, but at home she would let down and fall apart. "My parents were extremely helpful. My father emphasizes being happy. Once my mother took my physics book, threw it across the room, and said 'Stop this! It's not worth you feeling this badly!'" Danielle appreciates her parents trying to combat her perfectionism. But she allows that her parents' values are at the root of her focus on achievement. "Both my parents work hard, and their message always was, 'Your job is to be a good student.' That came easily for me. I'm scholarly. My younger sister is more social, so it's difficult for her." Excellent academic that she is, something is missing for Danielle. "I wish I knew my passion," she said, as she embarked on college, planning to try pre-med. "I could have had more overall fun in high school."

"Whose Life Is This?"

Parental expectations weigh heavily on girls. Be conscious of the effect your hopes for your daughter have on her. Keep in mind that her experience of high school will shape and change her in ways that neither of you can know. Briana feels that her mother's wish for her to excel in school has nothing to do with who she is. "My mom got married and had kids after college; she didn't have a career. Now she wants me to do what she didn't do. But I have no idea what I want to do, and her pressuring me to get better grades, to get more involved with more activities, only makes me want to retreat from her more. Why do parents try to mold children into something they are not? Let them grow up to be who they want to be. If they go through weird stages, ignore them." Briana's perspective does not take into account that some "weird stages" may be dangerous to her development. This is her mother's concern, but Briana and Carolyn are not communicating well enough to bridge the gap.

Some parents usurp their girls' lives. Fourteen-year-old Crystal confessed, "My dad is already looking at colleges for me and writing away for applications." Crystal understandably feels oppressed; she needs her life to be her own. She wants her father, Jareth, to support her interests, to enable her to grow and begin the process of college selection herself at the right time. By trying to manage her future, Jareth is exacerbating her stress. He is inhibiting her from being in the present, exploring her own identity, and finding out from her own mistakes and successes what she wants to do. Furthermore, Jareth's attempts to do the best for his daughter are alienating her from him. He will lose his relationship with her if he continues to try to control her life. "I just have to turn away," Crystal said.

Ask yourself, "Whose life is this?" Claudia had never lived alone or worked before she married and had children. She felt hampered by not feeling capable in the world and not earning her own money and vowed that her daughter, Valerie, would become self-supporting. She wanted Valerie to have the independence that she had never had. Valerie was aesthetically oriented, loved her electives in art, and despised her academic subjects. She had no intention of applying herself to subjects that she disliked in order to make a living some day. "I'll be a waitress to support my art if I have to, Mom. Don't bug me about my grades." Claudia obsessed about her daughter ending up as a starving artist and tried to force her to study more. Finally, she had to give up and put her energy into becoming more independent herself.

Neither you nor your daughter will be fulfilled if you unconsciously try to live through her. Even if you do not overtly steer her in a particular direction, if you have a bias, you will hang on her every failure and triumph. With this fixation on her life, you will avoid taking stock of yourself. Fairy tales like *Hansel and Gretel* portray the devouring aspect of a mother in the witch who seduces children with sweets, fattens them up, and then eats them. A girl whose mother "eats" her accomplishments learns to hide her triumphs or chooses not to succeed rather than provide fuel for her mother's vicarious living.

If you did not have your mother's support in high school in the way you wished or had a devastating experience academically or socially, sort out your feelings so that you don't project your unfulfilled wishes and personal needs on your daughter. Giving her opportunities to go against traditional gender assignments is vastly different from pushing her to do what you wish you had done. Instead, notice where her intiative and motivation lie and support her there. High school is a time for her to experiment and to test herself in those arenas that call to her. If she knows her own passions and develops the skill of meeting her own goals, she can easily change her mind and redirect her energy later.

Upping the Ante

Expectations conveyed in subtle ways have just as big an effect as those stated directly. Zena had been raised on stories of both her parents' achievements. Her African American mother, Carol, had been valedictorian when she graduated from Barnard College; her father, Lawrence, solved a forty-year-old problem in mathematics as a college junior at the University of North Carolina. "I grew up on stories like the one that my father had thrown off the curve in his high school math class because he only missed one on the final and everyone else got in the sixtieth percentile. The message was that I was supposed to surpass him." Seventeen-year-old Zena tried to escape the burden of these expectations when she volunteered to go to Zaire with a group in the summer of sophomore year. "As I worked digging a latrine that summer, I felt a tremendous sense of relief. It was the first time I was valued for what I could do rather than held up to an ideal I could never fulfill. Surprisingly, being in Africa also showed me that I do belong here. I really am American." Accept the reality of who your daughter is and work with that rather than with who you want her to be. Adolescent girls fervently want to *be* and *be seen* for who they are, not just what they do.

Is She Speaking Her Own Mind?

Girls who are voicing their own feelings and thoughts to you and to their teachers and mentors are those who have the best chance to succeed in life. Understanding and believing in her own feminine power makes it easier for a girl to speak her own thoughts and to trust her intuition and feelings, even if she is faced with an often rigid system of education that does not value spontaneity or any deviation from the already-known. It also helps her stand up to the belittling that she may experience from boys in her class who habitually express themselves in a competitive, put-down mode.

As she enters high school, be alert to changes in her that involve putting boys' opinions first or hiding her intelligence or talents because it's not "cool." For example, if she always spoke up in middle school, and now her teacher's comments say that she seems self-conscious and shy in the classroom, pay attention. It may be that during this transition she needs to observe before she regains her confidence in speaking out. But after you read her progress reports, talk with her about them. Ask her what she thinks about the teachers' observations and whether she deems the feedback valid. How does she feel in the classroom? Does she understand her poor performance or failure in a particular class? Does she feel uncomfortable in the class where everyone else seems to have the right answers and instant comprehension? Does she need more help from one of you at home? If neither of you is available or qualified, consider a tutor for her in that subject. You can't be everything to your child; outside help can be a blessing.

Does she feel demeaned or ignored by a teacher? If her teacher is a man, is he being flirtatious with her? This will be confusing to her and will undermine her confidence in the classroom. In any case, it might be appropriate to speak to her instructor or to have a three-way conference. Let her know that you are on her side and want to assist her.

If she will allow it, interact with your daughter about her ideas by reading her papers. Proofread them for typographical and grammatical errors before she turns them in. You can contribute and have interesting discussions with her about the material. This will give you insight into her intellectual development and her writing skills. Do not, however, try to rewrite the paper for her or criticize her ideas. Leave that to the teacher. Be respectful of the content, and she will trust you to read her work. If you are critical, she will withdraw immediately and reject your overtures next time. Seventeen-year-old Yvette wants to continue this exchange with her mother when she goes away to college. "We're already talking about my sending my papers on e-mail as an attachment. I don't want to give this up."

The academic challenge for a girl is to remain authentic to herself instead of mistakenly or blindly conforming to school expectations and succumbing to pleasing teachers. Whether she shuts down and conforms to the system or speaks out against the rules that discriminate against her self-expression, she will suffer. She needs to learn to deal with different personalities in teachers, when to speak the whole truth and when only that part of it that serves the end she desires. But she will be happiest if she feels authentic in her responses to assignments. If she learns only to "work the system" or gives up on a system that feels alien, she will lose herself.

Throughout discussions with your daughter, keep in mind that gender inequality, though often subtle, has real and stressful effects on our daughters every day. It may be insidious. Help her become aware of her own strengths, capabilities, and coping skills. Bring all her options to her attention so that she doesn't feel trapped. Enable her to assess where she is seeing the results of her efforts.

Be sure you are not reinforcing gender bias in your home. Unfair division of chores is only one way bias manifests itself in a family. You may have other, hidden biases that will cause your daughter distress. Notice, for instance, whether you have a higher tolerance for your son's or other boys' aggressive behavior than for that of your daughter. If you shrug your shoulders when your son shouts, swears, and shoves and are scandalized when you hear your daughter doing the same, examine your own reactions. Why is he allowed to express himself fully and she expected to be ladylike?

In school, reverse gender bias is on the rise. Teachers intent on supporting girls in math and science often undermine boys in the humanities. Kate's friend Don asked the English teacher how he was doing in the class. Their young male teacher responded, "You're doing all right for a guy." Kate said she and her friends were shocked. "My school is liberal. I couldn't believe this was happening. I get the rap of being the smart, obedient girl who never goofs off like the disruptive boys in class." Empathy must to go both ways on the gender issues.

Your daughter needs to know and experience that any situation, no matter how traumatic it seems to her, has solutions. Take her concerns seriously, then problem solve with her. This takes some time and much patience from you as a parent. But it is well worth the effort.

The Juggling Act

Talk with her about balancing all the things she wants to do in high school. If you are a high-achieving mother, how you handle your stress will influence your daughter's way of handling hers. Mona is a successful lawyer who specializes in divorce cases. The conflicts she mediates often spill over into her family life on weekends, with phone calls and emergency consultations. Mona tries to keep appropriate boundaries between her work and her teenagers' lives. She discusses legal issues with Arlene, fifteen, and Justin, seventeen, as points of interest but does not disclose the details of her clients' lives with her children.

Mona, however, is sometimes overwhelmed with the demands of her work and keeping up with her children's athletic and school schedules. Her husband is a busy research physician who is out of town every other weekend consulting at hospitals. Mona noticed that she often has migraines on weekends. Arlene, a solid student whose passion is ballet, also began to complain of headaches. Mona doesn't know whether her migraines are related to perimenopausal hormonal changes or whether they are a sign of stress. She's concerned that Arlene is also developing a pattern of overachievement and that her body is responding with similar symptoms.

Arlene said, "I think my mom worries too much about me, but I do get headaches when I'm feeling like I have too much to do." Mona talked with Arlene about taking four hours every Saturday to do something relaxing together; they agreed on a two-mile walk and lunch. Without such a plan, Arlene is always practicing her pliés or doing homework, and her mother is answering phone calls, while they haphazardly fit in errands. And taking time out makes Saturday less of a rush to get everything done that does not get done on weekdays.

Observe your own patterns of response to stress and assess your coping skills so you can teach your daughter those skills. Reorganize your time if you find that your old ways aren't working for you. If your daughter is always up until 2:00 A.M. the night before a paper is due, you could talk to her about organizing her time to begin writing sooner in the week. If you are going to edit the paper for her, that may also motivate her to get it done ahead of time.

Time management and organizational skills are key to remaining healthy and continuing to grow during periods of stress. If she is taking a heavy load in school and is ambivalent about trying out for the fall musical, give her permission to let it go this semester by reminding her of the overload she felt last year during rehearsal week. Suggest she wait for the spring production, when the number of courses she is taking drops. Teach her that she doesn't have to be *doing* something all the time in order to feel productive.

Emphasize the importance of proper rest, eating nutritious meals, and taking breaks from periods of intensive work. She may not always listen, but if you are modeling that value, she takes it in. You are preparing the ground in high school for how she will negotiate being in a new environment away from home for the first time, either at college or in her first job. If you have taught her what she needs to know, she will internalize what you say and put it into practice when she leaves home.

Don't insult your teenage daughter by talking down to her. She may be wiser than you think. If you try to force your point of view on her, you will alienate her. Rae told me, "You're not as young as people think you are as a freshman. In our freshman orientation class, they assume that you haven't formed yourself, your ideas, and your feelings when you really have."

Are You Practicing What You Preach?

You yourself need to sort your priorities and problem solve if you want to help your daughter master managing her own life efficiently and productively. Joyce said, "One night I was carefully pointing out to my sixteen-year-old daughter, Margo, that she seemed to put her friends first, answering their questions about an upcoming test and solving their boy problems, then not having time to write her own English paper. Margo looked me straight in the eye and said, 'Mom, that's exactly what you do. You put all of us first, making the little kids' lunches, doing errands for Dad, dinner for the whole family, and then you have to stay up half the night preparing for your office meeting. And you're always frazzled.' I stopped talking and just stared at her. For a few minutes I struggled with conflicting emotions of feeling criticized, unappreciated, disrespected, and suddenly I realized she was absolutely right, and I burst out laughing. Then we sat down and talked about how we could both manage our time better."

Ellen talked about the multilevel demand of having three children at different ages. "Each child is changing all the time in a different way. It makes having one child seem like a luxury—easier for the kid and for the mother. My library career also means that I have to make sure that my needs go into the equation. We have family meetings and put everyone's activities and wishes out on the table. Then we figure it out." Ellen emphasizes looking at the whole picture. If Kate wants to go out to dinner on a school night, she has her consider her other commitments that week. Ellen also taught her children to use a calendar and put up a blackboard in the kitchen where they can write notes and reminders to each other. You are likely to be the organizing principle in your family. The more you take the whole family system into account, the healthier and more balanced your life will be.

Strategies for Dealing with Stress

The patterns of response to stress are being established during high school. Danielle's stress came out in her body when her menstruation ceased for months at a time. Yvette noticed that she just wanted to sleep and get away from everything. "If I don't take baby steps, the deadlines suddenly hit me. It feels like we work, work, work and then get sick; all my friends have lots of colds and flus during the holidays." Some girls become passive and withdraw in the face of stress. Others become angry and give up, either quitting a team or dropping out of school. There is a fine line between your daughter arriving at a decision because she knows an activity is not serving her well or because of physical injury, and developing a pattern of making commitments that she can't keep. Overscheduling is self-defeating. She always feels as if she isn't doing enough.

Help your daughter develop more productive ways of handling stress by watching her and trying to understand her worldview. Expect her to be difficult when she is under stress; be the center that holds in the midst of her tirades. If you see that she is trying to please you or others, or doing too much in her life, talk to her about what you notice; ask her if she notices the same patterns. Sparking her self-reflection teaches her to identify her moods and what triggers them. Be in a listening mode. What are her options, and what does she feel she needs? Reinforce her self-soothing patterns: the ways she reduces pressure and gets back to her own center. Keeping a journal, reading, talking on the phone, taking a walk, even watching TV, can be time-out for girls. Share with her your own self-soothing techniques.

Ellen's younger daughter Alta was moping around on a rainy Saturday. Alta was whining about feeling bored and restless. Ellen recognized the signs of irritability that came up for Alta when her basketball season ended. Ellen knew that her daughter needed exercise, but Ellen was walking out the door to do an all-day staff training at the library and didn't have time to work through Alta's rising temper tantrum. "Do you want me to drop you at the ice skating rink on the way to my program?" "I hate ice skating," Alta snarled. After a few more back-and-forth sallies that increased Alta's frustration, Ellen began to feel frantic. "There I was having to leave, feeling bad because my kid's upset and I can't make it right. Finally, I said 'You know, Alta, you better just go take a run in the rain, because I don't think you'll feel better until you get some exercise.' And I left, feeling terrible because she was still mad at me." When Ellen got home, Alta, who had gone running, cheerfully greeted her mother. Alta said, "I take everything out on my mother. I even get mad at her for things I don't tell her about. I can't help it. And I appreciate that she puts up with me." Physical activity is a great stress reducer. Ellen said, "I know it for myself, so I can see it in my daughters. If I go three days without either walking or stretching, I start to get irritable and antsy. Moving in my body helps me get back to my whole self."

Your daughter may also find a respite from her academic studies by choosing an elective in painting, woodworking, or ceramics. Working with her hands will relieve her overactive mind, and she may find she has dormant talents.

Feeling competent and empowered helps girls manage high school. Encourage your daughter to acquire real-world skills. Teach her to manage her allowance and to open a checking account, especially if she has a part-time job. Show her how to ride the bus or subway, get a cab, and take the train. Let her make appointments and phone calls to get information, for instance, about the lifeguard training class she needs to take. Be sure her computer skills are up to par and teach her (or find someone to teach her) to use e-mail and to search the Web for information on her school reports.

Community: Giving Back and Receiving

Although community service adds hours to your daughter's busy schedule, it can also be a stress reducer for her by putting her life in perspective. Seeing that others don't have the same advantages that she does may make her more appreciative of her life and of you. Community service hours are required of students in many high schools. Taking care of children at a homeless day-care facility, making dinners at a soup kitchen, or cleaning up the park can empower your daughter; she can see her efforts make a difference. After all she has received, she will experience deep satisfaction at being able to give.

Tammy joined a project her freshman year with students from other high schools to learn and practice effective citizenry. Girls and boys work with the city to set up places for teens to go and things for them to do. They are lobbying their city for a teen skate park.

The project helps teenagers like Tammy make a bridge to the outside world beyond high school. Whether teaching swim classes to underprivileged kids or doing a clothing drive for hurricane victims, girls learn skills that prepare them for adult life. Yvette, who wants to be a middle school history teacher, tutors sixth graders in history. "I love it. I'm already learning what works in teaching."

"My Life Is Over!"

Just as losing a friend or not making friends and plummeting grades can send your daughter into a tailspin of despair, being prevented from playing a sport she loves through injury often leads to intense disappointment, and sometimes depression. Kaylie twisted her ankle early in the fall cross-country season and was forced to give up running. It was after months of feeling defeated and at a loss that she decided in April of junior year to apply for the Amigos program in Ecuador.

Kaylie's mother, Viviane, said, "I trusted Kaylie's intuition that it would be good for her. She's always been responsible and self-motivated. I felt badly about her missing cross-country and being frustrated with her injury. I thought she needed something new after her demoralizing year. Our son, Kaylie's older brother, had done Amigos several years earlier, and we had his firsthand reports about the program. He thought it would be good for her, too."

Kaylie was already a mature young woman, yet it was a big step for her to leave her family for an extended trip. "I didn't really think about being away from home for eight weeks until the last minute; I cried a little saying good-bye." This was the beginning of a lonely and difficult but rewarding endeavor in which Kaylie had to learn to comfort herself, develop new social skills with her partner Midori (who was having problems of her own), and tolerate hunger, her own and others', for the first time in her life.

Kaylie said, "The hardest part was being away from everyone I knew. But I made a lot of good friends in Ecuador. The people were incredible—they were so generous. They thought we were there to change their lives, and we couldn't do that much, so I always felt inadequate to the need. I could never relax; I felt I had to be doing something to help every minute. But I think the goal of Amigos is for us to see the poverty, not to change it. I wrote in my journal every day and cried when I got letters from home. I plan to go back in two years. I would know what to expect and be more prepared. I'm so glad that I did it."

Be aware that sports injuries and other physical injuries create a particular stress for adolescent girls. A girl's body image and self-esteem often plummet when physical activity that has kept her grounded in her body is curtailed.

Your daughter's disappointment with the casting of the school play can be another devastating experience in high school. Help her work through her crushed feelings and encourage her to put her energy into making the role she did get the best it can be. If she didn't get a callback and is intent on making a career of acting, sympathize and gently remind her that she will have many auditions in life and that she has to expect rejections. Encourage her to talk to the director about his perceptions of her audition. Perhaps she needs to prepare more thoroughly for the next one. Emphasize her honing her skills as a result of experience.

When your daughter runs into a rejection, injury, or any glitch in her life, be prepared to help her stop, take stock, and redirect her energy even as she mourns the loss of her previous strength. Try to communicate a balanced attitude about life's vicissitudes to your daughter. Illness, not getting the part, not winning the game or the competition are the shadow side of experience. Emphasize her doing her best rather than winning the prize. Yvette said, "My parents both come to all my Irish step-dancing competitions, but they have never had expectations of me. They're happy for me when I win, but not uncomfortably happy, so it doesn't put pressure on me. We enjoy ourselves."

Day-to-Day Friction

Repetitive cycles of bad feeling between you and your daughter are also stressful for both of you. Instead of going through the same angry or nagging scenes over and over again, be smart enough to see how the system works between you and take steps to break negative patterns. Valerie, Claudia's fourteen-year-old, stayed up late at night talking on the phone to friends and couldn't get out of bed in the morning. Claudia went in three or four times to try to wake her. "I would get so angry, morning after morning, and she would yell back at me. I hated having this conflict every day, but I felt trapped. Finally, I realized there was something wrong with this picture."

Claudia still considered it her job to get Valerie off to school on time. If she didn't succeed, she felt like a bad mother. As she tried harder, she was doomed to fail because Valerie needed to be taking more responsibility, and Claudia needed to become more independent from her daughter. She pulled herself together and sat down to talk with Valerie. "I hate us going off with terrible feelings in the morning, Valerie. What can we do to solve this problem? You're old enough to get yourself up with an alarm clock, and you'll have to explain yourself to the school if you're late. I can help you by taking the phone out of your room and giving you a cutoff time at night for using it. What do you suggest? How do you feel?"

After arguing and resisting for a while, Valerie said sheepishly, "Mom, I know I'm a pain in the morning, but I actually like you getting me up. It reminds me of when I was little. How about if you just call me once and I'll work on getting up right away? You're right, mornings are a drag now—I'll try to be better about it."

Claudia said she would give her a chance, but that the first time Valerie went back to sleep they would move on to another option. Their conversation was a starting point for breaking an entrenched pattern. At different times, Valerie had to use an alarm clock, give up her phone, and even be late to school. But Claudia and Valerie were able to work out their behavior by talking it out instead of staying stuck in the same unconscious rut.

Your daughter, like Valerie, will have conflicting needs of autonomy and closeness. Valerie wanted her mother's care in the morning, but she was also exploring relationships with friends on the phone. She didn't yet have her own boundaries in place about getting enough sleep in order to fulfill her morning commitment. She wanted her freedom, and she wanted her mother, too. By connecting to one another, their relationship improved as her mother honored both sides of her adolescent needs. Claudia also freed herself a little to pursue her own life. As she gave Valerie more responsibility, she could admire her daughter's artistic bent and look for a way to empower herself.

Day-to-day friction may arise with your daughter over her doing her homework. Have your fingers on the pulse of her academic life, but don't try to micromanage her studies. She needs room to choose what your involvement with her will be. Yvette said, "The good thing is that I'm in control of my schoolwork. I set the standard for myself with grades. I don't want anything lower than a B, but if I get a C, my parents just ask if I need help. Grades are a big self-stress for me. I'm very self-disciplined."

You don't have license to look over your daughter's shoulder as she works. But you want to be engaged with what she is studying and thinking about. It's best to establish a flexible relationship that allows you to respond when she asks for help. Routinely asking whether she has finished her homework does not accomplish anything. At the beginning of freshman year, continue to enforce basic rules about weeknights being for studying, not for going out or watching unlimited television. By senior year you will probably have to relinquish her to her own judgment entirely.

The issue of time spent with the family can become another source of stress. Parents often assault their daughters with accusations: "We never see you. You're always out. It makes us feel like you don't love us or appreciate us." Be positive: "I miss you. Let's you and I do something special together this weekend or plan a family outing." If your daughter is fighting every opportunity to spend time with her family, explore the basis for her rebelliousness. What is troubling her? Perhaps she is experiencing some conflict that she has not felt free to share with you. Or perhaps she is furious with your rules and does not feel she can challenge you and her father. Try to draw her out in a loving, sympathetic way.

Family Problems

When your family is struck by serious illness, marital problems, death, or divorce, you can prevent a catastrophic fallout for your daughter. To avoid deep-seated resentments and unresolved anger, discuss what is going on. Let her in on the process. Seventeen-year-old Kaylie said, "I think my confidence got shaken in seventh grade when my mom got breast cancer. She lost her hair after chemotherapy, and I used to be embarrassed when she'd pick me up, if she didn't wear a hat. I feel bad about that now; I didn't understand then, and I didn't really know much about what was going on with her. I tried to keep it away. Then the cancer came back in the other breast, so she had them both removed. It all went on for three or four years." Fortunately, Viviane is healthy again, and Kaylie is now securely established at college.

Girls need information about illness. Err in the direction of giving them too much rather than not enough. With a life-threatening illness like cancer, whether she can put her dread into words or not, information is power. If you share your feelings, she can work through hers. Describe the medical procedures and prognosis with her as you go along. She needs to have a forum for talking out her fears and concerns and coping with the outcomes.

If you and your husband divorce during your daughter's high school years, you will have to sort out your own feelings of anger, hate, resentment, and loss. It's important to tell your daughter your feelings in a considered way. If you don't tell her, she will know them anyway and have to bear the responsibility of her knowledge; that will interfere with your relationship. On the other hand, don't make your daughter your confidante about all the details of your alienation by calling your husband names and ranting and raving about his shortcomings. Naming your feelings of sadness and distress is different than taking those feelings out on her or trying to get her on your side. Being slanderous and cataloguing grievances means you have unfinished business with him that you need to work out in therapy or with your close friends.

Preserve your daughter's relationship with her father if you possibly can. On the other hand, if he isn't paying child support on time and you are hampered in taking care of her needs, tell her in as non-loaded a way as you can manage. You don't have to cover for his failure to take responsibility. Answer every question that she asks as honestly as you can while still maintaining a boundary of respect for her father. When Rae's parents separated between her freshman and sophomore years, she was shocked. "Everything was fine, then in one month my dad moved out for good. By the end of sophomore year, my mom and I had moved three times. I got a lot more independent, more into my schoolwork, and into theater. My theater coach outside school helped me a lot. When I felt bad, I called her and went to her house. One thing in particular she would say over and over, "Remember your feelings; use them later in your acting."

Rae learned to use her sadness, anger, frustration, and fragility in the service of her characters on stage and to be productive in her life. When things got heated between her mother and father, she had a concerned woman to turn to, a mentor. The worst stress for a teenager is when she is having feelings or thoughts that she cannot share with anyone. Trusted girlfriends go a long way toward being sympathetic to feelings, but when a girl knows the problems are over her head and heart, she needs a trusted adult to confide in. Rae works well under pressure: "When I'm busy, I do a lot better in school. I'm very self-organized. I know this hour I have to do this and I do it." But she did have an escape valve in her acting coach for the times when the chaotic feelings about her parents splitting threatened to overwhelm her. When Persephone returned from the underworld, wise Hecate became her companion and guide. Be sure your daughter has women in her life who care about her and model healthy attitudes.

College Bound or Not?

In junior year your daughter will begin to think about where she is headed. If she is college bound, her grades this year will count heavily for admissions. This may be a year to reevaluate her extracurricular activities and retain only those she loves. You will want to do a college tour of schools that already interest her. If you or your husband has a strong investment in which university she attends, you will only add to her stress. Researching colleges and doing exams, papers, and reading assignments during this year create a steady buildup of pressure that culminates in fall of senior year.

In the first semester or quarter of senior year, girls (and boys) are barely suppressed volcanoes of feelings threatening to overflow. You and your daughter will be narrowing the choices of colleges to which she wants to apply. Meanwhile, she will be acutely aware that fall grades are the last set that count for admission. Extensive applications for admission and financial aid are also due in December. The intense academic pressure to keep up or raise her grades, write a knockout entrance essay, and take the SAT or equivalent exam will be compounded by the beehive atmosphere of everyone in the class doing the same thing. She will be worrying, "Is my essay good enough? Are my grades good enough? What if I don't get in to any place I want to go? I can't wait for this to be over."

Yvette said, "I broke down, just went crazy in fall semester when applications were due. I had essays to write, semester finals, and a huge dance competition. I lost it one Sunday at dance rehearsal. I was sobbing. I couldn't dance, couldn't function. I had a nervous breakdown and freaked out at my mom, as usual."

Yvette's mother, Mimi, calmly stepped in and said, "It's OK, Yvette—it's only one rehearsal. Let's leave, go shopping, watch a movie, and forget about your work." Yvette said, "I screamed at her 'What are you talking about? I have so much more to do!' It was a totally impractical and irrational suggestion, but finally I gave in, and it worked. I gathered myself and took a deep breath. When I went back to my homework that evening, I could write the paper that was due the next day. I felt better."

If your daughter chooses not to go to college, you will need to have many talks about what she does want to do. Does she want to take a year off to travel with a friend or a group? How will her trip be funded? Does she want to work and get experience in something practical before she pursues further studies or decides what to do next? If she wants to remain at home in order to work or attend the local junior college, you will need to discuss new parameters for the living situation, now that she is an adult. You and she will also want to talk about how she will feel living at home while many of her friends go off to start new lives.

Respect your daughter's goals as they change. Girls continue to be influenced by cultural messages. She may feel that her life is in someone else's hands—especially, that she will marry and a man will take care of her. Or she may feel that she has to have a career *and* a family. Talk with her about what she wants for herself: career, family, children, travel, service to community, to country, to the world. Try to elicit her ideas, not just what you want to hear.

The challenge for your daughter is to develop autonomy and a sense of community and to follow her initiative, make choices, and design her own life. If she simply does the expected, she will remain dependent. It's important, therefore, that she act from her individuality and her passions. The *belief* that she can accomplish a particular activity, whether it's skydiving or sewing, begins with her being drawn to the activity, then trying to do it, and, finally, observing other women or girls in that field as role models. The same applies to studying, writing papers, doing math problems and science experiments, or playing tennis or chess.

You can reinforce your daughter's belief in her ability by encouraging her to try a variety of activities and finding women with whom she can talk and possibly share doing what she loves. Her yearnings in particular directions will lead her to mastering new skills in high school. This way she will have the capacity to deal with her choices when things are difficult along her life path, rather than feeling that she wasted time doing what her parents or feminism or society expected of her.

Support your daughter if she shows an interest in something that you never dreamed of. Her excitement and enthusiasm will strengthen her, if she can follow through and be successful. What she learns in terms of self-discipline and mastery is more important than the activity itself. If she wants to spend her free time trying to save the whales and you are an artsy family, laud her individuality and let her go for it. She may move on to something creative, but if she becomes a social activist and is happy, you will still be allied with her and you can learn from her social outlook as she learns from your more artistic one.

When the Stress Gets to Mom!

Your expectations of yourself in trying to meet your daughter's adolescent needs will also create stress for you. You may feel at a loss to understand your daughter's milieu, and sometimes frustrated and exhausted with trying to keep up with each new dilemma she springs on you. If you hated math and grew up thinking you couldn't do it because girls were not encouraged to do math, you may feel inadequate at being called on to solve an algebra equation for her. If you need nine hours of sleep a night, you will suffer when adolescent nightlife continually disrupts your rest. There will be times when you say, "I can't handle this any more!"

At other times, do not be surprised if you find yourself anguished, missing your daughter. Not only are you trying to help her negotiate this new, unfamiliar world, you're beginning to wonder who you will be without her and without your primary mothering role. This is a difficult emotional time, and your mood may swing from sadness to feelings of impatience for her to leave home.

In the midst of relating to your daughter, you may feel as if you are drowning in her needs, that you are so focused on trying to figure out what is going on with her, driving her around, and enabling her to live her life that you begin to lose a sense of who *you* are. When you begin to take everything she does personally, or cry at a minor rebuff or a casual joking criticism from her, this is the moment to step back and go do something for yourself.

Take a break; get some separation. If you find that going out with your husband or partner means that you talk the whole night about your daughter, you are not getting away from parenting. Agree with him to focus on other topics or on the play or concert you are sharing. Alternatively, call a friend and arrange to take a vigorous hike or attend a poetry reading that will re-center you and give you perspective. Spend some time alone reflecting on fantasies that you have secretly nourished, things that you have always wanted to do or have let slip during your preoccupation with mothering. Make yourself happy for a few hours a day. Refresh yourself, then reenter the fray. You can't do it for her, you can only be available for her when she needs you. Go back and forth between nurturing yourself and being there for her, and you will be able to stay on course and see her through these awesome adolescent years.

7

Daddy's Little Girl

"I can't talk to my dad. He doesn't listen or try to understand me. He just tries to reinforce his standards in every conversation," said Jade resignedly. Although she shines academically and athletically, seventeen-year-old Jade has still had to learn to work around her father, Howard, rather than connect with him. "It wasn't always this way," Jade added. "I used to be Daddy's little girl, the spoiled favorite one. I was sweet and got As." In middle school, when Jade began to argue with her father and no longer came running to jump into his arms every time he opened the front door, Howard had less and less to do with her. Over the next few years, whenever she asked him to drive her to a friend's house or a movie, he refused: "No, I can't. I promised Dexter [their dog] that I'd take him to the dog park." Jade said, "That really hurt me!" Howard is a hospital administrator who pushes Jade to achieve on his terms: to make money.

"Once in a while, he takes me skiing, but I can never talk to him about who I really am. There are certain subjects I don't get near. He won't understand and I'll get upset." Jade says that she knows her father loves her and didn't know what he was doing, but his rejection of her overtures did irreparable damage to their relationship.

Whether or not he is your husband, your daughter's father is your partner in parenting during these years. He will be coming from a different place and will see the world and his daughter from a man's point of view. You will differ on parenting strategies and gender issues. Collaborating with him will become another challenge, raising complex questions. How do you get her to understand her father and him to understand her? How do you and he differ in relating to your daughter? In what ways are your roles interchangeable? What can fathers and daughters do together to deepen their relationships?

Like the relationship between mother and daughter, even the best relationships between fathers and daughters become problematic at puberty. Your husband will respond to her changing body and startlingly adult behavior in different ways. When her body becomes more womanly, it often arouses sexual feelings in her father that are difficult for him to handle. Some girls talk about their fathers withdrawing from them at this age. Others talk about fathers who don't want them to go out with boys. A few have fathers who label them "bad" for their interest in dating and are hostile to their boyfriends. These responses are not helpful to an adolescent girl. He sends the message that there is something wrong with growing up, becoming a woman, something shameful about sexuality.

When there is a wounded relationship with her father or her father is absent, a girl is susceptible to pressure from men. If he doesn't reject her boyfriends, a father may get a vicarious charge from boys' attention to his daughter. He then unconsciously identifies with their sexual feelings toward her. In our myth, Zeus, Persephone's father, gives Hades permission to abduct Persephone. But Demeter's horror at losing her daughter forces Zeus to recognize Hades' crime. By standing her ground and refusing to let the land be fruitful, refusing to relinquish Persephone, Demeter gets Zeus' attention and reclaims her daughter. Although Hades tricks her, with the pomegranate seed, into consummating their marriage, Persephone is still reunited with her mother, her feminine self. Zeus, like Demeter and Persephone, changes in the course of the story. He represents the conscious pole of a man's psyche that respects the feminine; Hades represents the instinctual side, which simply takes what it wants. A father struggles with these opposites in himself as he meets his daughter in her adolescence.

Although he is naturally ambivalent about sharing his precious "little girl" with another man, you can help your husband stay connected to her. While she makes the transition from girl to woman he needs to listen to her feelings (and yours) in order to learn about the feminine, as Zeus did in the myth. The big challenge for him will be to relinquish his adoring daughter and spend more time with her in adult ways. If he was demonstrative with his love when she was younger, encourage him to continue to give her a hug or a kiss at appropriate times, unless she asks him to stop. If she does withdraw from physical contact with him, help him to understand that she is familiarizing herself with her new feelings and shape and that this is not a permanent rejection. She may be uncomfortable with touch for a while as her body develops. His sensitivity to and tolerance of her moods will contribute to her wanting his company.

If you notice that your daughter has subtly distanced herself from her father since she began menstruating, think about why this has happened. Many girls do withdraw for a while as they learn to adjust to their monthly cycle. But as she matures emotionally, notice whether her father is still treating her in babyish ways that irritate her or make her uncomfortable. Ask your husband what these shifts in attitude and behavior mean to him. How do they make him feel?

When a father feels protective and sweet toward his daughter, he often remembers what was going through his head when he was an adolescent. If he dreads the male focus on sexuality on his daughter's behalf and tries to shield her by warning her about the terrors of men's sexuality, he will only make her fearful. She may then lose him as a resource for learning how to deal with boys. Corey, dark-haired and impulsive, matured early. Plagued with learning disabilities, she struggled with school and making goals for herself. Beginning in middle school, she turned her focus to boys. Her father's unreasoned responses to her dating pushed her into flagrant acting out. Corey said, "I can't tell my dad anything about my love life. I'm always afraid he's going to go ballistic."

"Because I'm Your Father, That's Why!"

Patrick, Corey's well-meaning, research scientist father, admits that he tried to father Corey on the same authoritarian model that his parents used with him and ended up disastrously at odds with her. Frustrated and appalled when Corey experimented with drugs and ran away from home in the eighth grade, he waged battle with her as he tried to control her life. "I would say, 'You're not going out to that party!' She would respond, 'Yes, I am. You won't know. You'll think I'm out with the girls.' She was technically right. I was just laying down the law and not listening to her. My wife would say, 'You're being too hard. You can't act that way and expect her to want to talk to you.' I was too strict. It took me until her sophomore year fighting and angry to finally give up and try something new.

"I need a few more kids to figure this out. It's devastating to me when Corey's so ugly—using foul language and being hurtful. When I was a teenager, I never talked to my parents that way. If I ever did with my father, I'd be picking myself up off the floor. I was the good boy and conformed; I saved it until I got away from home."

When Patrick forbade Corey to date as a freshman in high school, she lied and went to friends' homes to meet boys. At sixteen, she got birth control pills from Planned Parenthood and is now dating a nineteen-year-old college student. Patrick has come around to accepting the inevitable and has decided to provide a safe environment for his daughter's relationship. He is intent on repairing the harm his rigid behavior caused. But he is saddened by how long it took him to learn to respond to who Corey is instead of who he wanted her to be. By trying to control her, he risked losing her.

Patrick now concentrates on controlling his own reactivity, and on compromising with Corey about her wishes. He religiously attends her swim meets and looks for other ways he can connect with her. Driving her to school in the mornings, he responds to her mood: sometimes silent, sometimes excited and talkative. He tries to share his own day-to-day feelings in a low-key way. With his knowledge of anatomy, he helps Corey with her biology homework. In order to participate this way, he had to make himself available. Maura, his wife, also had to agree to defer to his time with Corey.

You will have to make similar adjustments in your parenting strategy with your husband if you want to improve your daughter's connection with her father. If they don't spend time together, they will grow increasingly distant. As Patrick said, "Previously, I was in the secondary role. I could be ignored. There was no need for me. Her mother did everything. I felt really badly about being left out. But it was my own fault. When things escalated, I tried harder to change her. I feared losing her, and I also felt bad for her because she has learning disabilities like I do. But I was taking care of my fear in all the wrong ways."

Maura, a fourth-grade school teacher, was instrumental in helping her family weather the crisis of Corey's early teen years. Wracked by her own worry about Corey, she still stood by both her daughter and husband and tried to explain them to each other. When she realized they all needed more help, she sought family therapy. But she never gave up on Corey, and they have come through to a more understanding and harmonious family life. Do what you can to help your daughter and husband improve their relationship, and you will all benefit before she leaves home for college or her first real job.

Strike a Balance

You and your husband should try not to criticize the boys your daughter goes out with. Let her find her way. Remember, if you take a stand against a particular boy, she may feel she has to defend him and stay with him longer than she would have done without your intervention. When a father is too strict and possessive of his daughter, he risks pushing her into the very behavior that he fears.

A father needs to find balance in his reactions: to acknowledge his daughter's burgeoning beauty and her attractiveness to men and to appreciate her, as well as warn her about the dangers. If he shares stories about his own early dating experiences, when he felt vulnerable, his daughter will know not to see boys as more powerful and in charge. None of this can be heavy-handed; it needs to be part of an easy dialogue between a father and daughter. That ongoing conversation can take place when he is driving her to activities, working together around the house, or having lunch out. It takes planning to have a relationship.

If she and her father are connecting and he observes that a boy is being manipulative or controlling, he could make a comment: "I've noticed that Jeff always wants to go bowling and you don't get to see the movies you're interested in. How you do you feel about that? Is that OK with you?" If she doesn't answer, let it go. Openness and sensitivity to your daughter leads to intimacy. Just asking the question is enough to raise her consciousness.

Light humor can often be effective in a father finding this middle ground, but it should never include teasing her about her size, shape, or boys' reactions to her; he needs to faithfully support her love of her changing body. Appreciation, not sexual innuendo, should be the tenor of his responses to her. Being a loving, considerate man who admires and respects her will boost her self-confidence with boys.

Body Image

If a father expects his daughter to dress a certain way or look like his favorite movie star, he threatens to destroy her instinctual life. He must be aware of the highly charged issue of body image. If he slaps her on the back or, worse yet, on her fanny, and says, "Hey, you've gained a few pounds," he is not only being rude, he is saying, "You are not all right the way you are; you need to change." It doesn't matter if he intends it as a joke. She will hear an echo of the model-thin standard of the culture, which is not at all a joke. He will reinforce her fear that she is only pleasing or acceptable to men if she looks a certain way.

If you see her father behaving in this fashion, take him aside and talk to him about the effect he is having on his daughter. You can credit him with good intentions for trying to create a rapport with her by joking but explain to him the devastating, subtle consequences that such attitudes can have on girls. If it is her grandfather, uncle, or a close family friend who is too rigid or old-fashioned to take you seriously, try to limit your daughter's exposure to him.

Whoever the man putting her down, be sure she knows that you find his behavior offensive. Ally yourself with her openly and stand up to him, along with her, when he behaves inappropriately. Talk to her about not buying into these rampant sexist attitudes, and give her permission to walk away and not be polite about refusing such attention.

Your husband may be angry with you for taking your daughter's side. Keep your cool. Acknowledge his feelings. Explain her and your points of view. If you are able to hang in there and suggest alternatives that improve their communication, he may learn over time. If he has a weight problem himself and is trying to find a buddy, suggest that he invite her to go for a run, visit the gym, or play badminton with him and emphasize health, rather than weight loss, at least for her.

A father can be helpful not only in mitigating gender stereotypes and sending different messages about body image but in going against stereotypes in other areas of his daughter's life. The obsolete notion of girls needing to be dumb to get a guy still operates. There is sometimes pressure for a girl to not be as smart as she is, to not show her intelligence in front of boys. One girl told me, "I know I'm pretty smart, but I'm afraid if I say the answer in class the boys will think I'm a brain or a nerd. I'm afraid I won't be popular." If a father sees this attitude in his daughter, he can encourage her to be authentic, to change her attitude toward what's important in a relationship. He can make it known that he doesn't buy the old standards. He can tell her stories about his interest in the smart girls in his high school and assert his appreciation of her mother's intelligence. He can imagine with her what it would be like to maintain this deception for months and years to come, to pretend she's something she is not. Ask questions like: What would a relationship be based on in which you were pretending all the time?

An involved father can go against the traditional female injunction to protect male egos. Even strong girls like Kate, whose father recognizes her physical aptitude, have a bias toward saving masculine pride. "I know I can accomplish my dreams, but I still have these thoughts that I can't do certain things because I'm a girl, like throwing a ball or lifting something heavy. Even if a guy is skinny, and shorter than me, my first reaction would be that he would be the stronger. It comes up as 'He's a guy, he'll do it.' Then I'll think, 'No, I *could* do it, but he's a guy, so he'll do it.' I would let my boyfriend do it, so he wouldn't feel rejected as a guy." Kate's sensitivity wouldn't keep her from helping if she were asked.

A girl often succumbs to a boy's pressure when her social and academic demands conflict. In her first two years of high school, battling with her dad at home and sneaking around to meet her friends, Corey said, "I knew I was fucked up because whenever a guy asked me to cut school and go smoke or go to the mall, I went." During family therapy, when Patrick began to respond more to Corey, she let him in on her own anxieties about her behavior. Instead of threatening her with sending her to reform school if she cut class again, he could say, "It seems to me that you are really protecting your boyfriend by not speaking your mind in class or by not saying no when he wants you to give up your education." Corey felt enormously relieved to have her father take her side in a way that helped her grow.

Reassure your daughter that the older she gets, the more boys and girls will respect her intelligence. By senior year, when college is looming, everyone in a mixed group of kids will be cheering the smart girl beating two boys on the television program *Jeopardy!* instead of rating her on her looks. A father who can see the world through his daughter's eyes will be able to change and deepen the meaning of his relationships with all the women in his life.

Being in the Middle

Because your daughter is part of a teen culture that insists on its autonomy and rejects parental guidance, control issues with her father often come up. Many fathers, mimicking their own deficient fathering models, lay down the law without inquiring further. When her father is unfair, unreasonable, or overcontrolling and tempers flare between them, you as her mother may attempt to mediate the conflict by talking to each of them and sometimes to them together. Vi, the mother of three girls, remembers when her sixteen-year-old daughter, Sherry, was invited to the senior prom "at zero hour," ten days before the event. Because they often did sewing projects together, they excitedly pitched in to design and sew a dress of black taffeta and lace. When Sherry tried it on the day before the prom, the dress was beautiful but needed to be altered. "I had these wonderful fantasies of sharing this day with her: laying out the dress the night before, doing her nails and her hair, and giving her some of my special oil for her bath."

Suddenly, Sherry and her father, Dave, had a big blowup about an ongoing issue between them. Sherry had a habit of leaving her belongings strewn all over the house, which "drove her father crazy." In all the fuss of sewing, she had left her backpack, books, and athletic bag on the living room floor. When the fight with her father erupted, Sherry grabbed her new dress and its accessories and stormed out of the house. Struck to the core, Vi wept and begged her daughter to stay, to no avail.

Vi knew Sherry had gone to her best girlfriend's house, because Sherry had retreated there after altercations before. She did not expect to see Sherry again before the dance. Vi was devastated. "After Sherry left, I collapsed on the bed and cried and cried, furiously talking to myself. What did I do wrong? I was so sad."

Late the next afternoon, Sherry walked in and acted as if nothing had happened. Both Vi and Dave were able to respond to Sherry's cue, not bring up the incident, and let the prom take precedence. Vi had to sew Sherry into the dress in order to make it fit; her father took pictures of her and her girlfriends, who arrived dressed in their finery. "Finally," Vi recalls, "I watched them all walking down the street to another friend's house where the boys were going to meet them. I thought, Well, there she goes, we did it, even if it wasn't the way I wanted it to be."

At her next dinner date with her daughter, Vi brought up the conflict with Dave to air and validate Sherry's perceptions. Vi shared her own feelings of sadness and once again expressed the wish that

Dave could be more understanding and tolerant. Dave wanted to change but found it difficult to let go of control. When she asked Sherry how she felt, Sherry said, "I just had to leave. I can't stand him when he acts that way. Thanks for the support, Mom."

Even with everyone's best efforts, these explosions happen in families. In the aftermath, it's important for parents to follow through on helping their daughter succeed at the task at hand. Vi was able to alter the dress and prepare Sherry for the prom, honoring her daughter's need for her. Her father, too, got beyond his anger and joined in. Painful as it was for her, Vi had also respected Sherry's need to stay out the night before. Above all, she had been able to talk both to her husband and to Sherry about the conflict between them so that they understood each other better the next time.

Mothers often find themselves in the role of mediator between their husband or partner and their teenage daughters. Being the referee is valuable to them both because you as a woman may understand better than he does what your daughter is going through. But the role of go-between may also be painful, frustrating, and taxing for you, and you must be alert to your daughter trying to manipulate the differences between you and her father just to get her way.

Collaborating on parenting with her father, when possible, may help you avoid getting trapped in constant conflict between them. Discuss the values you both think are important and find fair rules and guidelines for your daughter to impart those values. If possible, present your conclusions to her together. After talking to Dave and Sherry separately, Vi also called a family meeting for the three of them (excluding their six-year-old son) to help bridge the gap after the disconnection. Dave was able to apologize for exploding, as Sherry was about dropping her belongings along the way, which helped them all feel better, even though they knew it could happen again.

Asserting your authority on behalf of your daughter helps her express herself. Beyond the personal values of fairness and remaining true to your feelings, your mediation has the larger value of helping to right the balance of power between men and women in our culture. Intervening on your daughter's behalf is strengthening to your feminine core and hers and affects other women's and girls' struggles to affirm themselves.

Sharing High School Secrets

Encourage your husband to talk to his daughter about his adolescent experience. Jim was afraid to tell Kate about his alcoholism in his teens and early twenties. He had put it behind him. Seventeen-year-old Kate said, "My father was very private about his past and his childhood. Little things came up, but I never felt comfortable asking. We were close in other ways. He's a musician, plays the guitar, drums, and piano, and he taught me to play the guitar." Jim took Kate to concerts and created a tangible bond between them, but she was completely unaware that he was going to therapy and involved in a process of healing his own deep childhood wounds.

One evening when the two were alone at home, Jim sat Kate down and told her about his abusive upbringing and his alcoholism from ages sixteen to twenty-nine. Kate said, "I cried off and on for a whole weekend about what happened to him when he was a kid; I felt so sorry for him." Kate was born when Jim was twenty-three years old. Hearing him talk about his suffering made sense of things she hadn't understood when she was younger and he was drinking. She said, "It helps our daily relationship now that I understand his past."

Ellen, Kate's mother, had worked through her husband's addiction and therapy with him. Not only does she know that this conversation will help Kate emotionally by relieving her of unnamed tensions from her childhood, but it will strengthen her relationship with her father, just as it strengthened their marriage. It also lightens

Ellen's burden of carrying his dark secret and makes Jim's rehabilitation all the more secure.

Jim's revealing his deep feelings to his daughter goes against the cultural stereotype. Most boys are taught to hide feelings of hurt or sadness, and grow up masking their vulnerability with anger. Because of her father's example, Kate will be able to see boys' humanity.

Healthy Boundaries

It is crucial that you keep your issues as a couple separate from your issues as parents. Do not go off on tangents, do not bring up your grievances. The clearer you can be about this, the better for all three of you. Helen, a homemaker, who was active in her church and Junior League, cultivated a social image. She cared most about what people thought of her. As a reflection of her own worth, she was invested in her daughter's being a model child. Fourteen-year-old Cassady, who had been a compliant little girl, began to complain about her mother reading her diary, getting into her drawers, and invading her privacy.

Helen had issues with her husband, Robert, about the extensive travel for his job with an investment company that kept him away from the family all the time. Instead of responding to Cassady's concerns for her privacy, Helen launched into a diatribe about what she perceived to be her husband's irresponsibility. Helen's invasion of Cassady's privacy stemmed from her not having her own emotional life. Cut off from her husband by his absences, she tried to live through her daughter. Avoiding marital issues, she attempted to mold Cassady in her image.

Faced with the facts of her displaced behavior, Helen finally got up the nerve to confront her husband, "I just can't go on with you being gone and our not having any intimacy." This began a series of confrontations that resulted in their seeking couples counseling. By taking up the problem directly, Helen took the pressure off Cassady and modeled a better way of relating to men for her daughter. This gave Cassady the way through to do the same with her father and kept her mother out of her things.

It will be more difficult to separate your issues as a couple from parenting if the behavior your husband exhibits toward your daughter is also the behavior you dislike when it comes your way. Marsha, a secretary in a real estate office, found the crude jokes about women told by her husband, Mike, insulting, and she had told him so repeatedly over their fifteen-year marriage. Mike, a small-town policeman, would stop for a while but would start up again if he'd had a few drinks or was watching a particularly provocative movie on television. He couldn't understand why Marsha took it so seriously. For Mike, it was just "guy talk"; he wasn't demeaning his wife.

When their shy daughter, Paula, became a curvaceous fourteen-year-old, Mike began to make little teasing comments about her and her girlfriends' bodies. Paula was mortified and withdrew from her father. Marsha was enraged and felt humiliated but used her empathy with her daughter to talk to Mike in a heartfelt way for Paula's benefit. Miraculously, hearing Paula's feelings from Marsha seemed to help Mike understand the issue differently than he had before. Marsha was also able to talk about boundaries and to say that he simply had to confine this kind of talk to visits with his male friends. Mike agreed to try. It helped that Marsha was able to place Mike's behavior where it belonged, in the male sphere, rather than condemn him for being a bad husband and father.

Paula was lucky that her father responded to her mother's plea on her behalf. When a father refuses to change sexualized or sexist behavior toward his daughter, it's crucial that you as her mother continue to stand up to your husband about his insulting conduct every time it happens. Clearly supported by you, she will avoid internalizing it as her problem and diminishing her self-worth. Let her know calmly that you detest this behavior in your husband. Difficult as it may seem, you can still be respectful of him in other ways without condoning his destructive behavior toward women.

Fathers need to be careful to not sexualize their responses to their daughters by telling off-color or sexist jokes or by treating her like a girlfriend or a "princess." You want her to define her boundaries with boys and men she is meeting outside your home, so the same boundaries should be clearly drawn at home.

Model Respect

Your daughter will be able to command respect from new men in her life if she has experienced this kind of respect from her father— especially if he listens carefully to her thoughts and feelings when she wants to share them with him. She will also be acutely aware of the regard, or lack of it, that he shows toward you, her mother, and toward other women in his life.

Girls are up against tremendous pressure to orient themselves toward men. A father who goes against the environment of sexism provides a powerful model for his daughter. Bombarded with media put-downs that say women need to lose weight, buy something, change the way they look, smell, or behave in order to be attractive to men, that daughter will hear her father's voice: "You are beautiful the way you are. You are intelligent, competent, and wonderful. I love you. Do what you want to do. Be who you want to be in every way you wish, and I'll support you in acquiring the skills you need in order to reach your goals." This kind of empowerment coming from her father can be stronger than the negative cultural input because it increases her core sense of self-worth.

A father's verbal message must be mirrored in his behavior toward her and other women. If your husband demonstrates respect for you, your daughter will take his cue in her relationships. Her relationships with boys may make you aware of ways in which you would like your relationship to her father to be more equal. Working through issues with a man in your life might be as basic as asking your husband to do some of the chores at home that he has never done. Simple as it sounds, it will have a big impact on your marriage and will model the possibility of change at any age for your daughter.

A father needs to affirm his daughter's autonomy and trust her decision making, even as he tries to protect her. If he screams at her when she opposes him, makes his support conditional on her agreeing with him, or ignores her, he will undermine his words of encouragement.

When the Family Is Complicated

Fourteen-year-old Tammy, the water polo enthusiast, has different issues to deal with in her relationship with her father, Joe. Joe, a high school science teacher, is twenty years older than her mother, Jean. Tammy has felt held back by her father's fear of letting her spend the night at a friend's home. "Overall, I'm OK with my parents' rules. But my dad has always been totally set on my not spending the night at friends' houses. My mom's cousin was raped by someone's uncle when she was thirteen at a sleepover. Then the kidnapping of a twelve-year-old girl in our state reinforced his fear. Finally, he and my mom gave in for sleepover parties, but I still can't just spend the night at a friend's unless my parents know her and her parents really well." This will continue to be a source of friction between Tammy and her father as she grows older and wants the freedom to make her own decisions about where she spends the night.

As the child of two devoted parents, however, Tammy has been raised to speak up for herself. She always feels heard even if she doesn't get her way. She has also had to deal with the unconventionality of her parents, who have been together twenty-three years and are not married. Tammy said, "The marriage issue is not important to me. I have a mutual respect with my friends about family stuff. My friend Delia's father overdosed when she was a year old. Her mother married her stepfather and had her sister; now they're divorced. Everyone has their own situation." This aplomb comes from being a child of loving, respectful parents who take care to explain to their daughter how they feel about their choices and to follow through with responsible behavior. Jean said, "I can only wish that Tammy will have as good a committed relationship as my partner and I have had for over twenty years."

To further complicate the family picture, Joe also has a daughter from a previous marriage. Tammy said, "I didn't meet my half-sister until I was six years old and she was sixteen. I had heard about her, but I couldn't see her, because my dad had a messy relationship with his ex-wife. He only saw his other daughter when I wasn't around." Jean said, "Joe's first child only lives three blocks away from us. He visited her, drove her home from school, and attended her class functions. His ex-wife was furious with him and us; she occasionally came screaming and pounding on our door and scared us. Joe took care of it when she made threats. It was a horrible time for all of us." Joe did the right thing by shielding his younger daughter from his previous wife's aggression, even as he continued to father both girls in everyday ways. Tammy was always assured of her safety and her love within the primary family framework.

If the Tables Are Turned

If you find that your husband and daughter are allied against you over an issue, be as open to exploring this dynamic with him as you would like him to be with you. Listen to their complaint. Ask yourself if there is truth in it. Although Helen sought couples counseling with Robert because she felt estranged from him, opening up issues with him also forced her to challenge her self-image as the tolerant parent. Snooping on Cassady revealed the unpleasant truth that she was the irrational, manipulative parent. Cassady could hardly bring herself to talk to her mother some days. Although they sometimes shared clothes and were ostensible friends, Cassady knew that her mother would get hysterical and suspicious whenever plans changed or any new independence had to be negotiated. Helen always saw Cassady as a reflection of her own image in the community. Cassady turned to her father to help her out. Fortunately, Robert took a more reasonable approach and was able to calm many of her mother's fears as they came up. But it was an ongoing source of stress for the family.

There are times when teenage girls want more from their fathers or find solace in their fathers and disown their mothers. This can be very painful and can trigger jealousy. Be aware of the part you play in the dynamic between your daughter and her father. Do you get between them because you're jealous of the attention he pays her? Do you bad-mouth him to her when you are angry with him and expect her to take your side? This is not good parenting.

If you find yourself in a triangle that is bringing up long-buried memories from the past when you were a teenage girl competing with another girl for the same boy, work through it. Perhaps you remember your own mother's jealousy of your relationship with your father. Separate your past from the present and use your experience to create a more constructive dynamic. Getting between your daughter and your husband will prevent her from relating to him and eventually turn her against you. Such unresolved patterns are destructive to your adolescent daughter, who wants both her parents' support for the task of growing up.

Try to get a handle on what is really going on. Helen's overinvolvement with Cassady caused Cassady to distance herself. Perhaps your husband is able to stay calmer in the midst of your daughter's storms than you are and she finds him easier to negotiate with. Perhaps he is able to relate to her academic life in a way that he hadn't before. Or she may be reaching out to him because she has been close to you as a girl and she wants to explore new territory. If your daughter must separate from you in a way that feels like tearing apart the close bond that you had before, comfort yourself with the thought that if you let her ally herself with her father, eventually she will return to you, too.

Mom and Dad in Sync

The girls who are healthiest are those who have worthwhile relationships with both their parents. Both Yvette's parents attend her Irish step-dancing competitions. Her father, Bernard, is a computer whiz and helps her with research for school papers. "One weekend when I had a dance competition that lasted both days, I wrote my paper longhand and he put it on the computer for me. It was so-o-o nice of him. I couldn't have done it. I was wiped out and had other homework due on Monday." Yvette was also grateful that her father had been active in her college search that fall. Knowing Yvette's love of dance and her goal of becoming a middle school history teacher, Bernard went on the Internet and collated the history and dance programs at schools that fit their budget, then figured out how the applications worked. "It helped so much!"

Jade's father, committed to a narrow vision and insensitive to his daughter's wishes, trespassed on her college application process. She described her tense college tour with her parents in spring of her junior year. "I ended up not speaking to my dad. He thinks the only two schools that are worthwhile are Berkeley and Brown. My mother went to Bryn Mawr and I kind of liked it there. My dad said, 'You don't need an all-women's college—you can hold your own with the men.' He kept pushing Brown; he wouldn't leave me alone." Jade decided she wanted a bucolic environment, not a big city. "I fell in love with Dartmouth, with the beautiful setting. I love the outdoors, nature, and beauty. He kept saying, 'But Brown's a great school.' I tried to go along with my mom, who was saying, "Just let him think you'll apply to Brown. But finally I couldn't take it anymore and I blew up at him. He thinks he's doing good; he just doesn't know who I am. I don't think he's capable of it." With her mother's support, Jade persevered and happily attends Dartmouth. But she missed the close, appreciative connection that Yvette had with her father about choosing a college.

Even girls like Yvette admit that they spend most of their parental time with their mothers. Yvette talks about having fun shopping with Mimi and accompanying her to exotic ethnic festivals and craft fairs. Yvette, an avid photographer, takes pictures at these colorful events. "My mom is always there for me," she said proudly. When she feels stressed, Yvette sometimes asks Mimi, an acupuncturist, for a treatment. But Yvette and her father share interests where Mimi plays no part. "Dad and I have always watched *Star Trek* together, and we go to see the new movies as they come out. Once we dressed as Star Trek characters for Halloween and had a blast." Eighteen-year-old Yvette, secure on the verge of college, draws on both her parents as resources for her developing identity.

You will find the combination of your internal pressures and conflicts with your daughter and your husband challenging, exhausting, exhilarating, and depressing by turns. But if you are willing to look at the friction honestly, you and your husband will learn a lot about your relationship and find new ways to handle differences. At the same time, you will be modeling problem solving for your daughter. When she begins to have intimate relationships, she will be both resilient and emotionally candid.

"Mom and Dad Can't Talk."

A high school girl caught in the middle between her parents' spoken or unspoken battles cannot reach out for the help she needs. Adventuresome and motivated, Jade sought experiences to further her strong inner drive to serve in the world. Sophomore year, she found herself in a predicament where she desperately needed her parents' support but couldn't connect with them. After a summer working intensively as an assistant in a medical clinic in French Guyana, she felt changed and disturbed in ways she could not name. Alienated from her friends, who seemed just the same after a summer securely at home with their families, and wanting to feel more comfortable back in school, she dived into the social scene and started drinking too much alcohol at parties. Feeling worse and more confused, she drank more. Jade knew she was in trouble and was scared as she found herself in dicey sexual encounters with guys she didn't know. But she said, "I felt at least I was defining myself instead of trying to live up to an impossible ideal." She wanted relief from her parents' expectation that she always surpass herself academically. "I did something self-destructive instead of going to the soup kitchen and helping people. I felt terrible. I thought, if only you knew that I'm not this perfect person. Pay attention to who I am!"

One night at dinner, alone with her parents, Jade tentatively tried to bring her feelings up, saying, "You know, I'm a teenager. I'm going to make some mistakes and learn from those mistakes." Howard jumped in immediately with the comment, "You're too smart to make mistakes." Jade said, "I shut up and didn't say any more." Sadly, her father's comment shut her off from both her parents. "I didn't think it was fair to make my mother keep secrets from him. I didn't want to put a strain on their relationship because I knew they were already having problems."

Later, after Jade had painfully extricated herself from her unsafe behavior, she said, "I couldn't go back and confide in them after I'd been lying to them about where I had been and what I'd been doing. I sort of dug myself into a hole." If you are not keenly discerning about your daughter and her new social challenges, she will retreat and tell you less and less because she will feel that you are clueless and wouldn't understand her conflicts.

Ultimately, each person is responsible for building his or her own parent–daughter relationship. If you can't talk to your husband in a constructive way, tell your daughter that you are there for her, no matter what, and that you will keep her confidences, even from her father. Teenagers protect their parents as often as they protect themselves. If Jade had felt able to share her distress with her mother and have her mother listen and accept her, she could have enlisted some support. It was up to her mother to decide how to handle the situation with her husband.

Frightened as she was by her own behavior, it would have been healing for Jade just to have a loving response. As it was, she felt categorized once again. She had to work it through alone, and her parents missed their chance, maybe not the only one but a significant one. Luckily, she is a strong, resilient young woman who was able to move on and continue her productive high school life. All girls do not have such resilience.

Fathers, as well as mothers, need to be able to sustain their daughters' emotional needs during this time instead of exploding or insisting their daughters make things easier for them by being nice, charming, or cooperative.

When Dad's the Soft Touch

If you are the parent who sets limits and her dad pays less attention and always says yes, she may seek his approval and pressure you to agree with him. Try to talk to him about the way this is undermining both your attempts to be consistent with her. This becomes especially difficult if the man who is always gratifying her is your ex-husband, who is less likely, in many cases, to respect your judgment. Leticia complains that her sixteen-year-old daughter, Brandy, has no supervision when she visits her father, Dion, every other weekend. Dion works six nights a week in a post office, sleeps in the daytime, and lets Brandy do whatever she wants when he is working.

Leticia throws up her hands in exasperation. "Then he treats her to expensive dinners, shopping sprees, and extravagant shows in the city when he takes a night off. Brandy perceives her dad as the fun parent, while she sees me as the drudge who not only works but inquires about her homework, sees that she get to school on time, and wants to know where she is going on weekend nights with whom." Leticia feels stressed trying to uphold her values in the face of being perceived as the taskmaster. She makes an effort to spend quality time with Brandy on the weekends she is home, but she cannot afford to lavish money on her. Dion stolidly asserts that he does the best he can. He loves his daughter and provides for her; he thinks that's enough.

Leticia knows, however, that Brandy shows her her real feelings. Whether she is angry with her mother, frustrated with school, or hurt by a friend's slight, she never hesitates to voice her mood. With her father, Brandy puts on her public face as her dad's happy, appreciative little girl. In the long run Leticia's willingness to accept Brandy's whole self will create a deeper bond and contribute more to Brandy's character than her father's permissive approach. The problem for Leticia is that Brandy may be getting into trouble running wild when her father is off working.

In this situation, for your daughter's sake, you need to talk to your ex-husband about your concerns. If you reach an impasse with him about his lack of limit setting, it is worth suggesting a few sessions of counseling with a therapist who specializes in adolescent psychology for the two of you to make an agreement on parenting your daughter. Single-parent fathers also may have problems with their ex-wives that warrant counseling.

Father-Daughter Time

Many fathers say, "The only time my daughter is nice to me is when she wants something." Realize that when your daughter needs you, she will probably try to reach out to you. See the opening and respond in a way that furthers your relationship. If your fourteen-year-old asks you to drive her to her friend's house while you're watching the baseball game, you can negotiate to go at the end of the inning or listen to an exciting moment in the car. Be good-natured and willing to help. These moments are short-lived and precious. There will always be baseball games. Say, "I'll take you to the mall and tomorrow I'd like you to go to the hardware store with me to buy furnace filters and help me replace them." Both do favors and teach her skills as you spend time with her.

Support your husband in connecting with your daughter and showing his interest. At dinner, give her room to talk about the day's events. You may have done this all through grammar school, but in high school, it will be different. A teenage girl may not want to talk to her family over dinner; she will eat quickly and ask to be excused. Other times, she will linger and enjoy this time of coming together in the day. Don't direct all the energy of the group at her and make your questions an inquisition. Share your feelings and thoughts about your own day.

When you do ask questions, make them specific about classes or activities or ideas. What is she reading in history, and how does she like it? Include her in the conversation in a matter-of-fact way, even if you do not get enthusiastic answers. But be sensitive to when she really doesn't want to talk, and back off. If she's sitting there, she's listening and absorbing what's being said. The ritual of being together is more important than her overt participation.

Encourage your husband to make time with your daughter on a regular basis, whether or not she asks for it. Make a date to go out to breakfast, shoot baskets, or ride bikes. Create a father-daughter night or day where the two of them do something special together. Rebecca told me, "Before I started driving, my mother drove me back and forth to school every day and we always had dinner together with my younger brothers. But my dad works late a lot at his engineering firm. We missed each other. So, he and I decided to go to a play or museum show once a month. It's great." Rebecca, avid about the arts, has a close, compatible relationship with Matthew and is happy going out with him. It gives them a chance to exchange ideas and enjoy each other.

Your husband can share his work and his hobbies with your daughter whether he is a lawyer, an accountant, a carpenter, a doctor, a gardener, or a psychologist. He can tell her what he likes and dislikes about his job. Not only is this important knowledge for her to have as she is considering different fields, it also acknowledges her increasing maturity. A father may feel uncomfortable entering into the teenage world but more secure taking his daughter along to his. Helping out with his work (or yours) either during school holidays or in the summer is a good way to introduce her to the realities of making a living. Bianca worked as a hostess in her father's restaurant the summer of her fifteenth year. She liked learning about the business and being rewarded for being responsible; she was able to save enough to buy a mountain bike that she coveted. Seeing the effort it took to make money made her appreciate her allowance more during the year. Her father noticed that she was proud of her bicycle and took care to maintain it.

"Maybe Later, Dad."

If her father asks your daughter to go the movies and she shrugs him off because she's waiting for calls from her friends, help him not take it personally. You both have to realize that at this stage her friends come first. She is becoming independent, but she also wants to be able to come back to you and her father. So don't shut her out just because she blows you off sometimes. Remind yourself and him that you want her to have her own life. If you honor where she is, she will come back to you and value her relationships with you both later.

By trial and error, Patrick found what kind of time his daughter Corey will spend with him. "I ask her to do something with me for an afternoon and it's pretty much limited to shopping. I go along and give her my opinion of what looks good on her. For her seventeenth birthday, I suggested we do something as a family. She just wanted money. I explained that I meant for us all to be together, and go ice skating or to a movie and dinner. She said OK, but it's slow getting her to participate with us and with me again. She ran the other way from my tyranny for so long."

Gradually, Patrick is building trust with Corey by first being willing to do it her way, to share in her world. It's working, and she is reconnecting with her family. Patrick has suffered enormously but now feels rewarded that his actions have turned things around. Through exercising good listening skills, patience, tolerance, and flexibility, he has demonstrated to Corey his willingness to relinquish control and see her clearly.

Athletics often provide an arena in which fathers and daughters can easily relate to each other. If he is interested in sports and knows a lot about them, he can be her fan by attending her games and by explaining both written rules and the more covert world of guy intimidation, like "trash talk" and "body blocks." From his own experience, he may also be able to coach her in soccer or basketball.

Corey has taken up working out like her father. Patrick had been a boxer and wrestler in his youth. Father and daughter banter good-naturedly when they go to the gym together. Corey is playfully competitive during their sessions, criticizing her father's style and strength. This has given them a place to blow off steam and connect.

Just as a coach, a father needs to not push his daughter beyond her own limits or try to bully her into playing the game his way. He cannot suggest that she lose weight in order to play better. He needs to guide and inspire her to good sportsmanship and to do her best. Jim, who bravely bared his soul to his older daughter Kate, played ball as an adolescent and coached a little in his twenties. Now, he plays tennis with his athletic younger daughter, Alta. He also attends all her basketball games and teaches her how to handle her perfectionistic coach's demands. Alta values her father's balance between fairness and competence. "He puts a lot of value on the character of a player or coach. He emphasizes whether you followed through on what you were supposed to do. This is a relief to me when my coach jumps on me for something I couldn't have known. I don't feel so bad." Alta feels her father gives her constructive criticism and support for playing wholeheartedly.

The World Calls

Look for ways to connect with your daughter. Involve yourself in her learning process. To the extent that she lets you, talk to her about what she is reading and writing. Both you and her father can help promote her critical thinking and self-examination by listening and responding to her ideas in an accepting way. High school may be a time when your daughter's relationship with her father deepens. Find the places where you have strengths to help her with her school work. Pool your resources. If your favorite subject in college was chemistry and her dad's was American history, you can each find pleasure in drilling her for exams or discussing concepts with her. The more input she has from both of you, the more solid her education will be.

Ask her about her social views of her country, the environment, the problems of the world. Discuss politics. If she's conservative and you're liberal, don't try to force your point of view on her. Many girls say, "With my mother I feel open to say whatever is on my mind; not so much with my father." Change this cultural pattern; be the father she can talk to. Let her have her ideas and learn to think them through. Enjoy engaging her about her beliefs. She will be discovering an intellectual identity, and it may change every few years. A father can respond constructively to his daughter's dilemmas. One girl said, "I turn to my dad when I want a more critical view. From my mom, it's always, 'You're the best.' My dad is more honest." She appreciates them both.

The world increasingly calls to your daughter as she moves through her adolescent years. As her father, be part of that call. Whether you are involved in social service, music, theater, sports, or travel, share the wider world with your daughter on an ongoing basis. Ally yourself with Zeus. The old truth "It's a man's world" is gradually but persistently crumbling. As her father, help her be part of making it a "woman's world" too. Your support will build her confidence and sustain her initiative to meet the world in college and beyond.

8 ⌒

*D*ays of Reckoning

CROSSROADS AND CRISES

Persephone is awakened from her enchantment with her own flowering by Hades' abduction. Forced to meet her fate, she is then initiated into the dark side of life. A girl's passage through high school likewise becomes an initiation. Seeking adventure, she takes risks as she explores the teenage world, away from her mother's watchful care. When Persephone returns, she is transformed: queen of the underworld, wife to her husband, a woman in her own right. Yet, still her mother's daughter, she experiences great joy in their reunion.

As your daughter pushes you away in order to express herself, she will also miss you. You will lose her and be reunited with her many times during these years. While she performs the tasks necessary to her journey, you can mark the crossroads that are way stations to adulthood. Your constancy and attention to her at these junctures will be the foundation of your relationship as adults.

Some crossroads can be anticipated, planned for, and celebrated: her first bra, first period, or getting her driver's license. The transitions from eighth grade to high school, from one grade to another, and from high school to college are all conspicuously stressful and exciting times. Others are the unplanned crises that arise from teenage experimentation, like her first trouble with the law, the first time she's caught drinking or smoking or sneaking out the window. Crises are necessary watershed experiences; she will learn from them. If you see these dilemmas this way, your relationship will be enriched. Both expected crossroads and unforeseen crises are important to her development. You should be prepared for both, then still expect to be surprised.

Celebrations mark the end of one stage of your daughter's life and begin to prepare her (and you) for another. They confirm the changes she feels and help relieve her anxiety. By bringing meaning and spirit alive, rituals effect transformation; they move you to recognize her new status. Rituals affirm your family's best intention of fostering healthy development in all its members, and give your community a chance to acknowledge and support your daughter's changing place at the table.

Crises are eruptions that alert you to invisible changes going on in your daughter. They are turning points that, if handled well, can solidify the values or ideas that will define her outlook on life. You will go back and forth between marking her progress and managing her acting-out or self-destructive behavior. If you respond thoughtfully to both crossroads and crises, you will promote her capacity to meet the unpredictability of life with equanimity.

Use your own adolescent memories of these critical moments to anticipate your daughter's feelings and plan accordingly. How did your mother handle those thresholds for you? If you recall shameful, embarrassed feelings about buying your first bra or getting your period, or if no one paid attention when you were invited to your first prom, got your driver's license, or graduated from high school, mourn your loss. Move on to make it different for your daughter. You will find yourself nurtured by the experience.

First Period

Foster a spiritual life in your daughter to sustain her through adolescence and into adulthood. If your religious tradition includes the Jewish bat mitzvah or Catholic confirmation at age thirteen, the ceremony will provide an ending to middle school and mark the threshold of high school. Many cultures have elaborate puberty ceremonies that specifically honor a girl's body at this pivotal time. Some churches are learning from other cultures and creating rites of passage for girls in early adolescence.

As her mother, you are the most important person to help her celebrate her first menstruation. This crucial passage is an opportunity for you to help her feel good about her body. Your daughter will be ambivalent about getting her period. Menstruating is a responsibility that demands self-care and a new self-concept. Affirming her healthy body with a ritual will influence her initiations into sexuality, childbearing, and menopause.

Depending on her feelings, you can do something quietly together or make a family celebration. In some families creating ceremonies comes naturally. Others prefer to let their daughter know in more low-key ways that she is being honored. If you think about it in advance and respect your daughter, you will be prepared when the time arrives.

Sometimes a spontaneous expression of joy can feel just right. Twelve-year-old Marilyn, an active, impetuous girl who spent hours outdoors observing insects and small animals, did not want to get her period. Over time, her mother, Terry, had shared the experience of her own periods and read a preteen book on girls' changing bodies with her daughter. But Marilyn preferred to avoid the subject. Terry was dedicated to celebrating Marilyn in some way but did not want to do anything that would embarrass her daughter.

Luckily, when the day arrived, Marilyn and her parents were on vacation with their extended family at the beach. As the word quietly spread, aunts, uncles, and cousins took turns coming to give Marilyn discreet hugs and good wishes. Their matter-of-fact understanding kept her from feeling awkward. Huddled around a bonfire as the sun went down, the warmth of her family's love and caring made this a memorable, comforting, and glad occasion for her.

Ann knew that her daughter, Nicole, shy and dreamy, would be mortified at being the center of attention when her first period came. When she saw signs of Nicole's body changing, Ann purchased a small moonstone necklace to keep for her daughter. The day Nicole got her period, Ann spent some intimate time with her daughter drinking hot herb tea and chatting about inconsequential things. After Nicole went to sleep that night, her mother put the decoratively wrapped necklace with a card she had written on her daughter's bedside table. Nicole will treasure that gesture for the rest of her life.

In another family who comfortably create ritual, Beverley talked to her daughter, Kendra, about her wishes for a coming-of-age ceremony. Kendra, a boisterous, artistic girl, wanted both her girlfriends and older women friends of her mother's to be present. Kendra loved to draw, write, and enact skits. Because her favorite time of day was morning, she and her mother decided on a morning storytelling circle; those invited were asked to bring a story to share (or act out) with Kendra that would offer her a bit of feminine wisdom. Beverley and Kendra prepared a bountiful lunch together with which to conclude the ceremony. Each of the guests brought small gifts to commemorate the milestone. If you have the time and resources, you could plan a long weekend (for sometime after your daughter's first period) to celebrate together at a hot spring, a spa, a campground, or a retreat center. Whatever you do, honor her body and make her feel special at this time.

Summertime Blues

The summer before high school starts is a good interval to plan a special experience for your daughter to boost her self-confidence before her most challenging year of adolescence begins. Ask her what she would like to do. Brainstorm and fantasize with her about what she might explore. One of your goals for this transitional summer is to challenge your daughter in a safe situation in order to prepare her for the stressful onslaught of freshman year. Another goal might be to spend time exclusively with her to make sure this year begins with complete understanding. You and she could get involved in your favorite charity's fund-raising run, participate in a beach clean-up day, or serve food to the homeless. If possible, arrange a month for the two of you to help build a house with Habitat for Humanity.

Try to find your daughter a new environment that both suits her, to insure her success, and takes her to an edge. Help her and a girl-friend start a small business putting on theme birthday parties for primary school kids. Dressing up as a clown or a fortune-teller is fun, and budgeting costs and her charges will help her learn to manage money. Joining a teen book club at the local library would give her an opportunity to meet new friends with common interests. If she loves to read, she could also volunteer to develop a storytelling hour for younger children. Find an avenue for her to paint a community mural or become a member of a teen group that speaks to junior high kids about the hazards of smoking cigarettes. Sign her up for a class in computer technology to broaden her skills.

If travel is part of your budget, let her help plan the trip and research some of the itinerary. Zoe finished middle school to a burst of applause for her role as Irma in a production of the musical *Anything*

Goes. She yearned to go to New York to see a Broadway show and visit the museums. As a graduation gift, she and Cassia planned a four-day trip, while her father and older brother remained at home. This celebration fulfilled Zoe's dream. It marked her successful completion of middle school and newly inspired her for a summer theater workshop. If you live in the suburbs, taking your daughter to explore the culture of a big city will always be a hit.

This may also be the summer when she can't wait to redesign her bedroom, putting away the memorabilia of primary school and plastering her walls with posters of new adolescent heroes and heroines. Other at-home activities could include making an article of clothing or a piece of furniture. Trying a new sport or performing art or doing special training in one in which she is already skilled will also help her feel optimistic about embarking on new directions or setting her goals higher for herself.

First Dance

The new freedom, more demanding classes, and intense social pressures of freshman year catapult many families into chaos. Girls feel intense anxiety and fear of not fitting in, not looking or acting "right." As one eighteen-year-old boy told me, "Girls have it rough in high school. For one thing, guys only have to worry about what girls think about them. Girls have to worry about both guys and other girls."

When your daughter hits her new social milieu, she loses her bearings for a while. The contradiction between her younger self (which you represent) and her insecure freshman identity often culminates in a disproportionate load of strong emotions coming out about her first dance of the year. For weeks in advance, she might be obsessed with what she is going to wear, who she is going with, and what she is going to do before and after the dance. In the midst of this frenzy, it is wise to talk to her about her tentative ideas as she goes along. Her plans will change many times, but if you can be even minimally part of the process, you have a better chance of heading off a dramatic conflict as she walks out the door. Not only will such a confrontation ruin the evening; you will also have to spend a lot of energy trying to get your relationship back on track.

On these social occasions, you need to consider her wishes and your expectations. Be clear about your limits. If possible, include her father in the discussions. Ask questions like, "Who are you going with? Who is driving? Where are you going to dinner? How are you getting home?" The controversial issue is always whether she is allowed to go to the after-dance parties, where many kids will be drinking and smoking cigarettes or marijuana. Decide how you feel about her going to these bashes, about the parameters for the night that the two (or three) of you can agree on.

If she is willing, help her get dressed. Even if it's not a dressy occasion, girls usually focus on clothes and makeup before going to a dance. Make her girlfriends feel welcome. Don't try to get in the middle of it all and be one of them. Keep to your maternal role: offer help and respond to requests. Be on the sidelines to provide towels, zip up, or advise on eye shadow or hairstyle, when asked. Finally, take pictures and wish them joy for the evening. Then go out to dinner with your husband, best friend, or a group of other parents and wait to see whether her getting home will be as successful an experience as your send-off was!

Trouble with the Law

One of the first crises that comes up for teenagers is a brush with the law. Being arrested for shoplifting, possession of drugs or alcohol, or reckless driving can happen to any teenage girl. If it does, you not only have to deal with the legal consequences, but you also have to help your daughter assess her motives. Ask yourself and her: Is this a one-time occurrence or part of a pattern of behavior?

One Saturday afternoon, Terry, who had some work to do for her job as a computer programmer, dropped Marilyn, now fourteen years old, off at the shopping center with a girlfriend, and agreed to meet them at the opposite end of the mall four hours later. When she drove up to their meeting place, a woman approached her car and asked if she was Marilyn's mother. Terry said, "Yes," and the woman identified herself as a security guard from Macy's. Marilyn was in custody for shoplifting, and the guard asked Terry to come to the office where her daughter was being held.

Terry was shocked. Her mind raced as she followed the guard back to Macy's: Does my daughter really feel so deprived that she has started shoplifting? How can it be? We have a tight budget, but Marilyn has a modest clothing allowance and has never complained that she feels less privileged than her wealthier friends. Worse yet, could I and my husband have missed that our daughter is seriously delinquent? It doesn't fit with who I know my daughter to be and how I feel about her on a gut level, but then what is going on?

When she arrived at the security office, Terry walked in to find a tearful, contrite Marilyn, who blurted out, "I'm really sorry about this, Mom. I don't know what got into me. I already called Dad and told him that I'm ashamed of myself and I'm sorry to have let you both down." Marilyn's regrets went a little way toward alleviating Terry's concern, especially when she heard that Marilyn had purchased a few items of clothing. But on the way out of the store, she had suddenly picked up a sample perfume bottle from the cosmetics counter and tossed it in her bag. When Marilyn was apprehended, her friend left and called her own parents to get a ride home.

The in-house guards gave Marilyn a warning: If she stole anything from Macy's within the next year, the police would be called and she would be charged. In long discussions with both her parents at home, Marilyn said she had picked up the sample on a dare from her friend. This relieved her parents' worry, because they knew her to be an impulsive child. It made sense to them that it had been a random, one-time act. They did, however, forbid her to go to the mall for several weeks, to help the lesson sink in.

It is wise to use incidents like shoplifting or malicious pranks to get to know your daughter in a deeper way. The way you handle the crisis determines how it will affect her character. Marilyn's parents knew their daughter well enough to feel certain that it was an unpremeditated act. It also reassured them that, although goaded by her friend, Marilyn took full responsibility for her behavior. In one way, her parents were glad that it happened: she could learn from her bad judgment and rash action without more dire consequences.

Marilyn's parents used their relationship with her to understand the situation and impose a fitting consequence. The spontaneous celebration of her first period on the beach was one way in which that relationship had been forged. This crisis provided another chance to strengthen their bond. If they had been punitive, instead of connecting with their daughter, they would have risked reinforcing her acting out.

Be fair and considered in these situations, and the crisis can become an important crossroad. If you find, however, that there is a persistent pattern of theft or substance abuse or of any antisocial behavior, then you need to get help for your daughter and yourselves. Seek family therapy to help you find alternative environments in which your daughter can take healthy risks, instead of destructive ones.

In this case, Marilyn's shoplifting marked a new passage for her and her parents. It was sobering to have to face not only her parents' shock and disappointment but also the possibility of police action. The incident curbed Marilyn's freshman bravura and made her reflect on her behavior. She felt ashamed of betraying her personal values and frightened for her reputation at school. Not going to the mall for three weeks was a minor inconvenience compared to the threat of acquiring a police record that might affect her adult ambitions. And being abandoned by the other girl had shaken her trust in their friendship. The serious conversations at home also influenced Marilyn's eleven-year-old brother, who watched his older sister carefully.

Summer Camp

Summer camp can be a lifesaver for girls who are having trouble socially at school. It gives them a chance to start over in a new setting and to make friends in a more carefree place. Without academic pressure and the feeling of being trapped in a social fishbowl, a girl's confidence can be bolstered by a summer camp experience. Renee, a dedicated student, had been lonely and miserable during a freshman year in which she couldn't connect with girls in her class. She followed the routine of going to classes and doing her homework, feeling left out and gawky. Tall and skinny, she had yet to start her period, and shied away from any interest in clothes, boys, music, or dances. She still preferred going to movies on weekends with her parents or younger brother. Yet she knew she was missing out with her peers. Her parents' support gave her relief at home but did nothing to solve the problem. Concerned about Renee slipping into depression, her parents looked for a summer camp that thrived on camp spirit and cooperation in a natural setting.

At first Renee resisted the idea of going away from home. But assured that, if she hated it, her parents would come to pick her up after a week, she agreed to give it a try. Fearing that no one would talk to her, Renee said, "I was nervous before I went. But the good thing was, it was all fresh. No one had an idea of who I was before. No one saw me as the brain. I just got to be me and see how people responded. I made several girlfriends easily just hanging out in the cabin and going to meals. I found that it helped just to ask a lot of questions, to show my interest in someone. I tried to be natural, in-

stead of trying to be like them. The counselors made a big difference, too. They made sure that no one was left out. When I got back
to school for sophomore year, I thought, I can't be that bad! It gave
me the confidence to look elsewhere at school for friends than the
original group who had rejected me as a freshman."

If your daughter is having trouble socially, seek alternative environments where she has the chance to reinvent herself. As she gets
older, she can also begin to train as a counselor for a summer camp.
Having a position of responsibility often makes it easier to make
friends. Renee was fortunate to have parents who recognized from
their own childhood experience that summer camp can provide
hope for the desperate times in a girl's social life.

Sophomore Slump

Sophomores are no longer the freshman darlings, the new students,
whom everyone is interested in and eager to help out. And they are
not yet upperclassmen who have clout, drive cars, and are revving up
for the real world. Sophomore year, however, is the year of the driver's
license. By the end of sophomore year, most girls will be sixteen. It is
a crucial year of many transitions. Your daughter's desire for more
freedom will explode. If there is no car available in your household,
she will have friends with the use of one. If you live in a city where
subways are the norm and entertainment pulses all night, she will
fight to be able to choose her own curfew, or none at all. Sixty percent of American girls are sexually active by age sixteen, so the im-
petus toward more adult freedom will be overwhelming.

Early in her sophomore year you will still be driving your daughter everywhere. Even if you are sick of being a chauffeur, look at this
stage as the last months of her life that you will spend this much time
with her. By her sophomore year, Nicole's shy nature had been bolstered by excelling at swimming on a community team. Ann, who

tended to shyness herself, told me, "I relished the months in sopho-more year that Nicole would still call me at 1:00 A.M. to come pick her up at a girlfriend's house because she wanted to sleep in her own bed. The streets were quiet at that hour; Nicole was so grateful and would tell me more about her evening than if we had talked the next morning. We felt close alone late at night. I knew these days were numbered—her friends were beginning to drive, and the next sum-mer she herself would have her license. I knew from my older daughter that once Nicole drove, I would see much less of her. She still kept a lot from me; she had her own life. But I saw that I could trust her judgment, that when she was tired she would come home, and that she wasn't off the deep end with drugs or alcohol. She was having a good time, and she set sensible limits." With a cherishing at-titude and a willingness to be inconvenienced, Ann enacted a ritual good-bye to Nicole, who was taking another step toward indepen-dence.

The Big Threshold

Learning to drive "changes everything" for girls in the suburbs. Talented, bouncy Rae said, "I wasn't spending the kind of time I had spent with my mother when she had to drive me, but the best thing about my mom is that she stayed involved in my theater." In spite of a messy divorce and going back to work in sales full-time, Joelle continued to support and encourage Rae's acting. Rae continued to relate to her mother as she found her new independence. This is the challenge for you as well.

After your daughter gets her license, her sudden soaring feelings of autonomy and entitlement may provoke you. Kendra, now seven-teen and given the privilege of driving herself to school every day, increasingly resisted every limit her parents tried to set. She no longer came directly home from school and did not call or ask permission for her new freedom. On weekends, she ignored her curfew, avoided doing her family chores, and would never commit to a family dinner. Her vociferous attitude was, "I'm grown up. I need to be with my friends, and I don't have to be responsible to you. You can't make me do it." Beverley and Kendra's father, David, had to find a way to connect with their daughter and not become angry themselves. In her grammar school years, they had set good limits and had fair expectations for Kendra, but they were caught unprepared when Kendra simply started disappearing. Beverley was hurt because Kendra shared her car and was not being considerate of her mother's needs. United in their concern, one Friday night as Kendra rushed out to a jazz concert, her parents told her that the following afternoon, the three of them were going to have a talk. This family meeting had to happen before Kendra did her homework, made phone calls, or left the house.

Kendra grudgingly agreed to meet. "I didn't want to sit down and talk about anything. I thought it was stupid, that they were treating me like a baby. I wanted to make my own decisions about my life. But I knew I had to." Beverley and David told Kendra that in order to have the privilege of driving their car, they all had to negotiate some new guidelines for its use and for her family time. They agreed to work out a later curfew and check-in time on weekends if she would talk to them about her wishes and what she thought was fair. They emphasized their concern for her safety and their need for her to do her share in the family.

Kendra said, "The thing I like about my mom and dad is that they listen to my side. I told them that as a junior I had to be out later because my social life doesn't start until eleven at night. I wanted to use my own judgment about what to do and where to go with my friends. And they listened and compromised—I got a curfew of 2:00 A.M. I didn't like hearing what they said about my chores and all, but I knew they were right. I'm better about it now.

It's just that I get so caught up in what's going on with my friends, my schoolwork, and jazz band that I hardly have time to think about anything else. I kind of appreciate my parents caring enough to make me stop and think about what I was doing. I know they love me."

If you were not good at setting limits when your daughter was younger, you will have to work harder at it now when she is driving and moving out of your charge altogether. Even though Kendra was basically amenable, Beverley and David made it clear that the consequences of her not abiding by the new rules would include not driving the car, no money for gas, and restrictions on going out. What is important here is that you stay calm and reasonable and remain flexible but also be firm where consequences for her actions are required.

Resist letting yourself be drawn into your daughter's hysteria. You have every right to put fair sanctions on her behavior and to ask for cooperation. She needs the freedom to be with her friends and to move into her own life as she becomes more independent. But she still has a relationship to her family, and privileges accompany responsibility—they do not supersede them. Kendra's resistance to having a sensible conversation with her parents about her behavior fell away as she let them in on her thoughts and feelings.

Beverley and David gave Kendra time to prepare herself for the family meeting by telling her about it a day in advance, which gave Kendra an opportunity to reflect on her actions. One of her mother's suggestions was that Kendra take an hour to spend time alone on Saturday mornings, to ground herself after her busy, extroverted week.

Kendra was pleased to discover that there was a way to have both sides: her friends and her own life and her family. She hated having her mom or dad angry with her; she wanted them to understand the demands on her life. But she couldn't figure out how to make this happen, because she was carried away by the intoxication of her new independence. Her parents had to show the way. The balancing of her individuality and her responsibility to her family or community is an important value to help your daughter learn.

As with all initiations, failure causes disappointment and frustration. If your daughter does not pass the driver's test, she is likely to be depressed. Some girls get depressed or angry and withdraw; some express their disappointment by acting out. You need to support your daughter in not giving up or acting out but instead persisting in mastering the skills she needs. The driver's test is the first of many such challenges.

Out the Window

Another common crisis arises when your daughter simply disappears from her bed one night. Kate said, "I was with four friends one night in my sophomore year at one of their houses. We just locked the door, climbed out the window, and walked downtown because none of us could drive yet. We got picked up by two surfer guys who took us to a senior party. We were all drinking, and a couple of my friends were "getting together" with guys—it was gross. We were drunk— wasted—and the guys who had picked us up wouldn't take us home. We had to walk at 3:00 A.M., and it was pitch-black and scary. It was the stupidest thing I ever did and I've never done it again." Kate did not get caught, but she learned a hard lesson.

If you suspect that your daughter is taking this kind of risk or catch her in the act one night, you need to intervene. Sit down with her and have a serious conversation about what is going on. Your biggest concern should be why she is being so careless with herself. Girls out on the street in the middle of the night are prey for kidnapping, rape, or murder. Is she, like Kate, trying to be cool by going to parties? Or is she angry at what she perceives to be your overly strict rules?

If your daughter regrets having exposed herself to danger, as Kate did, you have a good chance of influencing her to be more careful in the future. But you cannot take her behavior lightly. If you ascertain that your forbidding her to go to the school dance or another normal event with her friends prompted this behavior, then realize your mistake and admit that you were wrong. Tell her that you will be more open and negotiate a curfew for the next time.

On the other hand, if you feel your limits are fair and she has gotten in over her head with a group that takes dangerous risks, giving her a time-out from her peers by grounding her while you all evaluate the situation would be advisable. She needs to be lovingly held while you work through what is bothering her. You will need to do a lot of talking, soul searching, and negotiating for her to earn your trust again.

Summer Service

During the months between sophomore and junior year, your daughter may be ready for a bigger independent adventure than she has had in the past. As with all thresholds of change, it's not that you should expect this of her, but rather that you need to be aware of how her development is unfolding and what she yearns for. Some girls need more time with the family before they are ready to branch out on their own; others can't wait to explore the world. Be attuned to your daughter's character, and support her in doing what feels right to you both.

The summer after her sophomore year, Riane went to Nepal for six weeks on a program with Global Roots. "This was a life-changing experience. We built a bridge and it was great to find out that my fantasy of helping people had some basis in reality. Once, we were trekking out six days away from the nearest road. A boy followed us for two days, begging us to give him medicine that would prevent his younger brother from dying of amoebic dysentery. Our group leader couldn't give him the antiparasitic because she had an obligation to us; we still had weeks to go on the trip, so she had to keep the medicine on hand. It was sad. I cried and cried—I felt so bad for him. I decided then that I wanted to be an epidemiologist."

When Riane returned, she felt overwhelmed by culture shock. She needed to acknowledge what she had been through to help with the transition back to high school. After a few days at home washing clothes and getting her pictures developed, her mother, Judith, took Riane on a weekend trip to the mountains where the two of them hiked, looked at her photographs, and talked about her trip. Judith created a ritual experience that helped Riane integrate her feelings. She chose to take Riane away because Riane's best friend was still gone and Riane couldn't face talking to other friends immediately.

You can help your daughter regroup after a challenging summer and enable her to retain her new, wider horizon even as she eases back into her normal routine. An in-between period at home after such an experience can include showing slides, telling stories, making home-cooked meals, and giving your daughter some guidance about helping those who are suffering in her own community. Sometimes, the impact of such shattering experiences induces a feeling of helplessness that goes underground, only to emerge in destructive ways. With the help of her mother, Riane was able to direct her strong feelings of wanting to help people into doing volunteer work at a homeless shelter.

Riane's intense exposure to people who live on the edge between life and death also gave her a heightened sense of life. It was a shock to return to the world of the privileged middle class. Riane said, "Three days after stacking rocks we volunteers were dragging and complaining; we wanted to do something more exciting. Then the whole village came out to help and started singing songs. We joined them, learned their songs, and taught them American songs. It completely changed our mood."

Expect your daughter to find her normal high school life superficial, flat, and depressing after such an experience. Although she endured hardship in her Amigos program, Kaylie made friends and learned to value differences in people. After sacrificing two comfortable summer months at home to work with Ecuadorean families, she returned to begin her senior year. She said, "When I came home, I was changed. I noticed things in detail and was more observant. I was open with my best friend; I liked myself. But in a larger group of kids, I didn't feel like talking. Nothing had changed for them. You don't say what you're really thinking here. Now after a month I'm more the way I was before. I kind of regret not feeling the way I did when I came back." Kaylie loved being with her family, but she had partially outgrown her friends. Working in Ecuador gave her a different look at social inequality.

Kaylie spent a lot of time at home when she returned from Ecuador. Talking to her parents helped her sort out her feelings and learn how she had been changed by what she had lived. For many months, she was not interested in socializing on weekends with her friends. Viviane didn't see Kaylie's behavior as worrisome. She stayed available and let her daughter find her own way in her retreat. Sometimes girls need to withdraw and cocoon while changes solidify.

Junior Year: Temperature Rising

In junior year, things begin to heat up again for students. As noted earlier, sophomore and junior year grades count for college admission. And by now, most girls are not only driving but looking beyond their class and their school to the larger world. They have gained new emotional and intellectual strength and practical skills. But more is also being asked of them academically and emotionally, and there are new, potentially dangerous thresholds to cross.

For parents of newly licensed teenagers, junior year is harrowing. Even if you know your daughter is a good driver, you cannot predict what she will do with the distraction of four other teenagers shouting over a blaring car radio. And you have absolutely no way of assessing the driving skills of her friends.

You will be fortunate if your daughter's crises with driving are restricted to accidents such as gently rear-ending another car at a stoplight, scraping a post when she is parallel parking, or getting a speeding ticket in your neighborhood during her first year of being licensed. These minor collisions raise her awareness of cars' potential to do damage and teach her to improve her driving skills. Help her make a police report, deal with the insurance company, and get the car fixed.

If she is cited for any driving infraction, she will have to go to teenage traffic court to answer to the judge. When you accompany her to the hearing, you will be gratified to have the authority of the law meting out a fine or restricting or suspending her license. These are important lessons that you can reinforce by having her earn the money to pay for the damage to your car and her court fines. Coming up against these hard social realities will influence the care and quality of her driving. You would be wise also to have her drive with you for a few weeks, as she did when she had her learner's permit, in order to hone her skills and reestablish her confidence.

Junior-Senior Prom

Speeding and drunk driving among teenagers cause fatal accidents every day, but parents' anxiety is heightened on occasions like the night of the junior-senior prom. The prevalence of drinking among adolescents has resulted in the practice of limousine rentals to escort teenagers to and from the dance and pre- and post-prom parties. All the students' families share the cost. While school rules strictly prohibit appearing at school functions "under the influence," what happens at the pre- and post-parties is a different story.

If your daughter or her date drives to the pre-party, ask in advance who the designated driver is. To ensure a safe evening for your children, consider collaborating with friends to host a pre-prom party with a buffet dinner or hors d'oeuvres, either catered or potluck, for your daughters and their friends. Invite all the parents to join you and bring their cameras to take pictures. Make it an alcohol-free party or have a separate station for wine or beer to assure that no underage drinking goes on. Limousines can pick the teenagers up at your home. Celebrate your daughter and her friends dressed in their glittering gowns and sharp tuxedoes as a marvelous community event.

Hosting the all-night post-prom party will be a more heroic endeavor. Either you or your husband will be committed to staying up most of the night to shut off the alcohol flow, make sure no one leaves the house, and be responsible for sending the kids home the next morning. But your energy and generosity will be appreciated by all the families in your group. If kids have nowhere to go, they end up in a public place for post-prom merrymaking.

Proms are the highlight of class celebration in junior and senior year. Your daughter's first prom is laden with suspense and anticipation. Preparing her for it can be a rewarding mother–daughter ritual. Who will ask her, or who will she ask as her date? (Girls also go together in groups of three or four.) Once that is in place, you can indulge in adorning her. Share the search for the perfect dress, shoes, and wrap—shopping will take time and budgeting. Will she have her hair and makeup done? Or just a manicure and pedicure? Does her date know what color her dress is so he can order the right corsage? What about his boutonniere for his rented tux? Delight in helping your daughter transform herself into a radiant young woman for the evening.

The Quinceañera, a coming-of-age ceremony in many Latin American communities, and "Sweet Sixteen" parties, which have recently enjoyed a resurgence, celebrate girls at the threshold of womanhood. In the Quinceañera, in honor of her fifteenth birthday, a girl is presented as a "woman" to her community. She is dressed and adorned in the company of her mother and female relatives and friends. Showered with attention and gifts, she is blessed in a religious ceremony in the Catholic Church and goes on to dance and rejoice with her guests at a large party. Sweet Sixteen parties usually do not have a religious or spiritual dimension but range from formal, extravagant bashes to theme parties. Teens are sometimes invited to come dressed from an earlier decade, like the sixties. If you decide to have a special celebration for your daughter on her sixteenth birthday, she will make her wishes known. The important thing is that she feel honored.

Group Initiations

Keep in mind that you have many outside resources to supplement your own efforts to teach, protect, and provide guidance to your daughters through their adolescent years. If you feel that your daughter needs to be more self-sufficient and less reliant on what her peers (or you) think of her, consider a wilderness program as a rite of passage. Be sure to investigate the program thoroughly, because some of them can be punitive or abusive. Backpacking trips with other teenage girls can be a powerful booster of self-esteem. Toni, a guide for such a program, says, "Being in the outdoors is a key factor to a girl's positive body image. I just came back from a trip with three friends and I didn't even look in a mirror for four days. We walked into the state park carrying forty-pound backpacks. When we go through the ritual of setting up camp, lighting a fire, preparing meals, and cleaning up, we all get closer. There's always something new to talk about as we watch the sun go down behind the rocks or gaze at the stars." If your daughter has been hanging out with a destructive crowd or having trouble with peers, choosing a positive, girl-oriented program in nature can go a long way toward restoring her sense of self.

Senior Year: The Big Push

The fall of senior year is as tumultuous as fall of freshman year. For better or worse, your daughter has to start thinking about leaving and moving on once again. The question of what she will do next looms large. If she decides to remain at home and go to the local community college, the pressure to excel academically senior year will be reduced. But the issue of staying close to home while most of her friends go away will make other emotional and practical demands on both you and her. She may feel "less than" because she didn't go away. Some teenagers feel that only the kids who couldn't "cut it" stay home. If you can't afford to send her away this first year, she may feel ashamed of or resentful about her family.

If you plan for her to live at home, you will need to consider her new adult role in the family. The challenge for both of you will be for her to grow up while living under the same roof. Will she be a participating member of the family or a boarder? What are your expectations in terms of the household? Will she do housework, cook, or drive a younger brother or sister to help out? What about her independence in terms of sexuality, drinking, drugs, and bringing friends home? With all these new relationship dynamics to work out, parents who can afford to do so often decide to say, "Let's help you get a place of your own with other students, even though you'll be close by." If she is motivated to work part-time, that may be the best solution for your family.

If your daughter is applying to a four-year college or university, her anxiety (and possibly yours) about her school performance and the application procedure will sometimes verge on hysteria and result in emotional meltdowns on all sides. Taking SAT and college placement tests, making decisions about which colleges to consider, writing essays, and filling out forms in an atmosphere of stiff competitiveness combine to produce a tense family environment.

Teachers, parents, and advisors will also stress a last strong push for superlative grades the final semester or quarter that may count on applications. This is a good time to plan as little as possible in terms of family events that are going to cause additional pressure.

Those girls who have their heart set on a particular school may opt for "early decision." This means that if they are accepted by mid-December, they have committed themselves to attending. Riane, set on becoming a doctor, applied to Princeton "early decision" and was overwhelmed by the pressure. "It's not like the normal process, because you have to get the application in extra early. Then if you don't get in, not only are you crushed but you only have more applications to look forward to. It's an awful time because so many of your friends are upset. I tried hard not to worry, but on December 15, I drove my mom nuts. She was waiting with the envelope and I took my time coming home, ran errands just to avoid having to confront it. I kept telling myself not to hope. Then my mom was sitting there with this big envelope that we knew meant I had gotten in. I started crying and shrieking and so did she, and we hugged and hugged."

Graduation

Graduation from high school is the completion of one cycle and the beginning of another. It's a big day for students and parents alike. Kristin's valedictorian speech compellingly summed up one young woman's perspective on high school graduation as "the only truly modern, and truly universally American rite of passage." Both the school ceremony and the senior farewell party will send your daughter off with fanfare. She also needs her family's support and participation. Whether you give her a big party or have an intimate dinner out with the family, be sure that your daughter feels celebrated and filled with optimism on her graduation day by honoring her in a fitting way.

Ellen and Jim gave Kate a graduation party for their family and friends. On the invitation, Ellen invited each guest to bring some good wishes for the graduate. Kate's aunt brought a poetry reading on cassette that honored a young woman's coming of age. Her grandfather wrote and shared his memories of reluctantly going off to war after high school. He had been surprised at the kindness of the many different kinds of people that he met. His message to Kate was, "Wherever you go, you need to know that people will take care of you. Remember to take care of others." The guests took turns sharing their wishes for Kate. Ellen deepened the celebration by inviting this level of meaning.

Spirit and Meaning

Throughout all your daughter's rites of passage, be mindful that teaching her to nurture herself involves more than attending to her body. While monitoring her whereabouts so that she avoids dangerous situations, drunk drivers, and overdoses of drugs and alcohol is critical to her physical safety, you also need to teach her to nurture her soul. She needs a sense of meaning as she moves through adolescence into young adulthood. Paying attention to her dreams and fantasies, reading good books with female heroines, and keeping a journal all contribute to her rich inner life.

Spirituality helps your daughter form her core identity. Whether she is affiliated with a church, synagogue, or Buddhist temple or develops an appreciation for the sacred in everyday life, she will have a sense of a power beyond herself. Knowing her own soul and feeling grace and thanksgiving for her life will hold her during the difficult times. Share your spiritual traditions with your daughter, but if she shows an interest in other paths or philosophies, support her search for what is meaningful to her. In this time of change and intense peer interaction, a Catholic girl might go to a Jewish synagogue for services with her friend or an Episcopalian girl might attend a sitting at the ashram to which her boyfriend's family belongs. This is a time of exploration; the only sacred energy that sustains a girl is one that touches her personally in a deep way.

In many Chinese homes, there is an altar that marks sacred space, often with a statue of the goddess of compassion, Kuan Yin. In this way the family pays attention to the feminine spirit of love and caring. Try to incorporate some aspect of the feminine into your family's spiritual orientation. Whether it be the Madonna in Catholicism, the Shekinah in Judaism, or the spirit of Mother Nature, a feminine presence mirrors a girl's divinity.

Feminine Spirituality

Feminine spirituality acknowledges both body and spirit. A girl takes naturally to ritual making; the body-mind experience of menstruation inducts her into marking time in a periodic way. She looks for meaning because she is monthly in touch with forces beyond her individual control; her period comes when it will. With intention, time alone can become sacred. Whether she retreats to her room or to a favorite spot, she can feel a sense of grace in her own wholeness.

By nurturing herself at a deep level, she may experiece grace through meditation, or in personal feminine ritual like adorning, dressing, and bathing, or in being creative. However she chooses to access her feminine self, she will be able to renew herself when she feels depleted. Toni's sacred spot was in nature. "When I was young, there was a creek down the street called Serene Waters. I used to sit there and collect myself. I could feel my body in the wildness." With self-reflection and self-nurturing, a girl discovers what gives her life meaning.

Fourteen-year-old Amanda, bright and well read, lives in the country. Deeply immersed in books that explore the nature religion of Wicca, she creates rituals with her girlfriends. "I find love in the sacred," she said. She has an imperative need to process the vivid physical and emotional changes that she is going through.

Amanda and her friends cast a circle, invoke the powers of the four directions, and share the meaning of their friendship and a feeling of union with nature that supports their day-to-day struggles with guys, sex, and schoolwork. When they focus on their feelings of helplessness with other peers, the girls do not try to change or oppress others in their rituals but to empower and protect themselves. "We don't do bad-vibe ritual or put others down," Amanda said. Amanda also works on getting along with her mother in a self-designed ceremony. She concentrates on changing her own "angry streak" into more cooperative energy with her mother. Amanda takes responsibility for her part in their friction and tries to meet her mother halfway because she wants her mother's love and support.

Magic

Your daughter may be watching one of the many television programs that feature girl or women witches practicing magic. This exposure to feminine sorcery is empowering girls and helping them to see that they have different powers than boys. Girls need to know that their intuition is powerful—a real force in their relationships and their creativity. If your daughter is interested, watch the programs with her and discuss them. If she is reading some of the books on witchcraft for adolescent girls that are being published at an amazing rate, read them and share your ideas.

Sometimes a single exposure to a tradition or ceremony that touches her deeply at the right age can inspire a girl to design her own meaningful ritual at an important crossroads. Fifteen-year-old Melissa spent a year creating a ritual for her sixteenth birthday party after she attended another girl's bat mitzvah. Melissa invited girlfriends her own age, and women her mother's and grandmother's ages to whom she felt close, to gather with her in the park. Sitting in a circle surrounded by flowers and food, each person gave her a special gift—a book of poetry, a jewelry box, a personal story or myth. As she gave Melissa the present, the giver talked about why she had chosen her gift. To the accompaniment of the guitar, Melissa told her guests what it meant to her to celebrate her birthday this way.

Coping with Grief and Loss

When Demeter is reunited with Persephone, she expresses her joy by giving the Greek people the gift of agriculture. There was another gift, too. Persephone's abduction and her reunion with Demeter symbolizes the pattern of death and rebirth in life. When the Greeks enacted the girl's loss and return in a fall ritual each year, they participated in this mother-daughter mystery. By ritualizing your daughter's crossroads and crises, you, too, are teaching her the deeper mysteries of her life.

Encourage your daughter to develop her own rituals for the difficult situations she will face in life. When fifteen-year-old Tavia's boyfriend, Kevin, committed suicide, she was devastated. For months she was depressed and stuck, unable to reach out to others. After three months, her parents took her to see Frieda, a therapist who counsels adolescents. Tavia mumbled, speaking in a monotone as she described finding Kevin's body and her horrible, disembodied experience of the funeral. "I miss him and I feel guilty, wondering what I did that might have spurred him to die." After Kevin died, Tavia had adorned herself with his jewelry and rings, and a choker with his name. Frieda could see that Tavia's holding on to Kevin was holding her back.

Frieda asked Tavia, "Have you thought of doing a ritual for yourself, to help you say good-bye? Perhaps you could create an altar where you put all the things that remind you of Kevin—the jewelry, his photo, and the funeral notice. Maybe you could find a sense of ending for yourself, so that you can go on with your life. It's not that you don't love him; you will still hold him in your heart." Tavia took to the idea immediately and made it her own. She set up an altar and wrote a powerful statement of all the things she loved about Kevin and burned it. All alone, she lit candles, danced, and sang. Nonlinear and nonthinking, it helped her to make her feelings for Kevin sacred and to access her grief. Deepened by the whole experience, Tavia was then able to rejoin her classmates and move on.

Hope's mother left the family when her daughter was three years old. Raised by her single father, Hope received no guidance about sexuality. Looking for intimacy, she fell into sexual relationships indiscriminately. From ages sixteen to eighteen, she used her diaphragm erratically and missed days taking her birth control pills. After three abortions, she was guilt-ridden and loathed her body. She desperately wanted some relationship with the babies, to make amends. "I felt so bad and so sad, that I was a bad person because I rejected these babies who wanted to be born." Hope also felt overwhelmingly helpless. She had no religious orientation to help her with her dilemma.

Audrey, Hope's therapist, asked her about her beliefs. "What do you think about spirits? Do you feel that you caused these deaths?" When they had thoroughly examined Hope's feelings, Hope and Audrey developed a ritual to "speak" with the infant spirit Hope thought was trying to get into the world through her. Hope said, "We created an altar with an egg, pictures of babies, seashells, water, my mother, and the ocean. I told the spirit, 'I'm not ready for you. I don't mean you any harm. I understand you want to be here. Later on, some day, I want you, too.'" Hope said this simple act gave her a lot of relief and helped her remember to use birth control. "I could never talk to my dad about sex or the way I felt. He was always out with his latest girlfriend. I know he cares about me, but he doesn't know how to be there when I need him."

With her pregnancies, Hope was trying to become the mother she never had. Luckily, she had Audrey as a maternal figure and role model to help her, and eventually, she was able to take better care of herself as she explored her sexuality.

Before fifteen-year-old Barbara's mother, Emilia, died of breast cancer, Emilia told her that she would be with her in spirit, that she would live on in her daughter, and that Barbara would always be able to feel her love. Emilia gave Barbara her good jewelry and her bottle of perfume as gifts, legacies of that love. After the funeral, Barbara created an altar in her room where she put the jewelry and perfume, pictures of her mother, herself, and their family, and other cherished objects. She often lit candles on the table to remember her mother and admit her feelings of loss, grief, abandonment, and love. Sometimes, when she was upset, she sat in front of the altar and talked to her mother as if she were still there. She often felt that she heard her mother's voice answering her questions and giving her advice as she had when she was alive. Her younger brother joined her now and then, although his grieving took the form of spending every hour avidly pursuing sports. Their father respected his children's need to mourn in their own ways and made himself available to talk about their loss whenever they wished. He expressed his own grief as well as comforting them.

The impulse to create ritual as a way of dealing with loss will sustain your daughter even after she leaves home. In mid-November of her first year at college, Kaylie received the news that her friend Alison, away at another university, had died. Kaylie screamed and cried, and regretted that she hadn't spoken to her friend since August. "I felt so bad. I kept obsessing about how I should have called her." Alison died from heart failure (possibly stimulated by excessive drinking); a heart condition had gone undetected. Kaylie, facing finals, could not come home for the funeral, and missed both the ceremony and being there for her friends.

When she did get home at Christmas, she spent time with friends talking and writing about Alison. At the end of December, their ritual farewell culminated in fifteen boys and girls convening in a beach town to have dinner on Alison's birthday. "A lot of us had to make sacrifices to go. We went to a beautiful restaurant, brought a birthday cake, sang 'Happy Birthday' and 'Remember You' by Sarah McLachlan, and reminisced. It was my way of saying good-bye and holding her in my heart. I also made a collage with pictures of her to take back and hang in my dorm room so I could see her and tell other people about her." Kaylie feels she learned a big lesson from Alison's death. "I have to show my friends I care, call them on their birthdays, and keep in touch, because you never know what's going to happen."

Seize the Moment

Don't ever miss an opportunity to celebrate your daughter as an individual. Laud her strengths, her accomplishments (basketball, performing arts, or community service), her thoughtfulness, her generosity; show your heartfelt appreciation with a dinner or lunch out or, for larger passages (graduation), a nice party. Reflect on the difficulties and the glories. Let her know that you care. Reward her achievement. Celebrate and honor your daughter and generate life-renewing energy for your family and your community.

Mom's Feelings

Your daughter's acceptance to a college will be a unique moment in your struggle with letting her go out into the world. Now she has a place to go away from home. Your maternal support will be critical for her at this time, yet you will also be facing losing her. In one moment you will feel that you can't wait until she is out of the house; in another, you will feel the empty space she will leave as a sinking sensation in the pit of your stomach.

This period of time with your daughter may also bring up some sticky issues for you about your adolescence. How did your family handle your transition from high school to the world? How did you select your college? If you did not have the opportunity to go to college or ended up following along with your peers because your parents were too preoccupied with themselves or with earning a living to pay attention to you, you may feel a sense of loss on your own behalf. If your family felt that only boys needed higher education, you may be envious of your daughter's opportunities, even as you are proud of her for taking advantage of them. Try not to take any resentments out on her. Your daughter cannot be perfectly appreciative just because you had less. She needs to be able to approach her future on wings.

9

"Get a Life, Mom!"

"When my teenage girls used to say, 'Get a life, Mom!' I hated it—I was insulted. I thought I *had* a life!" Narda said vehemently. Narda had given up her career as a lawyer to raise her four children, three girls and a boy. Outspoken, energetic, and articulate, she was phenomenally active in volunteer work, and indulged her love of fabric art by doing quilting. Thea, more reserved, maintained a practice as a psychologist as she mothered two girls and a boy and heard the same refrain from her teenage daughters. Thea said, "I couldn't believe how devastated I was the first time my older daughter, Clarissa, walked down to the local teenage hangout, a coffee shop, came home late, and didn't say a word to me. It was as if I didn't exist. I was an accomplished professional woman. I swam competitively, and I had a good marriage. But in that moment, I couldn't resist wailing, 'Honey, I'm not used to you going out and not talking to me when you get back.' Fourteen-year-old Clarissa rolled her eyes and stormed out of the room. That was my initiation into the emotional roller coaster of the next four years. I had to completely revise my expectations of my daughter and myself."

Whether you are a career woman or a stay-at-home mom, letting go of your daughter will be a challenge. She has represented and challenged your maiden-Persephone side for better or worse. Whether she is rebellious or compatible with you, with her movement toward adolescent individuation, you will have to find self-renewal. As she moves toward finishing high school, you will increasingly question your own identity. Where are you in your life? How do you anticipate growing and changing? What will you do with the energy that has previously gone into mothering? As you lose this child, what is the psychological growth that you can anticipate? And how will your creativity be expressed?

Warning Signs

By the time your daughter finishes high school, you must finally relinquish your wishes for her to be anyone other than who she is. If you refuse to allow her to move into her world, you will arouse tremendous antagonism. A girl who is naturally growing into maturity will not be thwarted by her mother's resistance. Instead she will go underground, find her way surreptitiously, and, often, feel forced to rebel in self-destructive ways. Letting go involves rethinking your emotional investment in your daughter as well as giving up control over her. You must let go of protecting her from all danger and cede your trust to her, and you must find meaning in other roles.

Girls usually are more ready than their mothers to let go. Women who do not move on to live a gratifying, self-nurturing, fulfilling life cling to their daughters. Others avoid their painful feelings by dramatically separating, pushing their daughters away. If you don't face this big transition squarely, you may find yourself acting out the change instead of productively living your own life. You may have an affair, get depressed, or go into overdrive and busy yourself with superfluous causes.

Don't get stuck depending on your daughter's life for your own identity. One sign of this is when you rush around doing things for your teenager while she is happily occupied with her own social life or extracurricular activities. If you have been a devoted mother, the temptation to clean up her room, wash her clothes, do her errands, or shop for the special things she loves to eat, instead of doing something for yourself, will be very strong. Refrain from doing the chores that she is able to do for herself, while continuing to show love and caring in ways that are meaningful at this stage of your relationship. Give her the responsibility for her care.

Think about the choices you are making. Some mothers hold on to maternal chores simply out of habit, others out of the wish to continue to be needed. The defining, all-encompassing role of motherhood can be both satisfying and fulfilling. It can also be a secure place to hide when you are afraid to move on in your development. Busying yourself with doing things for her keeps you from having to think about what you need now.

Jean, unassuming and self-effacing, prefers to stay in the background while Tammy shines. Jean admits, "I don't know if I will be able to muster the same energy for my own life that I have put into hers." She will find it a challenge to let go because she has always planned her life around Tammy's schedule and put her daughter's needs before her own.

Jean tried to compensate for their family's impoverished situation from the time Tammy was born. "I used to comb the newspapers for free events: stimulating library programs, an interactive naturalist center, a community singing group. I also constantly entered radio contests and often won tickets to plays and concerts. When Tammy was eleven, I won a trip for us to visit all the movie sets in Hollywood. My husband supported my finding opportunities to broaden Tammy's experience. I eventually interviewed for a part-time job as a columnist for our community newspaper, and I used my ad-searching and radio expertise to get the job." It was easier for Jean to foster her daughter's talents and creativity than her own. Her challenge will be to use the wisdom she has gleaned from mothering and apply the same skills to developing herself.

For both your sake and hers, begin to hand over the responsibility for the minutiae of her everyday life to your daughter. Strike a balance. Teach her the skills that she needs to function as an independent young woman. Do this in a thoughtful, gradual way. If you do not foster her independence, you will become resentful, she will feel abandoned, and you will feel guilty. She does need to be her own person. Although you still have to make sacrifices of time and energy on your teenage daughter's behalf, it is critical for you to turn your attention to yourself—your goals and your maturing identity as your mothering role diminishes.

Another subtle sign that you are having trouble letting go is if you find yourself either angry or depressed much of the time when your daughter is leading her own independent high school life, just waiting for her to come home. Demeter's anger, grief, and rage scorched the earth. You must acknowledge your loss as healthy for both you and your daughter. She needs to descend into the abyss and take risks in order to form her identity and come back as her own woman. She will return with many riches earned by her own experience. As long as you do not reject her—in order to protect yourself from your grief that she is no longer merged with you—you will be able to welcome her back joyously, whenever she seeks you, as Demeter embraced Persephone.

If your daughter has had an emotional crisis, physical injury, or disease that has required exceptional medical treatment, staying connected and letting go becomes more complicated. Thea's younger daughter, Charlotte, dark-haired, dark-eyed, and muscular, was diagnosed with juvenile arthritis when she was ten years old. "Charlotte's condition required ongoing hospital visits three times a week," Thea said soberly. "We ritualized our doctors' appointments and made it into mother-daughter bonding time." Coping with taking heavy medication, stringently following a diet, and doing special exercises was a lot of responsibility for a young girl. Out of compassion for Charlotte's suffering, Thea did not want her daughter to feel alone in having to focus on her health.

A practical, thoughtful mother, Thea suggested that she and Charlotte keep a journal together. Using one book, they each wrote a page a week, and set a goal for her physical or mental health. Thea said, "I would write down wanting to do a hike three times a week, or drink more water, or do my breast exam regularly. She would concentrate on eliminating sugar from her diet and swimming twice a week. Sometimes our objectives would extend to things like my wanting to call an old friend or her needing to have a talk with her math teacher. Once a month we would go out to lunch and talk about whether we had met our goals and, if not, what was getting in the way. We shared our process and learned from each other."

Now seventeen, Charlotte shows the positive signs of the sensitive mothering she has received throughout her ordeal. She is a strong, buoyant girl with a sunny attitude, but she still needs her mother more than a girl would who was not afflicted. Her energy level is low; she cannot stay out late or always count on her body to support her. When she goes to a prom, she is wiped out the whole weekend from preparing, socializing, and dancing. Drinking alcohol is strictly prohibited because of her condition and her medication. She and her mother have to take these realities into consideration when negotiating her life. Thea's upbeat attitude is, "Our goal has been to foster her living a normal life yet not to jeopardize her health and growth. We concentrate on doing yoga and swimming together. My big issue is, How do I separate? How much does she need me and how much do I need to be needed?"

Recognize the Loss

When a mother tries to protect herself from change and loss by maintaining a false image of her daughter that mirrors her own good mothering, the reality of her daughter's emerging differentness will break through. Heartache and soul searching ensue. Modeling herself on her own mother, Sidney, a cheerful, attentive woman, elected to be a stay-at-home mom with her three children. "I never felt bored or depressed. I loved being there after school and doing volunteer work. Sometimes, I did compare myself to my best friend, an ambitious career woman whose children were raised by a nanny. But I didn't think that arrangement was good for her children. My friend always tried to subtly influence me to do more, like to train for a marathon with her. She'd say, 'You'll be more fulfilled, your children and your husband will be more proud of you.' We're very close, godparents to each other's daughters. I did have a nagging doubt, but I was content."

Sidney was shocked out of her contentment when her family and two others spent a weekend together to attend a major league baseball game. The father of a boy came to Sidney and told her that their fifteen-year-olds had been smoking pot the night before. Sidney immediately blamed the boy, who was known to be the troublemaker. She was appalled to find out that her eldest, her daughter Laurel, had supplied the marijuana, which had been given to her by a girl at school. "I freaked out. I couldn't believe that my daughter was the instigator. I completely flipped and took it personally—I was such a good mother! Then I thought, I'm out of it! I don't have a clue!

"Disappointed and hurt, I felt like grounding Laurel for the rest of the year; I didn't even want to see her face. My husband was much cooler about it, more businesslike and analytical. For me it was a wake-up call. I knew I had to get better communication with my kids and find more meaning in my life. I sort of wallowed around in my feeling of depression for a year; no one seemed to notice or care."

Sidney took up her own search. She started to track Laurel's moods more closely, talked to her and tried to understand her. Sidney also got a part-time job in a local gift shop. Intimidated by art, yet drawn to it at the same time, she pushed herself to take art classes at the local junior college. There she met stimulating people and enjoyed doing watercolor landscapes in outdoor settings. "Then Laurel and I signed up for an art class together, and she discovered that she was really good at it. Art gave us new common ground in our relationship. I also took psychology classes that gave me a perspective while Laurel was taking risks in high school."

Move on from Regret

Girls' risk taking challenges mothers to think about themselves and their daughters in more complex ways. Women review their years of mothering as they disengage. Many feel regret, wishing they had done things differently with their daughters. Sometimes they feel overwhelmed by remorse. Adriana, a good-hearted, well-intentioned mother, said tearfully, "I know I reenacted my childhood fears with my older daughter, Gina. My own mother was such a witch; I felt she hated me, and I wanted so much to be loved by her. I see now that I wanted that love from Gina. When she was little, I tried to be the perfect mother; I did everything for her. But when she got angry or difficult, I felt as if I was being attacked by my rejecting mother. I couldn't set limits except when it was too late. I'd scream at her and I drove her away. My husband always took her side, which made it all the more confusing. Gina got into drugs and ran away from home. After doing many treatment programs, she's clean and self-supporting, but she still rages at me or avoids me. I didn't know what I was doing. I hadn't had a model. Now, realizing how much I made her my mother, I feel terrible!"

Finally divorced from a husband who also undermined her parenting, Adriana is developing the relational skills with which to reconnect with Gina. She consistently asserts her love by sending Gina supportive cards and stays open to their infrequent conflict-free times together—going to a movie or having lunch out. When Gina asks for a favor, such as borrowing her mother's car or money, Adriana is no longer manipulated by her desire to be loved and sets firm limits. Creating rapprochement with Gina is a long, painful, and rewarding process.

The pain of seeing that your best intentions have been thwarted by your own blindness is sometimes crushing. In order to relinquish your feelings of regret, you must accept that all parents make mistakes. We learn from experience. And, as we have seen, it is never too late to begin to repair the bond with your daughter. Your inner work at this time is to make peace with yourself, acknowledge what you or your family system did wrong, know you cannot change the past, and move on. You must forgive yourself in order for your daughter to be able to forgive, accept herself and her family, and grow up.

Think about your maternal strengths and honor them. Give yourself credit for the devotion and intention that went into raising your daughter. Applaud yourself for lying awake at night, suffering for her and with her in her adolescent experimentation. She has gleaned strengths as well as weaknesses from you. Now she must forge her own identity in the world. If you let her go, you have many more years in which to amplify and develop an adult relationship with her.

If your musing on the past or a tragedy forces you to realize that you have restorative work to do with your daughter, face it, and make amends as best you can, even as you begin to separate. Hallie always felt left out as a child because her mother, Opal, overtly favored her older sister, Jasmyn. Awkward, hurt, and resentful, Hallie was the scapegoat in the family and Jasmyn was "the winner."

Jasmyn's talents as a ballerina were fostered while Hallie's beautiful singing voice was left untrained. Hallie and her mother fought all the time. "I felt unloved and unwanted by my mother but loved by my father. Still, my sister and I managed to be O.K. friends." When Hallie was eighteen, twenty-one-year-old Jasmyn was killed in an automobile accident.

The family was devastated, and Hallie felt that she should have died instead of her sister. "I thought I deserved death because I was the bad one, the one who couldn't do anything right. I felt guilty that I had hated her sometimes; in my mother's eyes, she could do no wrong." Over the next few years, Hallie painfully told her mother how she felt. In the depth of their shared grief, Hallie and Opal were able to hear one other. Gradually, Opal faced the enormity of what she had done by idealizing her older daughter and making Hallie all bad. She acted to repair their relationship by giving Hallie ongoing singing lessons. Two years later mother and daughter found themselves weeping at the end of a recital in which Hallie's beautiful solo soared to outstanding applause. That triumphant moment held the anguish of the work they had been doing since Jasmyn had died. Mother and daughter were reunited.

No matter how flawed your raising of your daughter, if you do the work that you need to do on yourself as she leaves home, she will return to you. And as you and she change and need each other in more mature ways, you will have the chance to become friends.

The Empty Nest

For the moment, you have given your daughter all the tools you can to nurture and empower herself as an adult. As she grows into a happy, meaningful life, begin to enlarge your own life. Who are you now? Pilar, a Brazilian woman whose husband is American, had been a devoted wife and mother of two children for twenty-two years.

Self-conscious about her Portuguese accent, she gained confidence doing fund-raising for her children's schools. "I never understood the phrase 'the empty nest' until my daughter Mercedes' junior year in high school," Pilar said. "She was my last child. Suddenly, I began to feel turmoil in my body, a feeling that became more and more urgent; it felt like a hollow space, an emptiness inside. It intensified when Mercedes was accepted into college; my 'bird child' was flying off three thousand miles away. She was starting something new and I felt I also had to start something new, but what would I do? I knew it had to be something drastic."

Pilar's distress prompted her to rent a room in a neighboring city where she put a computer, a desk, and a sofa. She left the walls bare. The eighth-floor view looked out on the stained-glass rose window of a cathedral. "I called my room my 'office.' My husband had a very difficult time with this decision. I understood why; we have a nice home, and with both children gone there would be more space. I couldn't explain it; I just knew that I felt empty and desperate. My husband acquiesced and signed the lease because he loves me. My children seemed to understand my needing a physical separation. I didn't tell anyone else except my two best friends. I felt ashamed and afraid that people would misinterpret. How did I dare do something so irrational?

"Every morning I got up and went to my office. With no agenda, I napped, read, or delved into the computer. Sometimes I would just sit, stare at the rose window, and let my mind wander. I realized that I had created the nest, the hollow place inside me in order to hold my children, but now I needed to fill that emptiness with myself. My own unselfish love for the children turned inward—it was astonishingly healing. I marveled that it felt like being in love but no one else was there. In the evenings I went home to my husband where he had dinner waiting. Six months later my lease was up and I was rejuvenated."

Mercedes supported her mother's self-searching and kept in close touch. She knew that Pilar was learning to use the computer and e-mailed her with love notes from her college dorm. Mercedes gave her mother what she had been given—love, respect, and understanding. Pilar craved solitude, but she also absorbed the love and support that her family sent her from afar.

While Demeter searched for Persephone, she disguised herself as an old woman and became a nursemaid to a baby boy. But this did not assuage her grief for long. Some women replenish their empty nest with a new puppy or by becoming involved with their friends' young children. If you find yourself trying to fill the empty space in your heart with mothering others, ask yourself if, like Pilar, you might need to fill that void with yourself.

The Gift of Unplanned Time

You do not have to leave your home in order to find yourself again after your daughter leaves. Treasuring unplanned time or taking a break instead of filling up the space with activities may give you a chance to enjoy not being on call and feel your way to the next step. Thea mused, "When my older daughter, Clarissa, began to spend ten-hour days at school as a junior, my first impulse was to sign up for more volunteer work. But I restrained myself and kept to my flexible part-time clinical hours. On days that I didn't have clients, I didn't schedule anything. I woke up, got her off to school, looked at the weather, and decided what I wanted to do that day. It made me anxious at first to be so free. But I persisted. Some days I felt like staying in bed and reading a book until noon. Others, I wanted to go to the beach, take a hike, or garden.

"Slowly, my mind started to empty out. All the demands, the details of what I had to do for my children, my house, my husband, and my clients stopped rattling around in my mind. New thoughts and feelings came up. As I rearranged my priorities, possibilities began to emerge. If I had filled my free time immediately, I would have continued at the same compulsive pace that I had been operating at before. It was a precious experience for me to let myself flow with the aimlessness."

Having more time for yourself happens gradually. Try to build it in as your family evolves and your children become more independent. If you do it deliberately, you will have the emotional tools to face the feelings that arise when you have an "empty nest." Sentimentalizing your daughter or mindlessly staying busy blocks the door to this rite of passage. Instead, with self-reflection you can reap the reward this period has to offer and build on your insights for the next stage of your life.

During this period, stop for coffee, browse in a bookstore, or sit on a park bench for half an hour in between doing your usual errands. Go to a lecture, movie, or concert alone instead of with your husband, something that you have always wanted to do but could never fit in. No matter how simple it seems, it can dramatically change your perspective (and often your daughter's, too). Marianne had always been interested in trying yoga but spent her free time playing tennis with her husband. When her daughter, Cathy, was seventeen and spending time with her boyfriend, Marianne determined to extend her own horizon out from the known safety of her family and joined a yoga class. She found both the physical strengthening and the meditative focus invigorating and enlivening.

After a few enjoyable sessions, she shared her enthusiasm with Cathy and asked if her daughter wanted to join her. Cathy said, "No, not really, Mom. Thanks anyway. But you know what I've always wanted to do? To take dance." Marianne found a dance class for Cathy at the same time as her yoga class so they could go together and stop for a cup of tea on the way home.

If you track your development along with your daughter's, you may have projects lined up at work or at home that you can't wait to get to. You may be passionately involved in a hobby and delighted to have more time to devote to it. May, a member of Narda's quilting group, has a sixteen-year-old daughter, Marigold. Also a stay-at-home mother, May has a down-to-earth, no-nonsense manner and a sly sense of humor. "I call our group 'stitch and bitch' because for the last ten years we have talked and complained about our children while sewing quilts. A lot of good parenting came out of it, but now we're talking about the traveling we're going to do when the last one is out of the house." Unstoppable Narda says that she has always expressed her zest for life. In addition to fabric artistry, she looks forward to getting back to playing the piano.

Your daughter's commitment to her own pursuits may revive your curiosity in an activity or subject that you abandoned for the sake of mothering. Women traditionally give up work or a career to raise their children. Narda, who has not practiced law for twenty years, was recently asked to join a law firm and is writing her résumé, which includes the voluminous volunteer work she has done on behalf of charity and schools. She is feeling insecure about reentering her field after so long an absence.

At the same time, Narda's eldest daughter, Amber, is graduating from college. Amber is anxious about finding a job in her chosen specialty of government and journalism. At this critical juncture in her life, Amber told her mother that after graduation she is tempted to take a road trip with a friend through the United States. Narda said, "I told her I thought that was a great idea, that she is the most free she will ever be right now. She did a very difficult senior thesis and I think it's the perfect time to lighten up."

Narda shared her anxiety about her own upcoming interview with the law firm: "What if I say the wrong thing?" Amber replied, "I can't imagine you having trouble with an interview, Mom!" "She sounded," Narda said, "as if she were absolutely sure that I would get the job and should take it. It made me feel more confident to know that she saw me as competent." In their reciprocal relationship, Narda was giving her daughter permission to take a break from hard work, and Amber was encouraging her mother to take up a new, challenging job.

As you re-create yourself, this reciprocity will be evident in many ways. Angela laughs as she recalls her fear when, at the age of forty, she was faced with doing a lecture on Shakespeare to an audience of two hundred other scholars at a college association meeting. Elizabeth, then a self-assured sixteen-year-old, took her mother shopping for an outfit to wear. Angela said, "I remember being in the store picking out my usual conservative browns and grays. Elizabeth suddenly and authoritatively said, 'Mother, you can't wear these wren-brown clothes anymore!' She thought that I didn't stand up for myself enough; my 'wren-brown' was the perfect symbol for my reticence. I wound up buying a lavender skirt and a white silk blouse. I felt like a new woman. I've worn purple skirts ever since."

Back to School

Some women whose children are leaving the nest can't wait to go back to school. You may decide to complete a degree suspended for the sake of mothering or branch out into a new field. In middle age, you will know what to study and be more focused than when you were young. Toni said that her quiet, soft-spoken mother, Lorna, gained confidence by going back to school. "My mom worked for my dad in his plumbing business and raised us four children—it was difficult for him when she got interested in the world. At first he wanted her to stop thinking about intellectual matters and devote herself more to the home. As she studied, my mom got more boisterous and outspoken. Now she's proud of herself for earning her B.A. in sociology."

Toni feels new respect for her mother's self-assertiveness. In addition to sharing her own two-year-old daughter with her mother, she is now able to have conversations with Lorna about political and environmental issues. When Toni finished her college degree, buoyed by her mother's expanding horizons, she convinced the local recreation center to hire her to develop a nature program for eight- to twelve-year-old girls. Lorna and Toni energized each other.

If you do choose to go back to school while your daughter is in high school or college, be careful not to compete with her for grades or achievement. Treat learning as an adventure. Have a cooperative, mutual exchange of ideas as you are both studying and exploring new ideas. Validate her accomplishments and help her through the rough places; she will do the same for you. Narda said, "My teenage girls have challenged themselves intellectually and are technical wizards. Because of them I have pushed myself in both arenas, and I ask them to help me all the time."

Sport Psychology

Devote some of your new-found time to your own fitness program and enjoy your increased physical and mental stamina. Stimulated by her daughter's athletic excellence, May took up playing tennis. "Marigold runs on a champion cross-country team. She loves the discipline. When I compared myself as a teenager, I knew I missed being challenged athletically. I took up competitive tennis and learned a lot about myself. Sport psychology is amazing—the best and the worst in my personality comes out when playing. I can see how I handle pressure. Playing tennis has helped me be bold and think strategically across the board." Whether you join a volleyball team, climb a mountain, or take a walk every day in your neighborhood, you will benefit from taking up a physical challenge to mark your transition from mothering to your middle years.

Reclaiming Other Relationships

When your daughter leaves home, you will have more energy for other relationships. You may turn your attention to your younger children, or you may feel moved to spend more time with your aging parents. If your primary focus has been parenting, you and your husband may have neglected your relationship. Renewing your intimacy with him or, if you are a single mother, dating again can be exciting and rejuvenating.

Many women speak of taking a trip alone with their husbands for the first time in many years. Whether a long-coveted dream vacation, a drive up the sea coast or into the country for a stay at a bed and breakfast, or camping out in the woods, getting away can give you leisure hours during which to attune to each other again. Don't be surprised if being alone with your husband is difficult at first. You will both have changed, and your one-on-one intimacy will now include your patterns of years of parenting. This can deepen your commitment to each other but takes the same kind of careful attention you practiced with your daughter.

Often the intensity of the dislocation of having teenagers puts stress on marriages. Women have affairs or men leave their wives for younger women. Try to be aware of the emotional upheavals that occur at this threshold so that you make wise choices for yourself and your family. Be patient and take a wait-and-see attitude.

If unbearable difficulties in your marriage precipitate a divorce, your relationship with your adolescent daughter will become more unstable. Joelle, fragile yet determined, left her husband when Rae, an only child, was fifteen. Joelle said, "I'd been telling my husband I was unhappy for years. Suddenly, I had to leave. I never dreamed how much pain it was going to cause. I assumed he would be decent about child support and alimony. Instead, he left the state and filed for bankruptcy. Four years later, we're still not divorced, and Rae and I have moved three times to a smaller and smaller house. It was excruciating for Rae to lose her 'perfect family' with plenty of money, a generous dad, and a fun mom. Rae was bright and talented and gave a lot to her friends. I fell apart and so did she. But I had to find a way to support myself and her and deal with the lawyers. Finally, I went back to retail clothes sales, which I had done before I got married.

"It was hard for me not to complain to Rae about her father's lying and not paying court-ordered support. We both knew that I shouldn't put her in the middle. But when I couldn't pay for her schoolbooks or give her an allowance, I had to be honest and realistic. I also told her that in spite of his negligence, I knew he loved her. It's been a nightmare." Because Joelle was fair about Rae's father, mother and daughter were able to stay close. At forty-eight, Joelle says that she is proud of herself for leaving. She's self-sufficent, happier, and has a nice relationship with a man. "But," she adds, "if I had known how painful it was going to be for both of us, I don't know if I could have done it."

Breaking out of family patterns that keep you dependent on others' wishes and needs will be tremendously empowering for both you and your daughter. But it is never easy, and there is always an emotional price to pay. Joelle said, "I was amazed at Rae's ability to support me, even with her own suffering. I'm stronger, and my daughter says now, 'It's the best thing that ever happened to you.'" Your daughter will learn from the choices you make and know that it is never too late to grow.

Joelle still cries as she describes sending her daughter off to college three thousand miles away. "I cried when I took her to school last year. I cry every time she comes home and every time she leaves. Then I'm fine. It's not that I'm sad, exactly, just emotional. I'm so moved, happy for her, but in the transitions I'm flooded with tears."

Feminine Friendships

Your women friends can nurture you as your daughter becomes more independent. Seek other women to talk to about your feelings. Feminine bonds will help replace the closeness you once had with her. Going out of town overnight with a woman friend or group of friends may be a first-time experience for many mothers. Whether a trip focuses on river rafting or doing a retreat at a Buddhist temple, it creates solidarity among women who may have been isolated in nuclear families. Testing your skills in the wilderness or in meditation, you will have a sense of physical well-being and centeredness. Taking foreign language classes together or working on a political campaign can also expand and deepen your network of female friends.

Kaylie's mother, Viviane, a lawyer and nurse, combines her expertise in a high-powered job administrating the human resources division in a hospital. Her breast cancer has been in remission for five years. After Kaylie's first year of college, with only one of her four children left at home, Viviane is questioning: "Who am I separate from my work and mothering? For the first time, I'm asking myself, What kind of person do I want to be? Who is left behind when they leave? It's scary. How am I going to spend my spare time? I'm standing at the edge of a void.

"I'm not interested in sports or socializing. My husband, who works a nine-to-six job, has his hobbies—gardening, golfing, and sailing. I'm the caregiver who runs the household and tracks the kids. He has an adventuresome dream of sailing around the world, but I don't know. I'm more serious; he brings me laughter." Viviane's only glimmer of her new direction is that she longs for a spiritual life. No longer a practicing Catholic, she feels drawn instead to a humanistic path—to doing community service. Viviane envisions working with other women giving to the community or to charity, and feels she will find her sense of meaning there. She admires the way Kaylie handled herself in the tough situation in Ecuador. "Kaylie has the attitude, 'I got through Ecuador, I can get through anything.' I like to do things to take me out of my comfort zone, and I encourage my children to do the same."

Rededicate Yourself

With the help of women friends, create an initiatory ceremony that marks your passage from mothering to middle age. As you imagine what kind of ceremony would make you feel celebrated, look to your spiritual traditions or draw on rituals that you have created for your daughter over the years. One woman craved a weekend alone during her daughter's senior year and arranged to go off to a local hot spring. Immersing herself in the mineral baths, meditating on the natural setting, and writing down her thoughts was the ultimate treat for her.

When Adriana anticipated her younger daughter, Paola, going away to college, she was terrified. Living with Gina's self-destructive behavior and an unreliable husband and father, Adriana and Paola had turned to one another for refuge. Now Adriana would be alone. She asked her three closest friends to join her on a camping trip with the intent of helping her find the strength to endure her loneliness. Camping out in the dark within the loving company of other women, Adriana faced her fears. They all focused on her releasing anxiety, being in the moment, and illuminating Adriana's skills and resources. They promised to be there for her. Fortified by this ritual, Adriana was able to wholeheartedly prepare for Paola's departure and let her go, secure in the knowledge that they would both find their way.

Angela gathered a group of eight "trusted, deeply connected women" to celebrate Elizabeth's departure. "I invited women who had been there for me and asked for their ideas. I encouraged my

friends to come in their own uniqueness, not as mothers or part-
ners." In a remote corner of a botanical garden, Angela's friends surrounded her with flowers. Each woman brought an altar object to
share with the group that expressed something about midlife for
her—a piece of art, a story, a rock, a fetish. One woman brought her
airline ticket to Egypt, a place she had longed to visit and was now
free to do so. Angela remembered, "We ate simple food: fruit, home-
made breads, cheeses, and nuts. They toasted me with a delicious
sparkling elderberry juice. I told dreams about my daughter. The ritual captured the poignancy of this separation, both the loss and the
liberation. I felt like a gypsy—free from having to conform to cultural rules. I looked forward to not having to be so careful, to not
having to model the right way for Elizabeth at every moment. I
wanted to be more me."

Follow Your Dreams

Mothers losing their adolescent daughters reconnect to feelings that
they had before they bore children. Psychologically, they are connecting to Persephone, the young maiden in themselves as a renewal
for middle age. They need to touch that youthful wellspring. A
woman at this juncture often dreams of being back in her own adolescence: her first boyfriend, her first prom, a favorite teacher, an em-
barrassing moment, or a great conquest. Or she dreams of going
back and forth between being her daughter, herself as an adolescent,
and herself as an adult woman. Dreams of her daughter or herself
being kidnapped or disappearing echo Persephone's fate. If heeded,
these messages help a mother separate from her daughter and re-
claim a connection to herself.

An intuitive mother of two who loved to garden and cook, Cassia
took her dream life seriously. In her daughter Zoe's freshman year,
Cassia had a nightmare about driving a car with Zoe in the passenger

seat that went out of control and plunged over a cliff. Waking in a sweat with her heart pounding, Cassia began to think about the warm, sweet relationship that she enjoyed with Zoe. She sensed that she was in danger of clinging to her wonderful daughter and stifling them both. As the driver of the car in the dream, she was in control of their fate. She needed to be careful. For the next three years she carefully recorded her dreams and watched the interweaving themes of her daughter's adolescence and her own initiation into middle age.

In one dream, Cassia was in a sports car with Zoe and three of her girlfriends, all packed in together. "There was a strange sense of being both the adult I am now and of being a teenager again. I belonged but I didn't belong." Cassia remembered the excitement and adventure of riding in fast cars as a teenager. But in the dream there is almost no room for her left in the car. She had to give up identifying with youth through Zoe's life in order to cross her own threshold.

In another dream, Cassia was in an Italian beach town with fifteen-year-old Zoe, shopping at an outdoor market. They are looking at jewelry and trying to figure out the exchange rate from lire to dollars. "There was a feeling of girls having fun, being away from home." Cassia tries to explain their interest in pearls to the shopkeeper but lets Zoe take over because she is fluent in Italian. They take turns trying on pearl necklaces but suddenly get separated. At first Cassia is unconcerned, but as night falls, she gets more and more anxious and desperately starts to search for Zoe.

This dream showed Zoe's surpassing her mother in her ability to negotiate the foreign country of her own adulthood. Cassia does not speak Italian; Zoe studies it at school. Each has different gifts, yet they share the pearls of their close feminine relationship. The pearls would be a touchstone for both of them when Zoe went off to college.

Cassia entered an adventure of her own in a dream in which she was alone, nude, exploring a rocky island with golden sand. In her wandering she finds another woman doing an archaeological dig and immediately begins to study with her, poring over her books and artifacts. "I'm ecstatic with my find." Cassia felt this dream pointed to her need for self-examination and solitude now that she was launching her daughter. She felt tremendously reassured by this rich vision of her future.

Finally, Cassia had dreams of being pregnant. In one, she was living in a simple village with other women. "I am in labor. Many women are clustered around me like midwives, but then suddenly the contractions stop. I still have my hands on my distended, hard belly. The others say they are sending for the old wise woman. She'll know how to massage the belly to help the baby out. I have faith in spite of my anxiety." Although Cassia was beyond childbearing, she was gestating new life.

Many women dream of being pregnant when their daughters are adolescents. While you watch your daughter's body change, your own body also changes. You may be beginning menopause as you mother your daughter through adolescence. Be aware of your feelings and choices about your own fertility and how aging is affecting your body. You may have chosen not to have any more children or long to have another. As you watch your daughter's strong, smooth-skinned body, you may be wistful or dismayed about the loss of your once-youthful figure and the stamina that you enjoyed as a younger woman. You will be integrating these feelings and changes into your own self-definition as your daughter's body becomes more fertile. Menopause is a disruptive underworld experience for many women. Use your mood swings, sleeplessness, and hot flashes to assist you in reevaluating yourself. Your creativity will now take new forms.

If an inspiring lecture, a stimulating workshop, a beautiful piece of music, or an insight breaking through triggers you to explore your dreams, obey the call to turn inward. Let your energy flow there. Your dreams will fertilize you. Just before Elizabeth went off to college, practical, organized Angela dreamed of a beautiful blue bowl full of fresh eggs, speckled, cream-colored, and brown. Angela tried to crack the eggs and fry them, but they would not fry. A voice in the dream said, "Angela, these eggs aren't to eat; they are not to feed your children. They are about your own potential." The dream prompted Angela to recognize her selfhood as she resisted her deeply ingrained patterns of mothering.

Two years after Sidney, jolted by her daughter's marijuana use, followed her instinct to pursue art classes, she was offered the chance to administer a small art gallery. "By the time we went to parent weekend at college in the fall of Laurel's freshman year, I was on top of the world. I felt so up! I had an amazing dream that weekend that I was in my maternal grandmother's front yard, taking a bath in a big, old-fashioned tub. I was a teenager, aware of my body and my breasts, feeling very alive. I was secretly pleased—my mother and grandmother wouldn't approve of what I was doing. But I knew that I didn't want to repeat what they had done." Sidney and her husband both came from traditional families where the man worked and the woman stayed home. Sidney was breaking the mold by changing her role.

When you pursue your own outer and inner life, your daughter will be free to separate and pursue hers. Take your most intimate wishes into account and value your own instinct, ideas, and feelings. Express them in your unique way. Sharing your individuality with your daughter is your finest gift to her; it empowers her to cultivate her own uniqueness. Dare to be who you are in your fullness and anticipate the next stage of your life with excitement and zest, secure in the knowledge that your relationship with your daughter will continue to grow.

10 ∽

*W*rapping It Up

We have come full circle. As you become aware of the deep relationship with your daughter that connects you to your feminine heritage, you will find that the old adage "Like mother, like daughter" also means "Like daughter, like mother." If you have approached her adolescence in an engaged way, you have been enriched by what you have given and by what you have learned. As you have instilled woman-centered values in your daughter, you have also enhanced your own capacity for living a meaningful, happy life.

The myth of Demeter and Persephone celebrates the cyclical nature of the mother-daughter relationship. As Persephone is forced or seduced into the underworld of risk taking and suffering, her mother also suffers at her loss. But every spring they are reunited. As you struggle to connect with your adolescent daughter in the everyday conflicts about curfews, chores, homework, and her dismissiveness of you, you have realized that you are participating in this feminine mystery. Underneath her very real struggles with her body image—how she looks, feels, thinks, or adorns herself—is a deeper coming to terms with knowing what it means to be a woman. You have supported her in learning to appreciate her female body and its creative and pleasurable potential, and you have deepened your appreciation of your own body.

In her relationships with boys, your daughter has touched on the same questions that Persephone faced when plunged into the underworld: How can I bear the pain? Will I stay or go? Is this darker, less harmonious world fertile or death-dealing? Persephone was persuaded to eat the pomegranate seed, food of the dead and sexuality. No longer a virgin, she had to stay in the underworld for a third of the year. Your daughter, too, has tasted the delicious forbidden fruit of sexuality and has experienced relationships that will ensure that she matures instead of remaining a child. If you have examined your relationships with the men in your life and tried to teach her what you know, you will have empowered her. And she will be able to stand as an equal before men in the political, professional, and social arenas, as well as the more intimate ones she enters into.

Your warm connection with her has ensured that she makes good friends of other girls. She will continue to build female support systems that will hold her through the vicissitudes of her life long after you are gone. As she solidifies these relationships, she will go back and forth between you and them; each enhances the other.

Your understanding of her need to dabble in the underworld of drugs and alcohol while modeling a wholesome lifestyle has helped her negotiate the risk-taking environment of high school in a way that strengthened her. You have enabled her to take healthy risks by challenging herself athletically, intellectually, and artistically. She has developed a strong foundation.

With all the pressures and expectations of adolescent life, she has found relief in your continuing understanding. She has listened to your manner of problem solving when she was in over her head. When Zeus realized the enormity of Demeter's grief, he came to Persephone's rescue and arranged her release from Hades. Watching her father treat women respectfully has led your daughter to expect the respect of other men. Supporting her in her passions has given her confidence in herself and her chosen goals. She feels capable of pursuing them on her own now.

Celebrating with her at the crossroads and meeting her in her crises has helped her through them and given her life meaning. You have embraced her with compassion and wisdom as she returned from each exploration of the world. And you have awakened her spirit. Wise Hecate, goddess of the dark moon, will now be with her at all the crossroads in her life. Because you shared yourself with her, she will not have to reject you as you may have had to reject your mother. She will know you honor her for who she is and that you accept her for being different from you. Secure in her own individuality, she will be considerate of yours.

As she needs you less and less, you can return to yourself in a full, rich way, freeing her to get on with her life and showing her the rewards of your maturity. As you take up your life away from mothering, you will see that you are no longer always putting others' needs before your own. In this in-between place, you are poised on the edge of a great adventure, as she is poised to go out and encounter life on her own. During her adolescent years, you may go away for a week or a month, or have a work project that consumes all your time, but if you are connected, you will always come back to her with the same wild rush of joy that Demeter felt on seeing Persephone emerge from the underworld. In those instances, you will know that you are the one who has been in the underworld while your daughter patiently or anxiously waited for your return.

The love between Demeter and Persephone shows the way for

mothers and daughters to find vitality in one another again. Both are transformed while Persephone is in the underworld. When they re-unite, they renew themselves in each other. Trust this pattern of loss and return. She will go, you will wait. You will go, she will wait. But, if you have stayed true to your love, you will find each other, embrace, and renew yourselves again and again.

Suggested Readings and Resources ∽

Amigos de las Americas
5618 Star Lane
Houston, TX 77057
(713) 782-5290
(800) 231-7796

Bartle, Nathalie, Ed.D., with Susan Lieberman, Ph.D. *Venus in Blue Jeans: Why Mothers and Daughters Need to Talk About Sex.* Boston, MA: Houghton Mifflin, 1998.

Boer, Charles, trans. *Homeric Hymns.* Revised second edition. Dallas, TX: Spring Publications, 1980.

Brown, Lyn Mikel, and Carol Gilligan. *Meeting at the Crossroads: Women's Psychology and Girls' Development.* New York: Ballantine, 1992.

Brubach, Holly. "The Athletic Esthetic." *The New York Times Magazine,* June 23, 1996, pp. 48–51.

Brumberg, Joan Jacobs. *The Body Project: An Intimate History of American Girls.* New York: Vintage Books, 1998.

Daughters. A Newsletter for Parents of Girls Ages Eight to Eighteen. 1808 Ashwood Avenue, Nashville, TN 37212-5012.

Dexter, Miriam Robbins. *Whence the Goddesses: A Source Book.* New York: Pergamon Press, 1990.

The Diary Project
www.diaryproject.com
    Chat room that offers teens fourteen categories to write about, including relationships, drugs, friends, family, feelings, racism, school, and stress.

Dodson, Shireen. *The Mother-Daughter Book Club.* New York: HarperCollins, 1997.

Full Esteem Ahead
6663 SW Beaverton Hillsdale Hwy. #214
Portland, OR 97225
Kathy Masarie, M.D.
www.europa.com/~kmasarie
    A program dedicated to encouraging and preserving healthy self-
    esteem in teens, especially girls, as they enter and move through
    adolescence.

Gilligan, Carol, et al. *Women, Girls and Psychotherapy: Reframing
    Resistance.* New York: Haworth Press, Inc., 1991.

Girls Circle Association
A Project of The Tides Center
6 Knoll Lane, Suite F
Mill Valley, CA 94941
www.girlscircle.org
Beth Hossfeld, M.F.T. (415) 388-0644
Giovanna Taormina (415) 267-5224
    Facilitator Trainings and Curriculum Materials for service-
    providers of girls' programs.

Girls Incorporated
120 Wall Street
New York, NY 10005-3902
www.girlsinc.org
    Girls Inc. works with public schools across the country in partner-
    ship with programs like Operation Smart, Preventing Adolescent
    Pregnancy, and Girls Re-Cast TV.

Henkart, Andrea Frank, and Journey Henkart. *Cool Communication: A
    Mother and Daughter Reveal the Keys to Mutual Understanding
    Between Parents and Kids.* New York: A Perigree Book, 1998.

Theresa Hossfield
6 Knoll Lane, Suite F
Mill Valley, CA 94941
    Unpublished poems. 1999.

Melpomene Institute
1010 University Avenue
St. Paul, MN 55104
Publication: *A Journal for Women's Health Research*

New Moon Network. *For Adults Who Care About Girls.* New Moon Publishing. P. O. Box 3587, Duluth, MN 55803-3587.

The Ophelia Project
P. O. Box 8736
Erie, PA 16505
Mary Baird (814) 833-6499
Susan Wellman (814) 734-2539
A program dedicated to healthy adolescent development, with a focus on girls. Mentoring, support groups, and parent education.

Phillips, Lynn. *The Girls Report: What We Know and Need to Know About Growing Up Female.* New York: The National Council for Research on Women, 1998.

Pipher, Mary. *Reviving Ophelia: Saving the Selves of Adolescent Girls.* New York: Ballantine, 1994.

Ponton, Lynn E. *The Romance of Risk: Why Teenagers Do the Things They Do.* New York: Basic Books, 1997.

Rutter, Virginia Beane. *Celebrating Girls: Nurturing and Empowering Our Daughters.* Berkeley, CA: Conari Press, 1996.

Rutter, Virginia Beane. *Woman Changing Woman: Feminine Psychology Re-Conceived Through Myth and Experience.* San Francisco: HarperSan Francisco, 1993.

Sagan, Dorion. "Gender Specifics: Why Women Aren't Men," *The New York Times, Women's Health Section,* June 21, 1998.

Spretnak, Charlene. *Lost Goddesses of Early Greece: A Collection of Pre-Hellenic Mythology.* Berkeley, CA: Moon Books, 1978.

The Stone Center
Center for Research on Women
Wellesley College
Wellesley, MA 02181-8259

Sarah Weintraub
1601 Shoreline Highway
Sausalito, CA 94965
"Distraction." A one-act play. Winner of the California Young
Playwrights Project, 1998.

Wolf, Naomi. Promiscuities: *The Secret Struggle for Womanhood*. New
York: Random House, 1997.

Women's Growth in Connection: Writings from the Stone Center. New
York: The Guilford Press, 1991.

About the Author ᴄ⤻

Virginia Beane Rutter is a psychotherapist and Jungian analyst on the faculty of the C. G. Jung Institute in San Francisco. Her passion is studying ancient myths and rites of passage through art history, archaeology, and psychology and finding their relevance in women's and men's lives today. She is married and the mother of two adolescent children, a boy and a girl, and has a private practice in Mill Valley, California. Her previous books are *Woman Changing Woman* and *Celebrating Girls.*

To Our Readers

Conari Press publishes books on topics ranging from spirituality, personal growth, and relationships to women's issues, parenting, and social issues. Our mission is to publish quality books that will make a difference in people's lives—how we feel about ourselves and how we relate to one another. We value integrity, compassion, and receptivity, both in the books we publish and in the way we do business. As a member of the community, we sponsor the Random Acts of Kindness™ Foundation, the guiding force behind Random Acts of Kindness™ Week. We donate our damaged books to nonprofit organizations, dedicate a portion of our proceeds from certain books to charitable causes, and continually look for new ways to use natural resources as wisely as possible. Our readers are our most important resource, and we value your input, suggestions, and ideas about what you would like to see published. Please feel free to contact us, to request our latest book catalog, or to be added to our mailing list.

Conari Press
2550 Ninth Street, Suite 101
Berkeley, California 94710-2551
800-685-9595 • 510-649-7175
fax: 510-649-7190 • e-mail: conari@conari.com
http://www.conari.com